States and
International Migrants

States and International Migrants

The Incorporation of Indochinese Refugees in the United States and France

Jeremy Hein

Westview Press

BOULDER • SAN FRANCISCO • OXFORD

This Westview softcover edition is printed on acid-free paper and bound in library-quality, coated covers that carry the highest rating of the National Association of State Textbook Administrators, in consultation with the Association of American Publishers and the Book Manufacturers' Institute.

Copyright © 1993 by Westview Press, Inc.

Published in 1993 in the United States of America by Westview Press, Inc., 5500 Central Avenue, Boulder, Colorado 80301-2877, and in the United Kingdom by Westview Press, 36 Lonsdale Road, Summertown, Oxford OX2 7EW

Library of Congress Cataloging-in-Publication Data
Hein, Jeremy
     States and international migrants : the incorporation of
Indochinese refugees in the United States and France / Jeremy Hein.
          p.   cm.
     Includes bibliographical references and index.
     ISBN 0-8133-8541-5
     1. Refugees—Indochina.   2. Refugees—France.   3. Refugees—United
States.   I. Title.
HV640.5.I5H46   1992
362.87—dc20   92-32777
                                                                        CIP

Printed and bound in the United States of America

The paper used in this publication meets the requirements
of the American National Standard for Permanence of Paper
for Printed Library Materials Z39.48-1984.

10   9   8   7   6   5   4   3   2   1

For John Hein in the 1930s
and
Phea Rân in the 1970s

Contents

Preface

Research on international migration is expanding from its traditional focus on the cultural and economic dimensions of migration to include the political relationship between migrants and the host society. Two functions of the modern state—providing social welfare and regulating cultural pluralism—are particularly crucial for the adaptation of contemporary international migrants. I propose explaining types of state intervention in the adaptation process by examining variation in the structure of welfare states and nation-states. A state's response to international migrants also is shaped by the historical context of the migration, such as the presence or absence of compatriot communities when migrants arrive. The interaction of such historical and structural factors produces a mode of state incorporation: the national model implicitly guiding a state's management of international migrants' entry into host society institutions. In turn, I suggest that modes of state incorporation pose distinct challenges to international migrants' membership in kin and communal networks. One function of migrants' social networks is responding to state intervention.

If not for the tragedy of the Indochinese refugee crisis, one might say that the migration of Vietnamese, Laotians, and Cambodians to the United States and France since 1975 was designed for a study of state effects on the adaptation of international migrants. Through colonization and then communist containment, both countries took turns controlling Vietnam, Laos, and Cambodia. France and the United States failed in their missions, in the process transforming the Indochinese into *allied aliens*: foreigners who are the responsibility of an interventionist state as a result of foreign policy defeats. Indochinese refugees migrate to the United States and France because of this history, and the host states take a special interest in managing their initial adjustment. Demographic similarities between the two flows further enhance the comparison. Since the characteristics of the arriving refugees are similar, historical and structural factors provide better explanations for the different forms of state intervention in the United States and France.

Because I focus on the relationship between international migrants and host societies, this book is more than the study of one refugee population. I discuss at length the historical uniqueness of the Indochinese refugee migration for the United States and France. But I also examine the relative importance of history, that is, the degree to which historical factors are causes of state intervention in the adaptation process. Similarly, I devote considerable attention to how the American and French states supply Indochinese refugees with resources to promote their adjustment, another unique feature of their resettlement. Yet by explaining the structural causes of state actions, I reach conclusions about the link between the welfare state and the nation-state in a host society. Finally, analyzing how the state challenges refugees' bonds with kin and community has implications for immigrants who use social networks during the adaptation process. Chapter One explains in more detail the theoretical importance of studying international migration in close association with historical context, the welfare state, the nation-state, and migrants' social networks.

This approach to international migration removes some of the human drama from the Indochinese diaspora that I have experienced firsthand through work in resettlement agencies and personal contact with refugees. However, it leads to the resolution of some fascinating anomalies. Why do the French and American states manage the adaptation of Indochinese refugees in different ways when the arriving refugees have similar social characteristics? How could the American military, in the span of thirty years, place Japanese-Americans and Vietnamese refugees in camps for opposite reasons? What leads the French Ministries of Foreign Affairs and Social Affairs to treat arriving Indochinese refugees like repatriates from Algeria in 1962? Analyzing modes of state incorporation answers these questions, in the process revealing how states constrain the adaptation of international migrants.

Initially, the American and French experiences with Indochinese refugees seemed to provide a natural research design for testing theories of international migration. Such plans changed soon after I entered the French archives and began interviewing refugees in France. The push-pull theory versus the world systems approach and the ethnic resiliency perspective versus assimilation theory proved to be targets too small for the rich data uncovered by my cross-national research on states and participant observation of refugees' social networks. Instead, I decided to accept Charles Tilly's (1984) challenge to comparative historical sociologists to show that societies really exist, that they are not "grand names" lacking internal consistency.

The object of my inquiry is two host societies, and I use three factors to explain their response to the arrival of political migrants. Rather than test theories, I inductively construct a complex generalization about the relationships among history, states, and migrants' social networks. I pursue a variation-finding comparison to "make sense of social structures and processes that never recur in the same form, yet express common principles of causality" (Tilly 1984, p. 146).

The financial support of two organizations was vital to the genesis of this book. I could not have pursued five months of research in France during 1987–1988 without a grant from the National Science Foundation. While in France, Ida Simon-Barouh, François Bonvin, and Jean-Pierre Hassoun were exceptionally helpful scholars and hosts. Marie-Reine Jouffroy and Patrick Coquard at the Bibliothèque de la Documentation Française went well beyond their duties by teaching me how to access French government documents.

Upon returning to the United States, I had the good fortune to join a Ford Foundation project at its Chicago site: "Changing Relations in the U.S.: Newcomers and Established Residents." Robert Bach and Roger Sanjec, coordinators for the national project, advanced my thinking about the unique turns in contemporary American pluralism. I owe an even greater intellectual debt to Josef Barton, Charles Moskos, Arthur Stinchcombe, and especially Charles Ragin. They provided me with encouragement when needed and constructive criticism where warranted. Janet Abu-Lughod, Howard Becker, Al Hunter, Bill Sampson, and Allan Schnaiberg also will find their positive influence in this work. A special thanks goes to Peter Rose. In 1982, he channeled my personal interest in European refugees during the 1930s into the study of contemporary political migrants.

Jeremy Hein

Acronyms Used in References

American Council of Voluntary Agencies (ACVA)
France Terre d'Asile (FTDA)
Indochinese Refugee Action Center (IRAC)
Journal Officiel (JO)
Ministère de la Santé (MS)
Ministère de la Solidarité Nationale (MSN)
Ministère des Affaires Sociales (MAS)
Ministère du Travail (MT)
U.S. Commission on Civil Rights (U.S. CCR)
U.S. Congressional Research Service (U.S. CRS)
U.S. Department of Health, Education, and Welfare (U.S. DHEW)
U.S. Department of Health and Human Services (U.S. DHHS)
U.S. Department of State (U.S. DS)
U.S. General Accounting Office (U.S. GAO)
U.S. House of Representatives (U.S. HR)
U.S. Interagency Task for Indochina Refugees (U.S. IATF)
U.S. Office of Refugee Resettlement (U.S. ORR)
U.S. Senate (U.S. S)
U.S. Statutes at Large (U.S. SL)

1

Introduction: Comparing Modes of State Incorporation

Migration to avoid persecution is ancient, but during the 1970s and 1980s, mass flight became an endemic feature of the Third World (Sutton 1987; Smyser 1985). Decolonization and East-West rivalry were the underlying causes of refugee crises during the post-World War Two era (Gordenker 1987; Zolberg et al. 1989). Independence from a European power often led to ethnic conflict because colonialism used ethnic minorities as middlemen, and created national boundaries which did not match the cultural composition of the territory. Rapid political realignments also resulted from expansion by the Soviet Union into Eastern Europe and Central Asia, while human rights abuses in the former USSR created a permanent dissident population. American attempts to bolster allied regimes or subvert the political process in Asia and Latin America created acute political crises as well as long-run political instability in these regions. The Indochinese refugee crisis results from all the causes which have generated refugees during the twentieth century: decolonization, superpower conflict, and ethnic antipathies (Rogge 1985).

Since 1975, over 2 million Cambodians, Laotians, and Vietnamese have fled their homelands, and 1.75 million subsequently resettled in other countries, 80 percent in Western Europe, North America, and Australia. By 1992, some 200,000 Indochinese refugees remained in first-asylum countries in Southeast Asia, and 370,000 Cambodians were encamped on the Thai-Cambodian border as displaced persons waiting for repatriation. Countless refugees died during their escape. In seeking to cross into Thailand, 60,000 Cambodians, 15,000 Hmong, and 5,000 Laotians perished (Wain 1981). Estimates of the deaths among Vietnamese boat people range from 30,000 (Wain 1981) to over 100,000 (U.S. Committee for Refugees 1987).

Since World War Two, resettlement has been the least-used solution to refugee crises, and the transfer of 1.5 million Indochinese to western, industrial countries is particularly unique (Stein 1986). Of these countries, the United States and France share an extensive, historical presence in Indochina. The U.S. ranks first in the total number of Indochinese refugees resettled (see Table 1.1). France ranks fourth among the western countries, although between 1975 and 1979 it was the second leading resettlement country for the refugees. For both the U.S. and France, the people of Vietnam, Laos, and Cambodia are *allied aliens.*

Enemy aliens are citizens considered disloyal by their government on the basis of ancestry, such as the Japanese-Americans interned during World War Two. Conversely, allied aliens are foreigners to

Table 1.1. Admission of Indochinese Refugees to Resettlement Countries, 1975-1989.

Country	Number Admitted
United States	930,153
China	263,000
Canada	154,264
Australia	136,157
France	126,897
Germany, F.R.	32,654
United Kingdom	21,658
Hong Kong	9,985
New Zealand	9,773
Norway	9,732
Switzerland	9,181
Netherlands	8,040
Belgium	7,508
Japan	6,557
Sweden	5,767
Denmark	5,028
Italy	3,752
Austria	2,371
Finland	1,053
Spain	935
Ireland	329
Luxembourg	293
Greece	255
Other	9,857
Total	1,755,268
Total Number of Refugees From Indochina	2,217,756*

* Includes over 300,000 Indochinese, primarily Cambodians, in Thailand who are legally not refugees because they are not eligible for resettlement in third countries

Source : Refugee Reports 1989b.

whom a state extends protection because of their voluntary or coerced allegiance to the state's foreign policy objectives. Where other countries admit Indochinese refugees as part of "international burden sharing," the U.S. and France have profound political ties to the Vietnamese, Laotians, and Cambodians because of failed attempts to contain insurgency in their homelands from the 1930s to 1975.

The resettlement of Indochinese refugees in these two countries is a "natural experiment" in state responses to international migration. Both states go to extraordinary lengths to manage the refugees' economic and social adaptation, in the process creating "refugee assistance programs which assist in the effective assimilation of refugees" (U.S. Superintendent of Documents 1988, p. AIS-6). Examining these programs reveals distinctively French and American ways of placing international migrants into the host society. The demographic similarities between the two migrations mean that these different modes of state incorporation can be attributed to factors other than the refugees themselves. By holding constant the time of arrival, numbers, class, and ethnicity of the refugees, three factors emerge that explain the different actions of the American and French governments: the historical context of the migration and the structure of the welfare state and of the nation-state. In turn, these factors explain the constraints placed on the refugees' initial adaptation, particularly the function of their social networks.

Historical Links Between
Sending and Host Societies

The Third World is home to 95 percent of the world's refugees, and of these 16,600,000 people, 33 percent are in Africa and 59 percent in the Middle East and South Asia (U.S. Committee for Refugees 1991). Leading the list are refugees from Afghanistan and the Palestinians; their combined populations account for 51 percent of all refugees. Between 1975 and 1990, First World countries gave residence to over 2.5 million refugees and asylum seekers. Most of these political migrants came from Asia, Africa, and Latin America, the same sources for the flow of immigrant workers to Western Europe during the 1960s and early 1970s, and the continuing immigration to Australia, Canada, and the U.S.

The common geographic origins and destinations of refugees and immigrants reveals that both types of migration result from the dynamics of the world system (Portes and Walton 1981). Where the internationalization of state security produces refugees, the internationalization of the division of labor produces immigrants

(Enloe 1986). After the mid-1970s, when labor migration to Western Europe ended, two modes of permanent, legal entry became available to would-be migrants: family reunification and refugee status (OECD 1988; Salt 1989). During the 1980s, one asylum seeker arrived to France for every three immigrants, and Sweden had a ratio of nearly one-to-one. Canada and the U.S. admit one refugee for every five immigrants. Refugees and immigrants are different outcomes of a single relationship between core and peripheral countries.

One feature of this relationship is the flow of immigrants and refugees to host societies to which they have historical ties (Fawcett 1989). Since the 1950s, Caribbean, African, and Asian immigrants have migrated to former European colonial powers (Castles 1984; Salt 1981). Some went as laborers, such as North Africans to France (Belbahri 1982), while others went because of special immigration status, such as Jamaicans and Pakistanis to Britain (Peters and Davis 1986). Spectacular cases of post-colonial migration include the movement of Moluccans from Indonesia to the Netherlands in 1951, and the flight of Ugandan Asians to Britain in 1972.

The U.S. also receives migrants as a result of past political activities. The migration of Puerto Ricans, Cubans, and Mexicans took root after American "intervention undermined the social and economic fabric constructed under Spanish colonial domination and reoriented it toward the new hegemonic power" (Portes 1990, p. 162). Filipinos, Koreans, and of course Indochinese also arrive because American military intervention created pathways to the U.S. (Chan 1991). By the early 1980s, approximately 45 percent of foreigners in France were from former African and Asian colonies (Documentation Française 1982). Of the foreign born population in the U.S. (including Puerto Ricans on the mainland), about 40 percent are from countries in Asia and Latin America whose association with the U.S. began with American military intervention (U.S. Department of Commerce 1990).

These historically rooted migrations have been primarily interpreted as a unique source of cheap labor for western, industrial societies (Castles and Kosack 1985; Freeman 1979; Piori 1979; Portes and Walton 1981). The economic function of some elements of this migration is not in doubt. But migrants' political relationship to the host state is a distinct dimension of their adpatation. In the past, Asian immigrants' in the U.S. experienced better treatment if their homeland was a sovereign nation rather than a colony (Chan 1990). In France, assimilation became a major political issue in the late 1970s and 1980s when North African workers took part in strikes and the second generation began combating racism, although immigrants had been arriving since the 1850s (de Wenden 1987). Few studies have actually compared split migrations and subsequent adaptation of the immigrants in different countries (cf. Bailey 1990). Fewer still have been able to isolate the effects of political relations (cf. Pedraza-Bailey 1985).

The migration of Indochinese refugees to France and the U.S. provides an unusual opportunity to compare the affect of historical ties on the incorporation process. It is now recognized that international migrants invent, rather than transplant, ethnic identities in the host society. Ethnicity can be forged from class stratification (Geschwender et al. 1988), economic competition (Olzak 1989), and spatial proximity (Tomasckovic-Devey and Tomasckovic-Devey 1988; Yancey et al. 1979). Gender is another identity that is reshaped as men and women respond to the exigencies of migration and adaptation (Lamphere 1987). Indochinese refugees do reconstruct ethnicity and gender, but they also arrive with an identity that greatly influences their adjustment: for the U.S. and France, they are allied aliens.

In both countries, the refugees' political identity distinguishes them from other migrants. However, the American and French states attribute different meanings to this identity. Because the demographic characteristics of the refugees arriving to the two countries are quite similar, this variation can be attributed to the historical context of the migration. The distinctiveness of the refugees from other waves of international migrants; the presence or absence of Indochinese communities at the time of arrival; and positive or negative public opinion are three contextual factors shaping how the state uses the identity "allied alien" in the incorporation process. Other factors relate to two state structures: the welfare state and the nation-state.

The Welfare State and Social Citizenship

"International migration" is a bureaucratic concept that first emerged with the formation of the sovereign state (Dowty 1987; Mitchell 1989; Tilly 1978; Whelan 1988). Other than colonization and the slave trade, western states began regulating international migration in the mid-nineteenth century, when passports were first issued in Russia. Throughout history states have expelled ethnic minorities and outlawed emigration of skilled workers, but it was not difficult for migrants to find countries in which to relocate. Since the 1930s, refuge has become a scarce right closely guarded by states even when refugees face genocide (Wyman 1968, 1984). By the late 1940s, all western, industrial countries had created national agencies to manage international migration.

At about the same time that states developed the interest and means to control international migration, they also began formulating policies to aid citizens experiencing particular socioeconomic problems. The welfare state developed from the historical processes of democratization, industrialization, and bureaucratization (Flora and Alber 1987). But there is considerable debate over its exact origins. National ideologies of public goods (Rimlinger 1971; Ruggie 1984), class conflict and social protest (Jenkins and Brents 1989; Quadagno 1984), and independent state action (Skocpol and Ikenberry 1983; Weir et al. 1989) are among the primary causes (for reviews of this literature see Quadagno 1987; Skocpol and Amenta 1986). While origins remain open to debate, the outcome is clear; citizenship came to acquire rights associated with physical well-being and economic subsistence (Marshall 1964).

Since 1900, the state has rapidly extended control over both international migration and social welfare. By the 1950s, the arrival of foreigners, the duration of their stay, and the activities they could engage in were closely regulated by western states. Similarly, the provision of social security, health services, and education were all included, to vary degrees, in the western social welfare system. The result of this merging of international migration and the welfare state is degrees of citizenship (Brubaker 1989; Freeman 1986; Hammer 1990; Layton-Henry 1990). Thus as opposed to "citizenship" in the sense of nationality, "social citizenship" refers to the range of statuses between alien and full citizen that represent combinations of rights for different types of migrants.

Refugees offer a particularly useful case for studying this convergence of state control over migration and social welfare. Although states intervene to assure supplies of labor, such as Mexican migration to the U.S. (Bach 1978), refugees serve the political rather than the economic interests of the state (Charlton et al. 1988; Mitchell 1989). Foreign policy, domestic pressure groups, and fiscal concerns shape the state's selection of displaced populations for admission as refugees (Zucker and Zucker 1989). The ideological determinants of American refugee admission policy are well documented (Gallagher et al. 1986; Loescher and Scanlan 1986; Zucker and Zucker 1987). But political bias is present in the refugee policies of Western Europe (Rudge 1987), Canada (Dirks 1985), Australia (Parker and Alford 1986), Mexico (Wollny 1991), and China (Kerpen 1988). When a state creates a special status in its social welfare systems for refugees, it has effectively linked international migration with the welfare state.

It is historically rare for states to mitigate the hardships experienced by international migrants. To promote colonization, states assisted migrating citizens by giving land grants and self-taxing privileges, as in England's North American colonies during the 1600s (Bailyn 1986). States began providing relief to foreign populations following World War One, although this aid was primarily food and shelter (Marrus 1985). But in 1951, the U.N. ratified the Convention Relative to the Status of Refugees which accords legally recognized refugees most rights given to citizens of the host country, including public assistance, labor protection, and social security. Over one hundred countries have signed both the 1951 Convention and the 1967 Protocol, although the U.S. has only signed the latter agreement. Yet by establishing the "benefits" available to refugees the Convention simultaneously increased the symbolic and fiscal cost of admitting refugees. States now had to guarantee certain rights to political migrants, and governments became increasingly selective in their decisions about which of the worlds' uprooted would become "refugees." Despite the Convention, states initially turn to their social welfare systems to aid refugees because it is another way of extending privilege to groups whose international flight supports the state's national interests.

State assistance to Indochinese refugees is pervasive in resettlement countries throughout the world, although there are important differences among these resettlement systems (Chantavanich and Reynolds 1988; Joly and Cohen 1989; Neuwirth 1988). In Canada, the Employment and Immigration Commission subsidizes private sponsors and provincial governments for resettlement costs, funds language courses and subsistence allocations, and develops an annual plan to distribute refugees to employment centers in the provinces (Canadian EIC, Settlement Branch 1986; Lanphier 1982). In Britain, the Home Office funds private agencies to operate reception centers and outreach programs, while local councils work with municipal government in the areas of housing and employment (Majka 1991; Robinson 1985). The Australian Ministry of Immigration and Ethnic Affairs operates a network of refugee hostels, and the Department of Social Security provides income support (Viviani 1984). Between 1977 and 1979, China resettled ethnic Chinese refugees from Vietnam on state-owned farms supervised by the Ministry of Civil Affairs; special benefits for the refugees included cash payments and the right to have more than one child (Kerpen 1988; Refugees 1988). Underlying these diverse cases is the use of the welfare state to provide migrants with rights and resources.

The resettlement of the Indochinese in the U.S. and France provides a rare vantage point for viewing how states construct social citizenship for international migrants. The Indochinese are valued political migrants and both states create a special status for them in the social welfare system. But these statuses entail very different rights to resources. The role of the central government in the welfare state and the method for determining citizens' eligibility for aid explain why the U.S. and France invent different forms of social citizenship for the arriving refugees.

The Nation-State and Ethnicity

The western state's concern with ethnicity presumed the replacement of a king's religious mandate by the authority of a state based on the will of the people (Bendix 1978). The rise of the state itself required control over markets, armies, and international relations (Tilly 1975). But since the French Revolution, which legitimated the idea that the "indivisibility of the state entailed the cultural uniformity and homogeneity of citizens" (Smith 1986, p. 134), state control has extended to ethnic solidarity. In Central and Eastern Europe, common cultures formed before centralized states and ancestry became the basis for the nation. Conversely, in Western Europe and North America citizenship became the link connecting a preexisting state to a new nation.

The French and American states used citizenship in the wake of revolutions to give a collective identity to the society. Yet in both countries, waves of arriving immigrants in the late nineteenth century created a new function for citizenship: a bridge into an existing nation-state rather than between the state and the nation. For contemporary immigrants, citizenship has little to do with legitimizing state authority or providing a national identity. This secularization of citizenship was so apparent to the French government that in 1987 it established the Committee on Nationality to make recommendations for reinvigorating the naturalization process (Documentation Française 1988).

Many immigrants do not naturalize even when eligible. In France, 74 percent of Asian immigrants want to become citizens, but only 41 percent of black Africans, 30 percent of Iberians, and 16 percent of North Africans (Cornut-Gentile 1986). Among recent immigrants in the U.S., naturalization rates range from 53 percent among Asians, to 27 percent among Cubans, and 8 percent among Mexicans (Portes and Rumbaut 1990). Much of this variation is explained by immigrants' level of education, the distance of their homeland from the U.S., and the political or economic origins of their migration (Portes and Mozo 1985). However, these social factors matter only because the state created the status "permanent resident" between alien and citizen. A permanent resident is secure against deportation and has access to the social welfare system. Indeed, the primary benefit of naturalization is priority in sponsoring relatives to the U.S., voting, and eligibility for some government jobs. Contemporary citizenship for immigrants provides an entry into the state rather than into the nation.

As a result of this trend, race and ethnic relations shape the incorporation of international migrants into the nation-state more than the rights of residence and political participation. In the U.S., there is much variation in whites' social distance from racial and ethnic groups (Owen et al. 1981). Since the 1920s, Western European groups have consistently ranked near "eligible marriage partners," while Mexican-Americans and Japanese-Americans have slowly moved closer to being accepted as "friends." Prior to the mid-1960s, many whites wanted to exclude blacks from their neighborhood and even workplace. Today, most whites "believe that blacks deserve the same treatment and respect as whites, and that some degree of racial integration is a desirable thing," although few support government programs specifically designed to aid blacks (Schuman et al. 1985, p. 202). Ethnic hierarchies also exist in France (Girard et al. 1974). The French express less antipathy toward Iberians than toward Asians, but also less toward black Africans than toward Algerians because of peaceful decolonization below the Sahara and traumatic independence above it. Similarly, the public believes that North Africans have a more difficult time assimilating to French society than black Africans because the former are Muslim. Ethnic stratification, not citizenship, is the principle component of the contemporary western nation-state.

As the French and American ethnic hierarchies suggest, there is considerable variation in how each nation-state manages cultural pluralism. For example, French surveys ask respondents: "Which of the following immigrant groups are rather well or rather poorly integrated into French society?" Contrast this question about immigrants with one from an American survey: "Thinking both of what they have contributed to this country and have gotten from this country . . . [have they] been a good thing or a bad thing for this country?" A simple reason for these different perspectives on adaptation is that countries like Australia, Canada and the U.S. developed from immigration, while countries like England, Germany, and France developed from cultural cores (Glazer 1983). A more detailed analysis of differences among nation-states examines the interaction of state bureaucracies and cultural geography (Anderson 1974; Eisenstadt 1973; Rokkan 1975).

The American state has historically been weak, and not until after 1865 did it play the unifying role found much earlier in countries like France, which had an absolutist state. The French state absorbed regional cultures into the Parisian core over centuries; fought powerful neighbors for territory up to 1945; and imposed French culture in African and Asian colonies until the 1960s. The constituent elements of the American nation-state developed under different circumstances. The state killed or assimilated Native Americans until the 1920s; enforced second-class citizenship for African Americans until the 1950s; and limited immigration to countries in Northwestern Europe until the 1960s. These historic patterns of race and ethnic relations are more important to the incorporation of international migrants than the formal requirements for citizenship.

The arrival of Indochinese refugees to France and the U.S. provides an ideal case for comparing how two nation-states respond to similar waves of international migrants. It will not come as a surprise that the French state seeks greater assimilation of the refugees than does the American state. But in the U.S., the development of Indochinese communities is managed, rather than left to chance, while in France the state seeks complete control over some of the refugees while allowing others a great deal of autonomy. These unexpected findings are explained by how the Indochinese refugee migration interacts with different nation-states: one formed by a Parisian core and a "civilizing mission" in Africa and Asia, the other by free European immigration and subjugation of African-Americans.

State Intervention and Migrants' Social Networks

The study of social networks is becoming a definitive component of the "new immigration paradigm" (Boyd 1989; Tilly 1990). A principle feature of migration networks among legal (Lamphere 1987) and illegal immigrants (Massey et al. 1987) is chain migration: organizing movement between countries through kin and communal relations. Refugees also use social networks to navigate their passage to a host society. About one in five Indochinese refugees in Thailand were persuaded by relatives and friends to leave their homeland (Institute for Asian Studies 1988). Surveys of Indochinese refugees in the U.S. find that one-third joined immediate relatives and another third more distant relatives (Strand and Jones 1985; U.S. GAO 1983). Similarly, Cubans arriving to the U.S. during the 1960s and 1970s had, on average, nine relatives and friends already in the country (Portes and Bach 1985).

However, refugee migrations are more frequently composed of

families, while immigrant migrations are more often composed of individuals (Castles and Kosack 1985; Portes and Bach 1985). Indeed, the family preference system in American immigration policy presumes the serial migration of related individuals, where as refugee admissions are based on broad political and nationality categories (Reimers 1985). While state policies shape the demography of migration networks, the political causes of refugee crises often lead to the migration of cohorts. The Cuban migration to the U.S. became poorer and darker over time (Boswell and Curtis 1984; Gallagher 1980). Military and government elites comprised the first wave of Vietnamese refugees, while later waves were more representative of the class and ethnic composition of their homeland (Hang 1985). But the difficulties of escaping Vietnam also lead to many fragmented Vietnamese families in the U.S., augmenting their reliance on the ethnic community (Gold 1989; Haines 1988; Haines et al. 1981). Refugees and immigrants are enmeshed in social networks, but migration constraints shape the form of these networks.

The state is a second factor now recognized as influencing the adaptation of international migrants. After fifteen years in the U.S., documented and undocumented Mexican immigrants have similar social networks and work experiences (Massey et al. 1987). However, legal residents still use the social welfare system to a much greater degree. Cross-national research suggests that a state's immigration and social welfare policies shape how immigrants organize self-help activities (Jenkins 1988). Similarly, the host society's legal system can facilitate or hinder the opening of immigrant enterprises (Waldinger et al. 1990).

State intervention can also be more direct. In the case of Indochinese refugees, special public aid policies temporarily provide an alternative to working in mainstream labor markets (Bach 1988; Johnson 1988; Rumbaut 1989b). Government assistance also creates middle-class jobs in agencies that provide resettlement services (Gold 1992; Hein 1988; Indra 1987). In the case of Cubans, state assistance totaling $1.3 billion between 1962 and 1980 (Taft et al. 1980) enabled many of these middle-class refugees to avoid the severe downward mobility so commonly experienced by teachers, lawyers, and other professionals (Pedraza-Bailey 1985). However, research on the Cuban enclave has not examined the contribution of state intervention to the development of an ethnic economy in South Florida (Wilson and Martin 1982; Wilson and Portes 1980). For example, the fact that 66 percent of Cubans, but only 45 percent of Mexicans, believed that there were many opportunities for success in the U.S. is arbitrarily attributed to the Cubans' "lack of prior familiarity with American society," rather than the fact that a resettlement program existed for Cubans but not for Mexicans (Portes and Bach 1985, p. 270). Portes and associates argue that the state is simply one factor shaping the "context of reception" and "the reaction of the host community" to the migrants (Portes and Böröcz 1989; Portes and Manning 1986). I will demonstrate that states play a far more significant role in the adaptation process.

The migration of Indochinese refugees to France and the U.S. could be used to determine the affect of state assistance on the socioeconomic mobility of international migrants. However, existing American and French government reports and social science surveys utilize samples and coding schemes too divergent to allow conclusive findings from such a comparison (cf. Ajchenbaum 1981, 1983 with U.S. ORR 1985; cf. Bonvin and Ponchaud 1981a, 1981b with Caplan et al. 1989). There are indications that refugees in the U.S. have greater job and educational opportunities, but they also experience more poverty than their compatriots in France. Even if the data existed, searching for the economic gain or loss produced by state intervention would obscure a much less researched topic: how state action challenges migrant's social networks, establishing conflicts that shape relationships among kin, friends, and community members.

State incorporation represents the meeting of the western welfare state and indigenous forms of self-help developed in societies that do not have welfare states. Research on "bureaucratic encounters" (Hasenfeld et al. 1987) and "street-level bureaucrats" (Lipsky 1980) reveals that bureaucrats' power over resources conflicts with clients' norms of equal treatment. However, this literature assumes that clients and representatives of the state are natives and share a common culture. Indochinese refugees arrive to France and the U.S. with traditions of providing social welfare through kin and communal networks rather than government agencies. State intervention in the adaptation process varies in France and the U.S., and the refugees' collective approach to adaptation thus is challenged in different ways. In France, refugees' social networks confront a social contract, while in the U.S. they confront a social conflict.

Research Design, Methodology, and Data

Comparing French and American responses to the arrival of Indochinese refugees is a type of cross-national comparison that emphasizes the nation as object and as context (Kohn 1987). One goal of this study is to better understand these particular countries. They are key host societies for contemporary international migrants and thus

are of intrinsic interest. A second goal is to reach generalizations about
the operations of a social institution. Disclosing the conditions under
which the welfare state and nation-state undertake some actions
rather than others has implications for the study of states in general.

A research design that maximizes both goals is what Tilly (1984, p.
116) terms a variation-finding comparison: establishing "a principle of
variation in the character or intensity of a phenomenon having more
than one form by examining systematic differences among instances."
Following this research strategy, I conceptualize a state's response to
Indochinese refugees as an outcome or case. Some comparisons analyze
the presence or absence of a social phenomenon. The variation-finding
comparison analyzes types of social phenomenon, such as the American
and French modes of state incorporation. It seeks to demonstrate that
differences in one set of social factors, such as historical context, social
welfare systems, and race and ethnic relations, are systematically
linked to differences in another set of factors, such as state policies to
manage the adaptation of political migrants.

To establish this covariation between historical and structural
factors, on the one hand, and state actions, on the other, I draw upon
two methodologies from comparative historical sociology: historical
interpretation and analysis of causal regularities (Skocpol 1984). The
first method searches for the salient themes and patterns in the
unfolding of a significant event. Chapter Two examines the historical
context of the Indochinese migration to the U.S.: the novelty of
refugees arriving due to a lost war; the absence of Indochinese
communities in 1975; and negative attitudes toward the refugees among
the American public. Chapter Three explains how these historical
factors interact with the political and normative structure of the
American social welfare system to produce social citizenship for the
refugees. Similarly, Chapter Four shows how the historical context of
the migration interacts with the patterns in American race and ethnic
relations to constrain refugees' formation of ethnic communities. These
latter two chapters suggest that the structure of the welfare state and
nation-state determine the nature of state intervention in the
adaptation of international migrants.

To substantiate this thesis, I then turn to the French case. In contrast
to the historical and interpretive methodology of previous chapters,
Chapters Five and Six use a causal and analytic methodology to
explain why the French state pursues a mode of incorporation nearly
opposite to that of the American state. Chapter Five establishes the
political, temporal, and demographic similarities between the
Indochinese refugee migrations to the U.S. and France. Because of
these constants, I argue that different state responses can be explained

by historical and structural factors, rather than by the characteristics of the refugees themselves. Chapter Six points to variation in the historical context of the migration and variation in state structures to explain the French state's construction of social citizenship and regulation of ethnic community formation. These chapters on the American and French modes of state incorporation rely on data in primary documents from government agencies and social welfare organizations.

Chapters Seven and Eight turn from the analysis of states to the refugees themselves. These chapters link variation between the French and American modes of incorporation to the different responses of refugees' social networks to state intervention in the adaptation process. Each type of intervention produces a distinct challenge to migrants' ties to kin and community.

The data in Chapters Seven and Eight are based on field work in resettlement agencies and interviews with refugees. Chapter Seven uses data gathered from participant observation in a resettlement agency in New York City and another in San Francisco during 1983 and 1984. I assisted Indochinese caseworkers with their jobs, attended office meetings to discuss cases and policy, worked with agency records, and subsequently interviewed thirty-six caseworkers at fourteen agencies. Most Indochinese refugees' in the U.S. receive state resources for a period of time, but their encounters with the American state are episodic rather than continuous. Field work in a resettlement agency, or even studying a single social network, could not capture the full range of interactions between refugees and refugee managers. For this reason, Chapter Seven supplements the data from participant observation with first-hand accounts of refugees adaptation from primary documents, such as life histories and agency reports.

Chapter Eight examines the social networks of refugees resettled in France. Some refugees receive substantial state assistance while living in temporary settlement centers; others bypass the centers and receive little or no aid. The structure of the French resettlement system required a more ethnographic study of refugees' social networks. I lived in Paris for five months in 1987 and 1988, and developed an ethnography of a Cambodian kin network which had received little state assistance. For two weeks during this period I also lived in a city in western France. There, I closely studied a temporary settlement center by interviewing staff members and Cambodian families who had passed through the center.

This micro-level analysis of refugees' social networks reveals that the meaning of membership in an extended family or an ethnic community varies for refugees depending on whether they resettle in the U.S. or France. Chapters Seven and Eight extend the causal argument of previous chapters by explaining why the structure of the American welfare state and nation-state challenges refugees' social networks in one way, while the structure of these institutions in France leads to another type of challenge.

PART ONE

Indochinese Refugees in the United States

2

International Migration
and Historical Context

International migration occurs in a historical context: when migrants arrive can be more important for the adaptation process than the traits of individual migrants. The Indochinese migration to the U.S. began when pro-American governments in Vietnam, Laos, and Cambodia collapsed. This context introduces three historical factors that shape the state's incorporation of Indochinese refugees.

First, these refugees are the only allied aliens to arrive to the U.S. due to failed American military intervention. The case of Cuban refugees provides a close parallel, but as discussed below, the Cuban migration resulted from an American strategy rather than a strategic failure. Second, Vietnamese, Laotian, and Cambodian communities did not exist during the peak years of the migration. No other migration to the U.S. occurred with such rapidity: the Indochinese population grew from 18,000 to over one million between 1975 and 1991. Finally, the refugees arrived simultaneously with large numbers of immigrants, undocumented aliens, and other refugees. Increased migration to the U.S. during the 1970s and 1980s eroded the allied alien qualities of the refugees for the American public and many Congressmen, giving rise to nativism.

These contextual factors explain some of the differences between the incorporation of Indochinese refugees in the U.S. and France. In contrast to the American case, Indochinese refugees were not unique within twentieth century migration to France; Cambodian, Laotian, and especially Vietnamese communities already existed when the refugees began arriving; and the French public had an overwhelmingly positive response to these refugees even though nativism toward immigrants was rampant.

The Lost War with Communism

American intervention in Indochina began with support for Vietnamese guerrillas fighting Japanese occupation during World War Two. But when France resumed control of its colonies after 1945, the U.S. provided financial and military aid for France's war against Vietnamese nationalists. After France conceded defeat in 1954, leaving Vietnam partitioned, the U.S. Navy helped transport 800,000 Vietnamese from North to South Vietnam. American efforts to contain communism then began in earnest. Nation-building programs sought to modernize South Vietnam and support a Vietnamese president chosen by the American government, although Ngo Dinh Diem would be assassinated during a U.S. backed coup in 1963. During the early 1960s military aid increased to pro-American regimes under siege from indigenous communist movements. Large numbers of U.S. troops entered South Vietnam in 1965 and bombing runs began over North Vietnam; aerial bombardments laid waste to Laos and then Cambodia during the early 1970s. The Paris Peace Accord of 1973 ended direct American intervention in South Vietnam, but the U.S. continued to supply arms and economic aid after its troops withdrew. Despite the cost in human lives and political duplicity, U.S. backed governments in South Vietnam, Laos, and Cambodia fell in April and May of 1975. As Zinn (1980, p. 460) concludes: "From 1964 to 1972, the wealthiest and most powerful nation in the history of the world made a maximum military effort, with everything short of atomic bombs, to defeat a nationalist revolutionary movement in a tiny, peasant country—and failed." The Hmong of Laos and Vietnamese employees of U.S. government agencies are microcosms of the larger process by which American foreign policy and military intervention transformed Indochinese into American allied aliens.

After first contacting the Hmong in the late 1950s, Washington gave serious thought to ending support for counterinsurgency activities when the Laotian civil war came to a brief halt in 1961. But according to a former CIA agent who worked in Laos, the decision to continue assistance was in part based on refusal to abandon an allied population (Blaufarb 1977). However, by 1970 the U.S. war effort in Laos was clearly a losing effort. Numbering some 400,000 in 1960, ten years later about 40 of the male Hmong population had been killed, and 25 percent of the women and children were casualties (U.S. S 1970). American officials once again confronted the fate of this group.

One worker with the U.S. Agency for International Development had enough foresight in 1970 to perceive the depth of this foreign policy crisis: "We have got to either resettle these people in Thailand or bring this whole issue over to the American people; maybe we should resettle them in the hills of Colorado" (U.S. S 1970, p. 38). Over 1,300 Hmong lived in the Denver area by the late 1980s. Another worker described American responsibility in even more profound terms:

> I will be the first to agree that our policies in Southeast Asia have been tragically wrong. And I further feel we should disengage militarily as soon as possible. But I feel, at the same time, that it is of paramount importance that we do not compound our mistakes by not, in some form, showing a continuing commitment to those people who over the years have shown the greatest loyalty to our presence (U.S. S 1970, p. 27).

Just what this continuing commitment would be was not resolved until 160,000 Hmong and other highland groups allied to the U.S. fled to Thailand, thousands dying during the escape from attacks by the Laotian Army. Some Hmong claimed they were bombarded with poison gas while in Laos, although the "yellow rain controversy" continues to be debated (Nichols 1988). However, the House of Representatives took the charge seriously enough to pass a resolution calling upon the president to take diplomatic action against Vietnam for using chemical weapons (Congressional Quarterly 1980). By 1990, over 100,000 Hmong had resettled in the U.S., although another 50,000 preferred residence in Thai refugee camps with the hope of someday returning to Laos.

Vietnamese allies of the U.S. did not suffer the catastrophic fate awaiting the Hmong. However, American accountability is even more acute because their plight was logistically more manageable. In the spring of 1975, Secretary of State Henry Kissinger and other foreign policy makers discouraged evacuation plans because they feared signs of imminent departure would undermine the morale of the Vietnamese army during a serious North Vietnamese offensive. Instead, Kissinger sought to negotiate a last minute settlement with North Vietnam that would have preserved a small portion of South Vietnam. The American Ambassador relieved of command a Brigadier General in the U.S. Air Force who secretly began evacuating his Vietnamese employees (Kelly 1977).

Even when it became clear that the war was finally lost, American officials failed to make adequate evacuation provisions for Vietnamese in danger of communist reprisals because of their association with the U.S. (Butler 1985; Dawson 1977). Two weeks before the fall of Saigon, 17,600 Vietnamese employed by the U.S. were targeted for evacuation should the need arise. Four days before the collapse the number increased to only 50,000 (Kelly 1977).

Through abandonment and incompetency, only one-quarter of the Vietnamese directly employed by American government agencies reached the U.S. within two years of the collapse of Saigon (Snepp 1977). Tens of thousands of others were considered only contract workers and thus were not part of any evacuation plan. Due to the hurried departure, the CIA failed to destroy thousands of files on "indigenous employees," providing evidence of collaboration for the new communist government. According to a former CIA operator in Saigon: "in terms of squandered lives, blown secrets and the betrayal of agents, friends, and collaborators, our handling of the evacuation was an institutional disgrace" (Snepp 1977, p. 567). Images of a lone U.S. helicopter lifting U.S. personnel from the roof of the American embassy in Saigon, while American Marines hold at bay masses of refugees, is a powerful symbol of the fate that awaited allied aliens in Vietnam, Laos, and Cambodia. American guilt over these events burst to the surface in 1989, when a military court convicted a U.S. Navy captain of failing to aid Vietnamese boat people in the South China Sea; the refugees resorted to cannibalism when their provisions ran out (Fritsch 1989; Refugee Reports 1989a).

The origins of the Indochinese migration in the spring of 1975 were thus shrouded in the legacy of the Vietnam War. The day after the fall of Saigon, Senator Eagleton charged that President Ford had "no constitutional authority to use U.S. armed forces to evacuate foreign nationals from South Vietnam" (Finney 1975, p. 15). He insisted that the Congress now approve the operation lest it establish a precedent for future presidents. The senator and others objected to the airlift of some 6,000 Vietnamese from Saigon by U.S. Navy and Air Force helicopters because they claimed it conflicted with the War Powers Act of 1973, which sought to limit presidential control of the military in undeclared wars. In a reenactment of the Vietnam-era bouts between Congress and the Executive Office, President Ford continued to use military forces to assist with the evacuation. After the airlift on April 29, ships of the U.S. Seventh Fleet waited for forty-eight hours off the coast of former South Vietnam in order to safely escort some 30,000 refugees who initiated their own evacuation by boat (Binder 1975).

Past foreign policy also shaped the American reception of the refugees. In April, President Ford used $98 million in AID money targeted for "postwar reconstruction of Indochina" to pay the Defense Department for transporting and housing this first wave of Vietnamese government officials and army officers (U.S. S 1975a, p. 89). When Ford created an Interagency Task Force for Indochina to resettle arriving refugees, he chose for its directors representatives from AID, the Department of Defense, and the CIA (Taft et al. 1980). For eight months during 1975, the Task Force operated four mainland military camps which housed the refugees (Kelly 1977). It was highly symbolic, but probably unintentional, that the three branches of the U.S. military most involved in the Vietnam War—the army, air force, and marines—each received a contingent of the refugees in a state-side camp.

Many in Congress also viewed Vietnamese resettlement as the denouement of the Vietnam War. The Senate described the Indochina Migration and Refugee Assistance Act as "a positive step, a situation where the President and the Congress are working together to meet the last remaining commitment . . . our Nation incurred in that conflict" (U.S. S 1975b, p. 14,840). Resettlement assistance for the refugees was so enmeshed in the legacy of the Vietnam War that seventy-one members of the House of Representatives voted in favor of an amendment that would have provided aid to American draft dodgers who had fled the country and where now returning destitute (U.S. HR 1975b). Thus unlike prior refugee migrations, the "original Indochinese admissions program was perceived as a 'rescue operation' precipitated by military defeat, rather than a traditional 'refugee' situation involving demonstrated victims of past persecution" (Loescher and Scanlan 1986, p. 119).

The aura of the Vietnam War continued to surround Indochinese refugees through the late 1970s and into the 1980s. In 1979, Senator Hayakawa linked the war to the country's responsibility to assist arriving refugees with learning English and finding jobs:

> The conflict in Southeast Asia was a burden that was borne jointly by all the States. The refugee crisis that resulted from that conflict is also a burden to be borne corporately as a nation. . . . We must be prepared, as a nation, to provide the financial assistance the Indochinese refugees need to become self-sufficient members of our society (U.S. S 1979b, p. 23,249).

Thirteen years after the withdrawal of U.S. troops, President Reagan could still justify admission of Indochinese refugees on the grounds that "many had fought with us for the freedom of their homeland" (Reagan 1986, p. 2). In 1988, the U.S. Congress passed the Amerasian Homecoming Act, which will admit 40,000 Vietnamese-American offspring and their relatives. That same year, the State Department pledged to obtain the release of all political prisoners remaining in Vietnamese "reeducation camps" as a result of their ties to the former regime, a population numbering at least 85,000.

The roots of Indochinese refugees' admission to the U.S. lie in America's political and military failures in Vietnam, Laos, and Cambodia. According to the U.S. Department of State (1982a, p. 57 and p.60), "we accept only refugees of special concern to the United States, who meet our admissions criteria, for whom there are no alternative solutions, and whose admission is required by compelling foreign policy considerations." To leave no uncertainty which populations met these criteria, the State Department concluded: "out of the current major refugee groups, Southeast Asian refugees have the strongest association with the United States." As a result of this policy, Indochinese refugees account for 68 percent of all refugees admitted to the U.S. between 1975 and 1990. Addressing the first Indochinese Community Leadership Conference in 1986, Senator Hatfield responded to critiques of continued Indochinese refugee admissions by stating:

> Go back 15 years, go back to the U.S. bombs ripping the countryside of Vietnam and tell me the United States is finished in the refugee camps of Southeast Asia. . . . I cannot say precisely when the United States' hands will be clean of some responsibility for the turmoil in Southeast Asia, but I can say that this day has not yet arrived (IRAC 1986, p. 4).

America's First Allied Aliens

The arrival of Indochinese refugees challenged the American state to live up to an historic responsibility. Communism prevailed in South Vietnam, Laos, and Cambodia prevailed despite the intervention of U.S. armed forces and more than two decades of assurances from Washington that success was imminent. Compounding the defeat was the tremendous physical destruction and loss of life in the three countries due to the U.S. war effort. The American government was unable to change the societal fate of the 100 million people in former Indochina, but it could aid those who escaped the new regimes.

The arrival of Indochinese refugees is part of a larger, historical migration to the U.S. Between World War Two and the capture of Saigon, the U.S. received approximately 1.5 million political migrants (see Table 2.1). The American government admitted displaced persons to hasten the reconstruction of Western Europe in the aftermath of the war (Barnet 1983). Pressure from ethnic lobby groups (Dinnerstein 1982), as well as human rights concerns (Loescher and Scanlan 1986), also contributed to the decision. Beginning in the mid-1950s refugees, particularly the Cubans, started to be admitted for unabashed foreign policy reasons related to East-West conflict.

Although the Cuban migration also resulted from this struggle (Masud-Piloto 1988), the Indochinese were the first allied aliens to confront the American state.

There has been a nearly constant stream of Cuban refugees to the U.S. since the revolution in 1959, but most have not fled because of failed American policies to which they had directly or indirectly given their support. The Bay of Pigs invasion in April of 1961 approximates the close military relationship between the American government and a foreign population that developed in Southeast Asia. However, this CIA operation only involved a brigade of Cubans recruited from the U.S. and the operation's failure led to the death of 100 and the capture of 1,200 more. The loss of this allied alien population undoubtedly heightened attention to political prisoners in Cuba for a short period of time. But the American government realized that henceforth the Cuban exiles could only have a minor role in U.S. foreign policy toward Cuba (Scanlan and Loescher 1983).

Table 2.1. Principal Refugee Legislation, Groups, and Numbers Admitted to the United States, 1946-1978 (excluding Indochinese).

Date of Legislation	Group Admitted	Number Admitted
1945; 1948	Displaced Persons from World War II: Germans, Poles, Balts, Russians.	40,324 409,696
1953	Cold War Refugees: Germans, Italians, Greeks, Yugoslavs.	189,021
1957	Cold War Refugees: Chinese, Hungarians, Indonesians, Yugoslavs.	29,462
1958	Hungarians	30,751
1958	Portuguese from Azores and and Dutch from Indonesia	22,213
1960	Displaced Persons and Escapees: Yugoslavs, Romanians, Middle Easterns.	19,783
1965	Cold War Refugees: Yugoslavs, Russians, Chinese, Czecks.	116,397
1966	Cubans	664,603
TOTAL		1,522,566

Source : Díaz-Briquets and Pérez 1981; U.S. Congressional Research Service 1980.

By disaggregating the Cuban migration, it becomes apparent that only between one-third and one-half of all Cuban migrants in the U.S. by 1980 could be considered refugees in the most general sense. Table 2.2 shows six Cuban migration cohorts within the larger flow between 1959 and 1980. The "revolution and counter revolution cohort" left during the period when the U.S. sought to overthrow the new socialist government in Cuba, particularly by recruiting Cuban exiles. Many Cuban migrants in this period believed that the revolution would be short lived and that their migration to the U.S. was a strategic, temporary move. This hope faded with the failure of the Bay of Pigs invasion (Scanlan and Loescher 1983). However, Castro did not impose restrictions on the amount of wealth migrants could take with them until June of 1961, and regular commercial air traffic continued to the U.S. until the missile crisis in October of 1962 (Rogg 1974). Between 1963 and 1965, about 70,000 Cubans escaped or made their way to the U.S. through third countries.

In the fall of 1965, Castro announced that immigration between Cuba and the U.S. could resume for purposes of family reunion. Over the next seven years, some 260,000 Cubans flew to the U.S. through the Freedom Flight Program before Castro canceled it in 1973 (Zucker and Zucker 1987). Both governments selected migrants using family reunification as the primary criterion, essentially making the endeavor legal immigration between two sovereign states (Pedraza-Bailey 1985). The emigration restrictions on youth of conscription age

Table 2.2. Cuban Migration Cohorts as a Percent of Total Cuban Migration to the United States, 1959-1980.

Cohort	Year	Total Migration
Revolution and Counter Revolution	1959-1962	27
Missile Crisis	1963-1965	9
Freedom Flight	1966-1972	33
Escapees from Cuba	1973-1979	1
Third Countries	1965-1979	14
Mariel Boat Lift	1980	16
Total Cuban Migration	1959-1980	796,913

Source : Diáz-Briquets and Pérez 1981; Scanlan and Loescher 1983; Zucker and Zucker 1987.

and political prisoners further suggest the essentially nonpolitical character of this flow (Scanlan and Loescher 1983). Indeed, the American open-door policy for the Cubans was so extensive that 70,000 Cubans who had originally found refuge in Spain were admitted, and 38,000 more arrived from third countries after 1973 (Zucker and Zucker 1987).

The arrival of 122,000 Cubans between April and September 1980 through the "Mariel Boat Lift" increased the existing Cuban population by 19 percent. Some of these migrants were political prisoners, many were people seeking family reunification during a moment when migration was possible, and a small proportion were convicts and mental patients released by the Cuban government. The Mariel cohort is an ambiguous case. The migrants fled like refugees, but the reason for the flight was a moment of leniency in Cuban emigration policy. In fact, more migrants left than either the Cuban or American government had planned on. In mid-April, the American government agreed to take 3,500 Cubans and even the Cuban exile community expected only 10,000 to arrive. It was the Carter administration's poor "crisis management" skills which magnified the scale of the migration (Copeland 1983).

The fact that the Mariel Boat Lift occurred twenty years after the Cuban revolution suggests that chain migration and economic factors where at work rather than political factors. Indeed, by the mid-1960s observers of the Cuban migration had already concluded that "it is clear that time lessens the personal impact of the most difficult years of transition from capitalism to communism" (Fagen et al. 1968, p. 116). The close proximity of Cuba to Miami, and the rapid development of a Cuban enclave in the city, vastly accentuated pull over push factors. Talks between Cuban exiles and the Castro administration on the fate of political prisoners began in 1978 (Copeland 1983). Indeed, 100,000 Cuban exiles in the U.S. traveled to Cuba in the two years preceding the boat lift to visit relatives and friends (Reimers 1985). Both exchanges primed the pump of migratory expectations on the mainland and in Cuba.

The best evidence of the social rather than political roots of the 1980 cohort is the key role played by Cuban-Americans in transporting Cuban migrants to the U.S. Only 697 of the 122,000 Cubans who migrated during the Mariel period came by plane; the rest were ferried to Florida in boats owned or rented by Cuban Americans (Copeland 1983). Cuban leaders in Miami even refused a State Department request to restrain the boat lift, forcing the U.S. government to accept more migrants than it had originally planned (Zucker and Zucker 1987). While most migrants in the U.S. eventually become involved in local and national politics, the political power of the Cuban community dramatically augmented the flow of migrants from Cuba.

By the end of 1980, the Cuban migration to the U.S. comprised six different cohorts. One cohort arrived as a direct result of failed U.S. foreign policy: the revolution and counter revolution cohort between 1959 and 1962. The missile crisis cohort between 1963 and 1965 fled during a period of heightened political tension and may be considered an analogous case. Combined, these two groups accounted for 36 percent of the 1980 Cuban population. Those Cubans who escaped after the Freedom Flight Program ended in 1973 add only 1 percent. Revolution, the political shocks following the Cuban missile crisis, and the ending of legal emigration between 1973 and 1979 account for only 38 percent of all Cuban migration to the U.S. Nearly all of the migrants in this group arrived between 1959 and 1965.

Not only were most Cuban migrants not fleeing political persecution, but the Cuban government encouraged many citizens to leave. One motive for this policy was to use the migration to externalize dissent: "Unlike the majority of exile movements, the Cuban exodus to the United States was an organized one, based on mutual arrangements of the Cuban and American governments" (Pedraza-Bailey 1984, pp. 146—147). In addition, out-migration enabled the Cuban government to redistribute scarce resources, like housing and jobs (Boswell and Curtis 1984). Finally, Castro used migration as a political weapon. For example, by allowing the Peruvian embassy to be mobbed by would-be migrants in 1980, Castro punished Peru for its lenient asylum policy during the 1970s (Copeland 1983). Similarly, Castro used out-migration to create difficult domestic issues for the U.S.; 26,000 Cubans with prison records, of which only 5,000 were hard-core criminals, were channeled by Cuban authorities into the 1980 boat lift (Boswell and Curtis 1984). Altogether, only 10 percent of the total Cuban migration between 1959 and 1980 occurred during a period when emigration was banned by the Cuban government (the cohorts between 1962—1965 and 1973—1979).

The largest migration cohorts are the Cubans who arrived between 1966 and 1972; 33 percent of the 1980 population was composed of these migrants who resembled immigrants boarding planes for the U.S. rather than refugees fleeing for their safety. Moreover, 14 percent of all Cubans arrived to the U.S. after already having migrated to another country. Some 140,000 Cubans went to Europe between 1961 and 1977, again on regularly scheduled flights (Marrus 1985), and about one-half of them then moved on to the U.S. (Zucker and Zucker 1987); other Cubans came via Mexico. Combined, the freedom flight and third country cohorts account for 47 percent of the 1980 Cuban refugee population. Thus almost one-half came to the U.S. as part of a normal immigration pattern. In fact, of all the Cubans who migrated to the U.S. directly from Cuba between 1959 and 1977, only 63 percent entered as parolees, the legal equivalent of refugee under existing legislation (Taft et. al 1980). The remainder entered the U.S. in other ways: 15 percent with immigrants visas and 21 percent as visitors who never left. If half of the Mariel cohort is included with the two other "immigrant" cohorts, than 59 percent of the Cuban migration bears a greater resemblance to immigrants journeying to an adjacent ethnic community rather than allied aliens fleeing a hostile political regime.

In sharp contrast to the Cuban case, the admission of Indochinese refugees in 1975, and even into the 1980s, has had little immediate value in furthering U.S. foreign policy goals. At times the U.S. has encouraged refugee flight to tarnish an enemy state's image, such as the movement of civilians from North to South Vietnam in 1954 (Wiesner 1988). But after 1975, the admission of Indochinese refugees could in no way be construed as contributing to American foreign policy. For example, the loss of 5,000 fishing boats by 1979 due to escaping "boat people" had a crippling effect on the Vietnamese fishing industry, but this was not the result of an American ploy (JO II 1979). Rather, the admission of Indochinese refugees stems from failed foreign policy and the U.S. government is obligated to assist the refugees as best it can (Suhrke and Klink 1987). Thus with the arrival of Indochinese refugees in 1975, "there was surprisingly little attempt to exploit the propaganda value of the Indochinese refugees, particularly in comparison with the Eastern European and Cuban situations. The difference was in the perception of the Vietnamese evacuation as a 'rescue operation' precipitated by military defeat" (Loescher and Scanlan 1986, p. 113).

The refugee crises in Southeast Asia are burdens rather than benefits to the makers of U.S. foreign policy. In June of 1979, the State Department issued a warning to Vietnam because Vietnamese troops in Cambodia appeared on the verge of invading Thailand in pursuit of Cambodian guerrillas. Later that year Thai troops and Cambodian guerrillas exchanged shots over an alleged theft of Thai military supplies (Niehuas 1979, p. 195). The makers of American foreign policy also have to respond to resentment among Southeast Asian countries of first asylum. Since the beginning of the boat people crisis in 1978 and the flight of Cambodians in 1979, the U.S. has had to assure Thailand, Malaysia, and other countries in the region that they will not be left with a residual population of Indochinese refugees (Suhrke 1983; Sutter 1990). Some of these countries, particularly Thailand, are key American allies. When American admission of Indochinese refugees declines, tension with allies in the region increases. According to the U.S. Ambassador to Thailand:

> U.S.-Thai cooperation on security, narcotics suppression, and trade is buttressed by a warm and active people-to-people relationship. . . . There are some 10,000 Thai students in American universities, and thousands of Americans, including businessmen, Peace Corps volunteers, missionaries, etc., who live and work in Thailand, as well as a more or less permanent Thai community in the United States of 300,000 persons. . . . [A] deterioration of U.S.-Thai understandings and cooperation on refugees could set back our relations along a very wide front, indeed (U.S. DS 1988, pp. 4—5).

For more than forty-five years, U.S. refugee policy has favored those fleeing communist countries. Yet within this ideological bias there is much diversity in how the American state responds to refugees. As a result, political migrants have a variety of relationships to U.S. foreign policy. These relationships range from saving "freedom fighters" from certain persecution (Hungarians in the 1950s), to "bleeding" enemy countries of their middle class to bring about economic ruin (Cubans in the 1960s), to honoring historic obligations and ensuring the good-will of remaining allies in a strategic reason (Indochinese in the 1970s). Indochinese refugees were the first allied aliens to arrive in the U.S. as the result of an American military defeat rather than an attempt by the U.S. to undermine an enemy state. Indeed, the defeat in Indochina dealt a major blow to the principle of communist containment that had guided post-World War Two American foreign policy. Coupled with new policies of detente toward China and the former Soviet Union, the admission of so many Indochinese refugees indicates that the American state is motivated more by historic obligation than political gain. Ironically, the Indochinese eventually became the largest population of refugees from communist countries in the U.S. only several years before the end of the Cold War in 1990.

Absence of Indochinese Communities

The absence of Indochinese communities in the U.S. prior to 1975 augmented the refugees' status as allied aliens because there was no ethnic identity to balance their political identity. Vietnamese, Laotians, and Cambodians engaged in international migration prior to

1975, but they formed settlements in France rather than the U.S. Some 80,000 Vietnamese, 5,000 Cambodians, and 5,000 Laotians lived in France when the refugees arrived in 1975. France's lengthy rule in Indochina accounts in part for this development. But even during the American suzerain, the migration continued in its old channel.

Vietnamese came to the U.S. for military training as early as 1961 (Herring 1986). Between 1955 and 1974, 18,500 Vietnamese entered the U.S. as immigrants, three quarters in the five years prior to the fall of Saigon, although some also returned to their homeland (Gordon 1987). By 1975 there were 13,747 Indochinese immigrants in the U.S., in addition to 4,342 Vietnamese with American citizenship. Of this total, 90 percent were the wives of American servicemen (Taft et al. 1980). By comparison, there were more than 8,000 Indochinese associated with foreign embassies (U.S. HR 1976). Thus prior to 1975, the Vietnamese migration to the U.S. was composed of diplomats or war brides (see Hayslip 1989 for an autobiographical account of one such marriage).

This historical absence of Vietnamese, Laotian, and Cambodian communities, and then the rapid migration of the refugees after 1975, proved unique in twentieth century American immigration history. Since World War Two, international migrants arriving in the U.S. have been received by fellow countrymen. In many cases the ethnic community in the U.S. ensured the migration in the first place. Political migrants fleeing Nazi dominated Europe before the war, as well as displaced persons following the war, were able to gain admission because ethnic associations completed financial vouchers in their favor (Dinnerstein 1982; Morse 1968; Wyman 1968). Even groups lacking the numbers of the Jewish, Polish, or Russian communities still had larger preexisting populations than the Indochinese. The 1950 U.S. Census counted 705,000 Hungarian-Americans six years before the arrival of Hungarian refugees (Taft et al. 1980). Over 220,000 Cubans immigrated to the U.S. between 1871 and the revolution in 1959, although many also returned to Cuba (Pérez 1986). But there were 30,000 Cubans in New York, and another 8,000 in Florida, when refugees from the Cuban Revolution began arriving. More importantly, in Miami "the nucleus of little Havana had already been established prior to the 1960s" (Boswell and Curtis 1984, p. 74). While all migrants initially arrive as foreigners, the absence of ethnic communities in the U.S. meant that the Indochinese arrived as complete strangers whose sole identity was that of the allied alien.

Not only was there little Indochinese migration to the U.S. prior to 1975, but Indochinese populations had only limited contact with institutions representative of American society despite two decades of

American intervention. French colonialism was a mixture of political, economic, and even cultural penetration. American communist containment was overwhelmingly a military exercise with the sole goal being military victory. American economic development projects were extensive during the mid-1950s, but they never reached their potential after 1960 because of the escalation of the war. While France tried to transform Indochina, America sought to prop up allied governments through force. U.S. penetration smashed existing culture through the mass importation of consumer goods, created rampant inflation through spending by military personnel, expanded the markets for prostitution and drugs, and made traditional Vietnamese corruption more profitable than ever (Karnow 1984; Sheehan 1988).

The one dimensional character of the American presence is particularly exemplified in the area of education. Despite U.S. hegemony in the region, Cambodia and Laos retained French language instruction in public schools and government. South Vietnam switched to English in 1962, eight years after gaining independence from France. For Vietnamese, Laotians, and Cambodians, France remained the cultural pole in the west even after the American intervention. For example, in 1974 there were 3,000 Cambodian students in Paris compared to 300 in the U.S. (Meunier 1974). If 90 percent of the 18,000 Indochinese in the U.S. prior to 1975 were the wives of American service men (Taft et al. 1980), then there were at most some 2,000 Indochinese students in the U.S. at that time. Even Australia had proportionately more Indochinese students than the U.S. (Viviani 1984).

The narrow focus of American penetration was also true in the area of business. Billions of dollars in U.S. government aid poured into South Vietnam during the 1960s and early 1970s, but there was virtually no private investment (Sullivan 1978). France remained the second largest importer of Vietnamese products, and French businesses supplied 35 percent of the ships that carried trade between the U.S. and Vietnam. In addition, French enterprises controlled 90 percent of rubber production, Vietnam's prime export commodity.

Finally, American settlement in Vietnam was far more tenuous than that of the French. In addition to economic contacts, there remained a small population of Frenchmen for whom Indochina was still home (Sullivan 1978). In 1963, there were 1,700 French citizens in Vietnam, and despite the increasing intensity of the war by 1970 there were 10,271 (some were undoubtedly ethnic Vietnamese). In 1970, there were only 6,217 Americans not associated with the military, and 72 percent of them where men. Conversely, only 53 percent of the French population in Vietnam was male, suggesting the presence of families and thus a more stable community.

The American population in Vietnam at any one time was quite small given the arrival of 164,500 civilians between 1965 and 1969 (National Institute of Statistics 1972). Arrivals even outnumbered departures in each year except for 1968, the year the Tet Offensive shocked Americans into reevaluating their belief that the war was being won. Given this large volume of nonmilitary American migrants to Vietnam, the fact that so few stayed more than a few months suggests a weaker attachment to the country than among the French population. France, rather than the U.S., remained the primary lure for those Indochinese tempted to migrate to the west. Moreover, Indochinese migrating to the U.S. after 1975 had little or no contact with institutions representative of American society.

Nativism and Historical Amnesia

The Indochinese refugee migration to the U.S. began just as three other currents of migration increased: immigrants, undocumented aliens, and asylum seekers. The waves of international migrants arriving at the same time blurred the historic uniqueness of the refugees for American citizens and they opposed the refugees' admission. Thus it was traditional nativism, rather than a negative association between the refugees and the Vietnam War, that put pressure on the government to close the door to the Indochinese. Only by magnifying the refugees' identity as allied aliens could the government justify their admission in the face of public opposition, further embedding the refugees' political status into the American state.

Negative Public Opinion

American citizens were deeply divided over the Vietnam War until the Tet Offensive in January of 1968 broke their confidence that the war could be won (Karnow 1984). In August of 1965, 61 percent of the public supported American military intervention, but by May of 1971, 61 percent were against it (Zinn 1980). Even after the Paris Peace Accord ended the war for the U.S. in January of 1973, a poll showed that 59 percent of Americans thought the U.S. bombing of Laos and Cambodia that spring would lead to U.S. troop involvement again (Gallup Poll 1978a). By March of 1975, 78 percent of the public was against the American government providing $522 million in military aid to South Vietnam (Gallup Poll 1978b).

As the South Vietnamese army began to crumble in April of 1975, the American public continued to oppose military aid and only favored

humanitarian aid by 55 percent to 40 percent (Gallup Poll 1978c).
Moreover, 47 percent responded negatively, and 43 percent positively,
to the question: "Do you favor using U.S. troops to evacuate 150,000 to
200,000 South Vietnamese who have worked with Americans?" And
by a margin of 54 percent to 36 percent, Americans opposed permitting
these former allies to resettle in the U.S. Indeed, even those
Americans who favored humanitarian aid for South Vietnam were
evenly divided in supporting admission of Vietnamese refugees to the
U.S.

Opposition to the arrival of Indochinese refugees coalesced in
communities where the refugees initially settled (Stern 1981). In the
spring of 1975, Governor Brown of California petitioned Congress to
assure that Vietnamese refugees would not take jobs from Americans.
Officials in Seattle defeated a resolution welcoming the refugees.
Resentment was particularly pronounced among Americans near the
four military camps where the first Vietnamese were temporarily
housed. Fort Chaffee, Arkansas, was one site and residents of an
adjacent town actually picketed the compound to protest the location
of Vietnamese refugees in the vicinity.

It is plausible that the bitter legacy of the Vietnam War left
Americans with a negative disposition toward Indochinese refugees. If
true, then negative or positive attitudes toward the war should
correspond with negative or positive attitudes toward the refugees,
respectively. Yet a 1980 survey found that respondents who labeled
themselves "conservative" exhibited far higher antipathy toward
the Indochinese than "moderates" or "liberals" (Starr and Roberts
1982). Only 25 percent of conservatives, 33 percent of moderates, and 40
percent of liberals agreed with the statement: "As a people,
Americans should feel obligated to help refugees from Indochina." Yet
the three political perspectives only differed by five percentage
points in their current approval for U.S. military intervention in
Southeast Asia. This minor variation suggests that there is "no simple
relationship between political viewpoint, pro- and anti-war
sentiments and reactions to refugees" (Starr and Roberts 1982, p. 178).

Other surveys also found that self-labeled Republicans, Democrats,
and Independents did not differ greatly in favoring or opposing
admission of Indochinese refugees (Gallup Opinion Index 1975, 1979). A
study of church members who sponsored Vietnamese refugees concluded
that although most had supported the American military presence in
Vietnam, the war itself was not an important reason behind their
motivation to help the refugees (Fein 1987). What distinguished these
Americans from their compatriots was religious conviction,
humanitarian ideals, and membership in the college educated middle-

class, which tends to be more liberal on immigration issues. Americans' negative attitudes toward the Indochinese appear to stem more from nativism against foreigners in general, and racism toward Asians in particular, than from the legacy of the Vietnam War (Roberts 1988; Starr and Roberts 1981; U.S. CCR 1987).

Indochinese refugees did not receive a hero's welcome in 1975, and restrictionist attitudes among Americans actually increased in the next several years. Fifty-two percent of the public opposed taking the refugees in 1975, and 57 percent opposed the policy in 1979. Another poll conducted in the summer of 1979 found that 62 percent of those surveyed disapproved of President Carter's plan to admit 14,000 Indochinese refugees a month (New York Times 1979); other surveys also found opposition in excess of 60 percent (Niehaus 1979). Table 2.3 indicates that between 1975 and 1979, support for the refugees became more diffuse, and therefore of less utility to the refugees. Social and economic indicators that predict attitudes toward immigrants in general, such as city size and level of income, increasingly came to determine Americans' views of the Indochinese refugee migration.

Government officials believed that economic problems caused nativism toward the refugees (Donelly 1982). Between 1975 and 1979, unemployment and inflation began to rise, and the public perceived declining economic prospects (Stern 1981). Opposition to the admission of the refugees should thus rise from 1975 to 1979. In fact, the data in the Table 2.3 show that economic crisis had only a weak affect on restrictionist attitudes. Rising unemployment primarily affected the fears of the nonwhite, the low-income, and midwestern and southern residents. Yet nation wide the "opposed" rate only increased by five percent, of which one percent came from those previously undecided. Thus while flare ups between American minorities, regional ethnic groups, and Indochinese migrants could have been expected, overall economic decline did not dramatically increase hostility toward the refugees.

Neither the legacy of the Vietnam War nor economic conditions were directly responsible for the public's negative attitudes toward Indochinese refugees. More significant was the timing of the refugees' arrival; they began arriving just as nativist and anti-foreign sentiments increased in response to a rising number of immigrants. Changes in American immigration law in 1965 provided the opportunity for Asians, Latin Americans, and Southern and Eastern Europeans to more easily obtain visas (Reimers 1985). The law abolished the quota system for allocating visas and substituted family ties and, to a lesser degree, job skills as the criteria. The American public supported this liberalization, but the large numbers of arrivals

Table 2.3. American Public Opinion Towards Indochinese Refugees in 1975 and 1979 (in percent).

	Favor Admission to the U.S.		Oppose Admission to the U.S.	
	1975	1979	1975	1979
National Average	36	32	52	57
Race				
White	36	33	53	57
Nonwhite	39	25	43	56
Education				
College	46	42	45	49
High School	35	28	55	61
Grade School	28	27	52	60
Income				
$20,000 and over	37	39	52	52
$15,000-$19,999	39	30	53	64
$10,000-$14,999	38	29	51	61
$ 7,000-$ 9,999	43	24	45	63
$ 5,000-$ 6,999	30	29	58	55
$ 3,000-$ 4,999	33	29	50	55
Under $3,000	31	32	52	54
Occupation				
Professional and Business	44	45	45	47
Clerical and Sales	46	39	46	49
Manual Workers	36	25	52	65
Not in Labor Force	24	30	62	58
City Size				
1,000,000 and over	33	37	53	55
500,000-999,999	37	39	53	48
50,000-499,999	40	31	49	57
2,500-49,999	37	33	55	59
Under 2,500, Rural	35	26	51	63
Region				
East	41	39	46	50
Midwest	32	28	56	64
South	35	30	50	57
West	39	32	55	59

Source : Gallup Opinion Index 1975, 1979.

began to generate restrictionist attitudes (Simon 1985). In 1977, a poll found that 42 percent of the public favored decreasing immigration; only 33 percent held this view in 1965 (Gallup Poll 1978d).

The 1965 reforms also led to a dramatic shift in the sources of immigration because comparatively few Europeans took advantage of the new law. Europe sent 38 percent of all immigrants to the U.S. in

1965. But by 1977, 75 percent of immigrants came from Asia, Latin America and the Caribbean. The change in the composition of immigration to the U.S. was unanticipated and contributed to a restrictionist backlash among Americans. By the early 1980s, polls showed that two-thirds of the American public thought legal immigration should be curtailed, and Hispanic and Asian migrants were specifically targeted as being too numerous (Harwood 1986).

Increased illegal migration paralleled this legal flow (Passel 1986). By 1980, there were approximately two million undocumented aliens living in the U.S., and nearly half had arrived during the previous five years. These migrants came primarily from Latin America and the Caribbean (77 percent), but Mexico supplied 55 percent of the total with no other country surpassing 5 percent. Comprehensive legislation to prevent the migration and hiring of illegal aliens languished in Congress for four years until finally passed as the Immigration Control and Reform Act of 1986. While the government was slow to act, public opinion quickly demanded an end to perceived economic competition from illegal migrants. Beginning in 1977, surveys showed that "the American public consistently expresses overwhelming opposition to illegal immigration along with calls for strengthened enforcement actions by the government to stop the influx" (Harwood 1986, p. 205).

The flow of migrants coming to the U.S. for family and economic motives was compounded by a tidal wave of asylum seekers heading toward American shores from the Caribbean and Latin America (Huyck and Bouvier 1983). Socialist revolution and counter revolution in Nicaragua beginning in 1979, and death squads in El Salvador and Guatemala in the early 1980s, combined with underdevelopment to spur migration to the U.S. By the mid-1980s, approximately 10 percent of El Salvador's population was living in the U.S. and between 1983 and 1986, El Salvadorans submitted 25 percent of all asylum applications received by the Immigration and Naturalization Service (Zucker and Zucker 1987). In 1980, 125,000 Cubans came directly to the U.S. during the Mariel Boat Lift; by 1981 some 45,000 Haitians had also arrived by boat and that year the Coast Guard implemented the Haitian Migrant Interdiction Operation. Like the migration of undocumented workers from Mexico, the Cuban and Haitian migrations raised Americans' fears about the sovereignty of the country's borders. A 1980 poll found that 66 percent of the American public favored halting the admission of political refugees, while only 26 percent favored continuation of admissions (Gallup Poll 1981). For most Americans, traditional nativism overshadowed the historic origins of the Indochinese refugee migration to the U.S.

Ambivalence Among Politicians

The Vietnam War divided members of the American government as much as it divided American citizens. The first consequence of this division was a hesitancy among Congressmen who had long opposed the war to support the rescue of allied aliens in South Vietnam in April of 1975. But as more refugees began arriving, America's history in Southeast Asia quickly diminished as a factor shaping politicians' attitudes. Instead, political contentions centered on federal payment for resettlement costs and the ability of Congress to curb the presidential tendency to admit large numbers of refugees. In the long run, members of Congress were influenced by nativism to the same extent as their constituents.

The Executive Office proved to be the foundation of support for Indochinese refugees. President Ford authorized the admission of 140,000 refugees, and President Carter ensured the arrival of over 200,000 more. Almost all of the 360,000 Indochinese refugees admitted to the U.S. prior to mid-1980 (when new legislation was enacted) came under the parole authority of the Attorney General acting on orders from the White House. Altogether, ten separate parole programs were created during this period (U.S. CRS 1980). Each was an ad hoc quota to admit a certain nationality group based on a particular affiliation with the U.S. For example, in 1976 one parole program was created for 3,500 former military allies in Laos; in 1977 a special admissions quota of 2,000 was established for Vietnamese boat people on humanitarian grounds. In 1979, Carter doubled the monthly quota from 7,000 to 14,000, thus necessitating a new parole program (U.S. ORR 1988). That year Carter also ordered the U.S. Seventh Fleet, which patrols the South China Sea, on special alert with orders to rescue Vietnamese boat people (Niehaus 1979). In each case, the president decided that the country had an historic obligation toward refugees in Southeast Asia.

One reason American presidents took such forceful action was the support they received from newspaper editors, union and civil rights leaders, and human rights activists. In contrast to reactions at the grass roots, American elites exhibited a very liberal response to Indochinese refugees. In May of 1975, nearly fifty nonprofit organizations petitioned the Senate to provide generous assistance to the refugees (U.S. Senate 1975b). Newspapers and news weeklies were among the refugees strongest supporters (Simon 1985). During the 1970s, the *New York Times* devoted four out of nine editorials on immigration to championing the case for admission of Indochinese refugees. This support among secular newspapers was mirrored among newspapers with a religious orientation, such as *Commonweal*, a leading Catholic newspaper, and *Christian Century*, a Protestant newspaper. The news weeklies like *Newsweek* and *Time* published reports on America's obligation to aid refugees in Southeast Asia along side articles arguing that illegal immigration should be curtailed.

Another factor behind executive branch support was the Citizens' Commission on Indochinese Refugees, a private lobby group formed in 1977. The initial impetus for the commission came from Foreign Service officers who had worked in Indochina, were now in the State Department, and felt that American allied aliens should not be forgotten. However, the Commission was organized by directors of the voluntary agencies which had aided refugees in the past, and they recruited other influential Americans. Their efforts had decisive results:

> the Commission was able to dispel fears that the trade union movement, minorities, and civic groups would not react with generosity, compassion, and sympathy to Indochinese refugees because of economic and social concerns. The Citizens Commission secured support from numerous national organizations, including labor unions, ethnic associations, religious groups, and a wide range of other organizations (Loescher and Scanlan 1986, p. 133).

While the White House and political elites were unequivocal backers of Indochinese refugees, congressional support was far from unanimous. Table 2.4 provides the legislative record of congressional activity related to Indochinese refugees from 1975 to 1980. As evidenced by the votes on bills and conference reports, the Senate backed Indochinese refugees almost as much as the president. However, the House of Representatives proved to be a difficult constituency from which to win support for Indochinese allied aliens.

In the last week of April, 1975, President Ford asked the Congress for authorization to use the American military to evacuate South Vietnamese with close ties to the U.S. On April 29, Ford ordered seventy military helicopters and 865 marines to rescue 1,400 American citizens and 5,500 South Vietnamese, despite the fact that the legislation had not been passed (Fanning 1976). Two days later, the House voted against endorsing the President's action by a margin of eighty-four "nays" (Haley 1982). For some congressmen, voting nay was the parting shot of the Vietnam War era, a way of once more voicing opposition to American military involvement in the region. Other congressmen declined to give Operation Frequent Wind, the code name for the evacuation, their support lest it establish a precedent

Table 2.4. U.S. Congressional Action on the Evacuation, Admission, and Resettlement of Indochinese Refugees, 1975-1980 (in "yea"-"nay" votes).

Legislation	House	Senate
Use U.S. Troops to Evacuate Americans and Foreign Nationals From South Vietnam		
Bill:	230-187	75-17
Conference Report:	162-246	46-17
Authorize Money for Resettlement Programs for Indochinese Refugees		
Bill:	381-31	77-2
Conference Report:	No Objection	No Objection
Reimburse Local Schools for Costs Due to Indochinese Refugees		
Bill:	311-75	Voice Vote in Favor
Conference Report:	No Objection	No Objection
Increase Admission and Permanently Fund Resettlement of Refugees		
Bill:	328-47	85-0
Conference Report:	207-192	Voice Vote in Favor

Source : Congressional Quarterly 1976, 1977, 1980, 1981.

upon which future presidents could justify using the U.S. military to accomplish their own foreign policy objectives. Altogether, 60 percent of the House voted against the final legislation on the evacuation, a level of opposition significantly higher than among the American public (47 percent).

In this context, congressmen seeking support for the refugees had to invoke American immigration history, rather than the refugees' identity as allied aliens. The Senate passed a resolution "to welcome the latest exiles to our shores—the refugees from South Vietnam and Cambodia" (U.S. S 1975b, p. 14,842). In the House, advocates of the Indochina Migration and Refugee Assistance Act claimed that voting against "the funds needed for an orderly integration of the refugees into our society [would] in effect, be turning our backs on our heritage" (U.S. HR 1975b, p. 14,350). One congressman observed that the number of Vietnamese refugees expected to settle in the U.S. "only" equaled all the immigrants from South and East Asia the preceding year.

Yet in likening the refugees to the other immigrants, members of

Congress had already begun to focus more on migration issues than on the historic origins of the refugee crisis in Southeast Asia. During debate on the Indochina Migration and Refugee Assistance legislation, a congressman voiced a common belief when he stated that: "a large number [of the refugees] may wish to emigrate to France or French-speaking lands because of the strong French cultural heritage in their homelands" (U.S. HR 1975b, p. 14,355). The State Department argued that the comparatively large population of Vietnamese in France would attract some of the Vietnamese now in the U.S. It also counseled that refugees might relocate to former French colonies in West Africa (U.S. HR 1976).

Sentiment was so strong in favor of relocating Vietnamese refugees already in the country that senators talked of paying for the transportation of those refugees who wished to emigrate (U.S. S 1975b). The director of the InterAgency Task Force on Indochina even advocated paying countries that took the refugees the same sum allocated to American voluntary agencies which resettled refugees in the U.S. (U.S. HR 1976). In fact, the IATF used the U.N. High Commissioner for Refugees to solicit resettlement offers from countries in Western Europe and South America. Nearly 5,000 Vietnamese refugees in the U.S. were eventually relocated to third countries, primarily Canada and France. Some in Congress had hoped that as many as 20,000 refugees might take this route and negotiations commenced with dozens of countries around the world; offers even came from prerevolutionary Iran and Nicaragua. Had countries other than Canada and France shown an interest in receiving Vietnamese refugees, and had the refugees themselves felt greater attachment to these other nations, American officials would have eagerly transported them from the U.S. Thus as early as 1975, some politicians could overlook Indochinese refugees' status as allied aliens. Overtime, many in Congress came to view the refugees as just another type of immigrant, facilitating restrictionist sentiments among the American public.

But because President Ford had assured the arrival of 129,000 Vietnamese and 1,000 Cambodians, Congress had little reason to withhold funds for their resettlement. American citizens worried about the economic impact of the refugees, and local government was concerned with funding the social welfare expenses the refugees were likely to generate (Taft et al. 1980). Thus there was little controversy in passing legislation to reimburse voluntary agencies and local government for the several years of expenses to be incurred (initial legislation guaranteed funding through mid-1977). However, the legislation which would eventually become the Refugee Act of 1980 was more complicated because it included changes in both refugee resettlement assistance and admissions. The House was able to adopt the conference report by only fifteen votes.

Activity in the House deserves closer attention because of the controversy the refugees generated. Table 2.5 presents the votes by political party and region of the country against legislation affecting Indochinese refugees. The table also distinguishes the two dimensions of the legislation which eventually passed as the Refugee Act of 1980: admission to the U.S. and resettlement assistance after arrival. With respect to the evacuation in 1975, it was clearly northern Democrats who opposed using the U.S. military to save allied aliens. At this time, attitudes toward the war were associated with initial attitudes toward the refugees among elected officials, although not among their constituents. But resettlement assistance for the 1975 wave of Indochinese refugees was not particularly divisive for the House, and representatives do not differ greatly by party or region. Similarly, the 1979 legislation on the admission and resettlement of refugees contained an amendment allowing the House or the Senate to veto the president's annual refugee admission quota. With this safety valve, the 1979 bill was not controversial.

Table 2.5. Percent "Nay" Votes in the U.S. House of Representatives on the Evacuation, Admission, and Resettlement of Indochinese Refugees.

Legislation	Total	Republicans	Democrats	Northern Democrats	Southern Democrats
Evacuation in 1975:	52	42	65	72	49
Resettlement in 1975-1976:	13	23	16	11	24
Admission and Resettlement in 1979:*	13	23	6	2	17
Admission and Resettlement in 1980:**	48	76	31	18	61

* With amendment providing for House or Senate veto of annual refugee admission requested by the President in excess of the normal flow.
** Without amendment providing for House or Senate veto of annual refugee admission requested by the President in excess of the normal flow.

Source : Congressional Quarterly 1976, 1977, 1980, 1981.

When members of the House dropped the veto provision while preparing a conference report with members of the Senate, the entire package was thrown into jeopardy. Despite the fact that democrats comprised 62 percent of the House and President Carter had vigorously backed the bill for over a year, restrictionist sentiments nearly led to the legislation's defeat. Thus by 1980, politicians' responses to Indochinese refugees were shaped by factors affecting attitudes toward immigration in general, such as region of the country, rather than the politics of the Vietnam War (see Yarnold 1990 for a sophisticated statistical analysis showing the importance of political party and region on these votes). The fact that the refugees were American allied aliens did little to offset American nativism in a period of high immigration.

Conclusion

Indochinese refugees arrive to the U.S. because military and political defeats in Vietnam, Laos, and Cambodia transformed the populations of these countries into allied aliens. American efforts to replace the French presence in Indochina began with nation-building projects during the 1950s. In the 1960s, the U.S. turned to military force to prop up pro-American regimes until they fell in 1975. Since then, over 650,000 Vietnamese, 200,000 Laotian, and 150,000 Cambodian refugees have migrated to the U.S.

Three contextual factors reshape the meaning of this allied alien identity after the refugees reach the U.S.: the novelty of refugees from a lost war, massive arrivals without ethnic communities, and nativist sentiments. These factors are the historical components of the American mode of incorporation, and nativism proved the most powerful. Refugee advocates come from the human rights lobby, the Senate, and the Executive Office, but the American public and the House of Representatives have restrictionist sentiments. An ailing economy and bitterness over the Vietnam War are not the most important causes of these negative attitudes toward the refugees. Instead, increased immigration in general, and the non-European origins of these migrants, led to a resurgence of nativism. The result is historical amnesia. Key elites are able to use historical symbols to sustain the refugees' admission to the U.S. But nativism halts history at the American border, isolating international from domestic events, and past from present.

The ability of nativism to fragment the host society's response to these international migrants is surprising given the refugees' unambiguous symbolism. They are the first allied aliens to arrive as the result of a lost war. Unlike the Cuban refugees during the 1960s, the Indochinese are already an allied population because their migration stems from an American defeat. The admission of Cubans was an American ploy to topple a new socialist government through a variety of means: recruiting Cuban exiles for military operations; draining Cuba of its middle class and skilled workers; and discrediting the Cuban revolution by having Cubans "vote with their feet." American responsibility for the "fall of Havana" was never a key factor behind U.S. refugee policy towards Cuba, as American accountability for the "fall of Saigon" is for policy on Indochinese refugees.

The nature of American intervention in former Indochina is a second factor that might have mitigated the affect of nativism. Unlike French colonization, which had economic and cultural elements, the U.S. presence was overwhelmingly military. Even during the height of American involvement, there were comparatively few American civilians in Vietnam. In Laos and Cambodia, which retained French as the language of government and higher education, the American presence was limited to embassies and bombers. The arriving refugees' political and military relationship to the American state should have been unambiguous for the public and elected officials.

Finally, the absence of ethnic communities during the peak years of the migration might have heightened the refugees' political identity. Within five years of the last American bombing run in Southeast Asia, 475,000 refugees from Vietnam, Laos, and Cambodia arrived in the U.S. The rapidity of the migration meant that the American public and government knew that the refugees arrived as a result of military defeat. Without an ethnic history, the refugees' only symbolism for Americans and their government had to be that of political migrants fleeing countries that Washington has promised to support.

Despite the presence of factors which should have amplified and perpetuated the refugees' historic identity as allied aliens, nativism barred such external influences from the past and outside American borders. This left two domestic institutions to determine the incorporation of the refugees: the welfare state and the nation-state.

3

From Political Migrants to
Clients of the Welfare State

Citizenship has long been synonymous with nationality. The convergence of international migration with the welfare state since 1945 has added a second meaning: access to the social welfare system. Sustained immigration has forced western states to invent new combinations of rights for a range of migrants who are neither aliens nor full members of the host society. Such "social citizenship" is often determined by bilateral or international treaties, but the historical context of the migration also contributes. In the case of Indochinese refugees, the American state creates a form of citizenship to match their status as allied aliens. As a result, the social welfare system translates the refugees' political identity into rights and resources to promote their adaptation.

Yet the structure of the American welfare state constrains refugee advocates, profoundly influencing the refugees' new social citizenship. Two features of the social welfare system are particularly significant. First, the central government has a limited role in providing aid at the local level. Conversely, in Western European countries like France, the state assumes a prominent role. Second, American eligibility rules are restrictive and limit the provision of aid. In France, rules are encompassing and require citizens to meet many needs through public programs. Ultimately, federalism and anti-welfare attitudes determine the incorporation of Indochinese refugees into American society more than the historical context of their migration.

Managing Migration with the Welfare State

Constructing social citizenship for Indochinese refugees means giving them a distinct status in the American welfare state. The Indochina Migration and Refugee Assistance Act of 1975 provided for special one-time funding for refugees from Indochina, particularly the reimbursement to the states for the cost of the refugees' cash and medical assistance (U.S. SL 1975). Reauthorization of the Act in 1977 allowed Indochinese refugees to become permanent residents, added some new forms of domestic assistance, and, most significantly, continued federal funding (U.S. SL 1977). The Indochinese Refugee Children Assistance Act of 1976 reimbursed states at a higher level for the cost of refugee children's education and special language instruction, and authorized funds for the education of adult refugees (U.S. SL 1976). These initiatives eventually culminated in the Refugee Act of 1980, the first piece of legislation to codify the obligation of the federal government to assist recognized political migrants. Thus by 1980, "refugee" was a special status in the social welfare system, largely due to the arrival of Indochinese refugees.

Using the welfare state to manage the resettlement of allied aliens fused bureaucracies involved in foreign policy, international migration, and social welfare. This hybridization began in the mainland reception camps which housed the first Vietnamese refugees to arrive in 1975. Under the auspices of the Interagency Task Force for Indochina Refugees (IATF), the Departments of Defense, Labor, Justice, State, and Health, Education and Welfare all provided services to resettle the refugees. The IATF aptly describes this meeting of international migration and the welfare state: "Military officers . . . became concerned with profound human and social questions; HEW officials worried about Naval and Air Force transportation problems; Labor Department officials did consular work and Foreign Service Officers worked as employment agents" (U.S. IATF 1976, p. 614).

Other unusual relationships developed among organizations as the pace of resettlement increased. While operating in the camps, the State Department provided $400,000 to the Salvation Army, $3 million to the Immigration and Naturalization Service, and $46 million to the Department of Health, Education, and Welfare (U.S. IATF 1976). The Social Security Administration connected U.S. foreign policy to social welfare assistance when a commissioner justified continued aid to Indochinese refugees on the grounds that "we have certain obligations . . . because of the war, and because they are now new residents, to at least make this one-time attempt to give them a shot at being in the middle class, in the mainstream" (U.S. HR 1977b, p. 78). And the Commissioner of the Immigration and Naturalization Service turned his attention from visas and border patrols to pronounce that "the vast majority of Indochina refugees will prove to be . . . resourceful and will free themselves of the need for public assistance" (U.S. HR 1977a, p. 96). Such jurisdictional trespassing reveals how federal officials created a new form of social citizenship for Indochinese refugees, one which linked international migration with the welfare state.

Changes in the organization of the resettlement program provide additional evidence of the rapidity with which allied aliens from Indochina acquired rights and resources. The first director of the IATF, who came from the Department of State, testified in May that: "Resettlement is not really the proper role to be played by the [National Security Council] complex. It should be moved to a domestic agency" (U.S. HR 1976, p. 204). That same month, an official from the Department of Health, Education, and Welfare was appointed director of the Task Force. When the last reception camp closed, HEW organized a Refugee Assistance Task Force. In September of 1976, the Task Force was transferred to the Social and Rehabilitation Services, the social services branch of HEW that aids senior citizens, the handicapped, and Native Americans. The following year, the refugee program was relocated to the Office of Family Assistance in the Social Security Administration, which operates income maintenance programs (U.S. DHEW 1978). Each organizational move brought Indochinese refugees closer to the core of the American welfare state and further from their roots in failed U.S. foreign policy. The American state was so successful in creating a separate social welfare status for the refugees that when the Social Security Administration presented its proposed budget to Congress in 1979, the Indochinese Refugee Program was itemized separately along with Aid to Families with Dependent Children, Supplemental Security Income, and the Black Lung Benefit Program (U.S. HR 1979b). Four years after the fall of Saigon, Indochinese refugees clearly had a unique form of social citizenship.

The Refugee Act of 1980 institutionalized this link between a status in the hierarchy of international migration and a status in the welfare state. The Act established an Office of Refugee Resettlement (hereafter ORR) in the Department of Health and Human Services. The ORR funds public and private organizations to provide social services to refugees, and reimburses state governments for refugees' use of cash and medical assistance. To receive reimbursement, each state must submit a refugee resettlement plan, designate a state agency to administer the plan, and appoint a state refugee coordinator. By mandating that state governments organize refugee offices and develop resettlement policies, the federal government ensured that "refugee" now means both a form of political migration and a type of social citizenship. As stated in the Refugee Act of 1980:

The objectives of this Act are to provide a permanent and systematic procedure for the admission to this country of refugees of special humanitarian concern to the United States, and to provide comprehensive and uniform provisions for the effective resettlement and absorption of those refugees who are admitted (U.S. SL 1980, np).

A range of fiscal and administrative considerations shaped the domestic provisions of the Refugee Act. The Secretary of HEW reported that he needed a central office for refugee resettlement given the size of federal assistance to refugees, which totaled $2 billion since 1962 (U.S. HR 1979a). In addition, the existence of a special Indochinese program, along side the persistent program for the Cubans and a new program for Soviet Jews, led welfare state officials to question the wisdom of having ethnically specific forms of assistance (U.S. S 1979a). The House of Representatives sought more control over refugee resettlement by insisting that the ORR not be located in the executive office (U.S. HR 1979e). But despite these considerations, Congress developed the resettlement provisions of the Act to manage the adjustment of Indochinese refugees.

Congressional hearings and debates over the resettlement procedures overwhelmingly concerned the adjustment needs and public assistance rates of the 250,000 Indochinese refugees who had arrived in the preceding five years. In addition, the Act phased out the Cuban resettlement program, thus severing the federal government's responsibility for a refugee population that (in 1980) outnumbered the Indochinese population. Moreover, President Carter did not use the provisions of the new legislation to resettle the "Mariel Boat Lift" Cubans who arrived three weeks after he signed the act. Soviet Jews were the only other significant population of political migrants arriving to the U.S. at the time, and the Refugee Act continued a separate form of assistance developed in the late 1970s. The social welfare programs created by the Refugee Act of 1980—especially a new form of public assistance—were designed for Indochinese refugees.

The Benefit of Social Citizenship:
Lenient Criteria for Public Assistance

Federal officials use the American social welfare system to translate Indochinese refugees' status as allied aliens into resources of use in their adaptation. Since 1975, the most important resource has been public assistance. Most newly arrived refugees experience a period of unemployment. Generous public assistance policies diminish their poverty and allow them to take publicly funded language and employment training programs. The Indochina Migration and Assistance Act of 1975 required refugees to meet the economic eligibility criteria of Aid to Families with Dependent Children, but exempted them from the family composition requirements for two years (U.S. DHEW 1975). This provision allowed refugee mothers with husbands to receive aid in those states which normally restrict aid to single parents, and also enabled married couples to receive aid for families even when they did not have children. To incorporate Indochinese refugees, American welfare officials created a form of income support absent from the existing social welfare system.

The refugees' special status in the public aid system is temporary, but it represents a significant extension of social rights to a migrant population. Officials from public aid departments estimated that 40 percent of the Indochinese refugees receiving cash assistance in California would be ineligible if they had to apply under normal criteria. In Oregon the proportion was 62 percent, and in Texas it was 79 percent. The Department of Health, Education, and Welfare calculated that 45 percent of all the refugees in the country would lose their benefits if the federal government ended the refugees' unique status in the social welfare system (U.S. HR 1977b). As summarized by the Refugee Task Force: "Many Indo-Chinese refugees currently receiving public assistance would not be eligible if they were United States citizens" (U.S. IATF 1976, p. 661).

Welfare bureaucracies disliked the refugees' special assistance status, but they recognized its necessity given the structural inadequacies of the American welfare state. Although not known for social welfare innovation, the Department of Health, Education, and Welfare noted the difficulty of aiding intact families among the working poor. It concluded "that the long-range solution depends on a substantial reform of the welfare system that couples aid to needy persons, regardless of age or family characteristics, with strong self-support efforts and incentive" (U.S. HR 1977b, pp. 161—62). Congress also realized that assisting Indochinese refugees revealed the deficiencies of the American public assistance system. Members of the House of Representatives observed that only seventeen states had general assistance programs. Without new federal legislation in 1977, Indochinese refugees in the other states would be "without access to supplemental cash assistance, the very type of assistance that those working, but underemployed refugees need to supplement their present low incomes" (U.S. HR 1977c, p. 34,088).

Reauthorization of the Indochina Migration and Refugee Assistance Act in 1977 disclosed another right extended to the refugees; it allowed them to become permanent residents although they had been admitted as parolees. In eliminating this barrier to full citizenship the Congress exempted the refugees from criteria that immigrants have to meet, particularly two rules established in 1917 as the first effort at immigration restriction and which have never been removed. These amendments to the Immigration and Nationality Act enable immigration officials to exclude from admission to the United States immigrants "likely to become public charges" and who "cannot read and understand some language or dialect" (U.S. Code 1983, pp. 982—83). Although the literacy requirement did not pose a problem for most Indochinese refugees in the U.S. at the time, the public charge provision would have been a significant barrier had it not been waved. Officials from the Immigration and Naturalization Service testified that one-third of the Indochinese refugees in the country would be ineligible to become permanent residents under the rules normally applied to immigrants (U.S. HR 1977a). To resettle allied aliens from Indochina, the American state invented a new form of social citizenship to match the refugees' value as political migrants.

The Refugee Act of 1980 formalized refugees' exemption from the family composition requirements of public assistance by creating Refugee Cash Assistance. The law also required the federal government to pay 100 percent of these costs for a refugees' first three years in the country. Like natives, refugees receiving cash assistance must register with an agency that provides employment services. However, for refugees these agencies include nonprofit organizations which receive federal funds to teach English or job skills. By registering with these organizations, refugees do not have to submit to local public aid bureaus, which are less sympathetic to their adjustment needs. Moreover, the Refugee Act exempted refugees from any work registration requirements for their first three months in the country. In addition, the Act allowed the ORR to provide medical assistance to refugees who did not qualify for such aid under local income requirements for assistance, thus instituting a reform of the public assistance system for the Indochinese, but not for natives. Federalism and restrictive eligibility rules forced government officials to invent new programs as they constructed social citizenship for the refugees.

When the Refugee Act came up for reauthorization in 1982, Congress added several amendments to curtail refugees' access to social welfare resources (U.S. HR 1982b; U.S. S 1982). The amendments rescinded the sixty day waiver for registration with an employment agency, and barred refugees who were full-time college students from receiving cash assistance. Furthermore, the Act stated that refugees who refused a job offer should have their assistance terminated. Counties with high rates of public assistance among refugees also tended to have large numbers of refugees, and the amendments authorized the ORR to limit resettlement in these areas. Finally, several weeks prior to passage of the Act, the ORR reduced from thirty-six to eighteen months the period in which refugees were exempt from the family composition requirements of public aid.

But despite these more restrictive policies, refugees are still temporarily exempt from the family composition criteria of public assistance and the ORR reimburses the states for all forms of cash assistance for a period of time (by 1992, the reimbursement period had been reduced to eight months for Refugee Cash Assistance and zero months for AFDC). Thus, for a period of time, the refugees are the wards of the federal government but are assisted by local government. This paradox results from how the federalist structure of the American welfare state responds to the arrival of allied aliens from Indochina.

Federalism Constrains Social Citizenship

In the U.S., the federalist system of government allows the states significant autonomy in making social policy (Leman 1980). As a result, there is much divergence among regions of the country. Historically, southern states opposed passage of the Social Security Act in order to maintain a racially split labor market (Quadango 1984). On the other hand, fiscal strength and sufficient bureaucratization allowed states like Wisconsin and New York to be social welfare innovators regardless of developments at the national level (Amenta and Curruthers 1988). Under these conditions, the central government intervened only sporadically. Thus the American welfare state originated from a "big bang" in the form of the Social Security Act of 1935 (Leman 1977).

Nonetheless, the Social Security Act embodied federalist social welfare principles. The Act became the framework for all subsequent social welfare programs and insured that conflict between local, state, and national government would continue (Patterson 1986; Skocpol and Ikenberry 1983). Only old age insurance became a national program and it is based on worker and employer contributions. For noncontributory programs, such as Aid to Families with Dependent Children (AFDC) and General Assistance, the federal government provides a minimum level of payment, and matching funds up to a ceiling for the remainder of the payments made by state and county governments. State governments determine eligibility requirements and benefit levels within national guidelines.

Federalism posed the greatest barrier to the American state's use of the social welfare system to create a new form of citizenship for arriving allied aliens. Only by taking full fiscal responsibility for the refugees can the state ensure that other levels of government will carry out the reception plans made in Washington. The public's negative sentiments toward the refugees already put these plans in jeopardy. State and local government's autonomy in the realm of social welfare policy further curtailed the ability of refugee advocates to provide special rights and resources to Indochinese refugees.

Refugee advocates resolved this conflict by creating a new status in the public aid system—the refugee—and a new form of federal aid: Refugee Cash Assistance. These policy innovations temporarily allow the state to assist the Indochinese nationwide and to circumvent the diversity of regional welfare policies. During the 1980s, three-quarters of ORR's annual budget funded state governments' provision of cash assistance, medical assistance, and social services to refugees. Between 1980 and 1990, the ORR spent over $3 billion to cover the public assistance costs of all arriving refugees (66 percent came from Vietnam, Laos, and Cambodia). Federalist politics in combination with the refugees' status as allied aliens led to a more centralized social welfare program than is typically produced by the American welfare state.

But federalism also places Indochinese refugees in the center of an intense, historical conflict between federal and state government over the payment of welfare costs. Public assistance expenditures on refugees reflect existing benefit levels, and the presence or absence of Aid to Families with Dependent Children—Unemployed Parent at the state level, and General Assistance at the county level (Berkeley Planning Associates 1982a). Easing public aid eligibility rules allows a larger proportion of arriving refugees in all states to go on the welfare rolls. Although there is no cost to states during the federal reimbursement period, once this period ends the refugees become their responsibility. It is at this point that the federalist politics of the American welfare state shape the boundaries of Indochinese refugees' social citizenship.

Conflict between the central government and the states over the supply of resources to Indochinese refugees began within days of their arrival in 1975. The director of the IATF wrote all fifty governors to assure them that "State and local authorities will suffer no direct fiscal hardship and little indirect hardship from the influx" (U.S. HR 1975a, p. 13). The concentration of Cuban refugees in Florida spurred fears in Congress that some states might also develop a large population of refugees from Vietnam. Indeed, Congress did not use the

Cuban refugee program to resettle Indochinese refugees because the Migration and Refugee Assistance Act of 1962 stipulated that federal support was only for states with large numbers of refugees. According to one congressman, the resettlement of Indochinese refugees "was to be different than the resettlement of the Cuban refugees because you get to the problem of equitable redistribution of these refugees" (U.S. HR 1976, p. 366). Dispersing Indochinese refugees among many states did more evenly distribute resettlement costs, but it also ensured that conflict between federal and state government would not be confined to a single state, as with the Cubans in Florida.

The problem of managing international migration with a federalist social welfare system reemerged in 1977 during the debate on the reauthorization of the Indochina Migration and Refugee Assistance Act. Noting the increased taxes residents of California would have to pay should federal reimbursement to the states end, a senator stated: "The Indochina refugees are essentially a Federal responsibility. . . . Until the impact of the arrival of the Indochina refugees has been absorbed, the cost of assisting them should be borne largely by the Federal government" (U.S. S 1977, p. 33,067). When other Indochinese refugees followed the first wave Congress pointed to the assistance for the 1975 cohort as a precedent. In 1977, one congressman observed that an additional 15,000 refugees were slated for admission and the "Federal government cannot deny assistance to these refugees who will be arriving over the coming year" (U.S. HR 1977d, p. 34,089).

Demands for federal payments were not simply rhetoric. Congress delayed reauthorizing the Indochinese Refugee Migration and Assistance Act, and federal funding for the resettlement program expired for six months in 1977—1978. During the hiatus, eleven states suspended financial support for the resettlement program rather then spend their own funds (U.S. GAO 1979). California, which contained 27 percent of the Indochinese refugee population at the time, was among the insurgent states.

The passage of the Refugee Act of 1980 greatly reduced the fiscal uncertainties in the resettlement program that result from the federalist politics of the American welfare state. The Act provided for full federal payment for refugees' public assistance costs for three years. But this period represented a compromise (U.S. S 1979a). The director of Oregon's Department of Human Resources advocated reimbursement for five years. The county of San Diego argued that because federal policy had admitted refugees in need of social welfare programs "those state and local governments so affected should be fully reimbursed by the federal government for the cost of meeting such demand for so long as such demands exist" (U.S. S

1979a, p. 171). During the Congressional hearings on the act, the governor of Minnesota gave an articulate statement of these local sentiments:

> In order to assist refugees in adapting to American life, there must be a range of financial, social, educational, and employment services available. Refugees are here as a result of national, not state, policies. Further, the relocation of refugees into states is controlled by the State Department and national private agencies—not the elected representatives of the states that ultimately are responsible for providing services. Therefore, there is a continuing federal responsibility for funding refugee assistance (U.S. HR 1979a, p. 380).

Although the conflict between the states and the federal government diminished after 1980, the states still perceive the refugee program as a Washington initiative. A local welfare official described the relationship between federal and state government as

> a game of chicken: if you don't give me the money by a certain time I'm going to cut off the programs. That is exactly what happened in Oregon in 1981, when the third quarter ended and the federal government had not given the state its appropriation for refugee cash assistance for the fourth quarter. A conscious decision was made from the governor's office and from the Director of Human Resources that we could not spend state dollars with the promise that the federal government would pay us back. . . . We sent out notices to the clients in their own languages advising them that as of a certain date all of the refugee cash assistance would be terminated (Pullen 1986, pp. 50—51).

Another backlash occurred in 1982, when the ORR reduced from 36 to 24 months the period of reimbursement to state governments for refugees' use of public assistance. Refugee Coordinators from Oregon and New Jersey suggested that states only receive new refugees on the basis of their proportion of the total U.S. population (U.S. HR 1982a). Some states immediately cut from the welfare rolls those refugees who now became their financial responsibility. The cuts were so large in the state of Washington that the State Refugee Coordinator diverted nearly one-third of its social service funding to "impact aid for refugees cut off aid," which in addition to skills training and economic development, included "emergency services" (U.S. ORR 1983). Although Indochinese refugees' social citizenship is inscribed in law, the federalist politics of the American welfare state permanently jeopardizes their access to social welfare resources.

The fiscal dilemmas posed by federalism are paralleled by conflict between state and local government. The U.S. Conference of Mayors surveyed fifty-two large cities and found that 63 percent reported that refugees were overloading municipal services, such as health and education (U.S. Conference of Mayors 1982). The mayor of Santa Ana, California, believed that "by allocating funds directly to states, the new impact aid program overlooks the immediate needs of the local governments which serve the refugees most directly" (U.S. HR 1982a, p. 246). In response, the ORR created a social service grant termed "targeted assistance" to directly fund resettlement programs in about forty counties where some 200,000 refugees resided (U.S. ORR 1984). Between 1983 and 1990, ORR allocated over $365 million to targeted assistance counties. Although a new form of social citizenship had been created at the national level, the structure of the American welfare state—especially the division of power among levels of government—requires persistent intervention by national refugee advocates to ensure the flow of resources to Indochinese refugees. Yet the refugees pay a second price for their resettlement under the auspices of the welfare state: becoming stigmatized by using public assistance.

Welfare and the Work Ethic

The Social Security Act institutionalized restrictive eligibility norms by establishing a means-tested, rather than universal, form of income support (AFDC) for the poor of working age (Skocpol 1989). In Western Europe, aid to the low-income is accomplished through a Family Allowance, a program that covers all families, although benefits rise as household income decreases (Gordon 1988). These countries also have national health care so that all classes participate in the same medical program. By contrast, the American system even includes nonmonetary assistance for the poor, such as Food Stamps, which is very rare in Europe. In the U.S., segregating aid to the nonelderly poor from other forms of aid stigmatizes recipients (Glazer 1986).

Recipients of AFDC must register with a local government employment office. This stipulation applies to all men, as well as to women with children over six years old. But medical coverage is tied to enrollment in the program, providing a strong disincentive for recipients to find employment. Medical coverage is ended once recipients reach a specified income threshold, and employers do not provide medical insurance for many entry level jobs (Patterson 1986). Yet the belief that poverty is caused by a combination of welfare use, broken families, and lack of the work ethic is pervasive among Americans (Smith and Stone

1989). Americans support for the welfare state, particularly for means-tested programs like AFDC, depends on whether they prioritize a belief in the work ethic or the value of social rights (Hasenfeld and Rafferty 1989). Higgins (1981, p. 67) concludes that in the American welfare state "many services are strictly means-tested, are punitive and designed to deter 'undeserving' applicants."

Public assistance is the basic resource offered to refugees by the resettlement program; such aid mitigates their fall into poverty and also allows some to take full-time language and job training courses (Haines 1985a; North 1983). But government officials never anticipated that the majority of Indochinese refugees would receive cash assistance during their first years in the U.S. These officials were particularly shocked by the figures in Table 3.1: accelerating public assistance rates as the refugee population grew, and declining case size indicating the reliance on aid even among small households. A rising proportion of refugees from rural areas arriving during a national recession caused this increase in public assistance rates (U.S. HR 1982a). By 1982, 80 percent of the refugees who had been in the U.S. for one and one-half years or less were receiving cash assistance (U.S. ORR 1983).

Public assistance continues to be a vital source of income for Indochinese households in the country less than five years (see Table 3.2). Furthermore, these rates are highest in California, Minnesota, and Massachusetts, states with large refugee populations (see Table 3.3). When California is excluded, the national average of public assistance among Indochinese refugees drops to only 35 percent, suggesting that use of cash assistance is not pervasive. Nonetheless, even this level of use violates the restrictive norms of American social welfare.

Table 3.1. Indochinese Refugee Receipt of Cash Public Assistance, 1975-1980.

	1975	1976	1977	1978	1979	1980
Total Population*	92	138	147	162	223	388
Percent Receiving Cash Assistance	12	30	35	33	37	45
Average Number of Persons per Case	3.26	2.90	3.10	3.08	2.95	2.89

* In thousands.

Source : U.S. ORR 1981.

Table 3.2. Sources of Income in Indochinese Refugee Households 1985-1988 (in percent).*

	1985	1986	1987	1988
Work Only	34	31	32	35
Work and Cash Public Assistance	26	24	21	19
Cash Public Assistance Only	40	45	47	46

* Among Indochinese refugees living in the U.S. for five years and less in each year.

Source : U.S. ORR 1989.

Table 3.3. States with Largest Indochinese Refugee Populations and Refugees' Receipt of Cash Assistance (in percent).

State	Indochinese Population*	Receiving Cash Assistance**
California	37.1	88.5
Texas	8.1	14.6
Washington	4.6	44.0
Illinois	3.6	40.0
Pennsylvania	3.5	57.0
Minnesota	3.2	63.8
Virginia	3.1	30.4
New York	3.4	42.2
Oregon	2.5	51.3
Massachusetts	2.3	69.8
U.S.	659,000	52.2

* In 1983.
** All refugees in 1983 residing in the U.S. three years or less (rates for Indochinese refugees alone would be slightly higher).

Source : Refugee Reports 1984; U.S. ORR 1984.

As migrants from the Third World, the Indochinese have numerous traits that hinder their entry and success in the American labor market: languages quite different from English, few transferable job skills, large families, poor health, and traumatic experiences (Haines 1985b; Stein 1979). However, unemployment and cash assistance rates vary among the several ethnic groups in the Indochinese population (Haines 1985c), the migration cohorts (Montero 1979b; Nguyen and Henkin 1982), and between men and women (Haines 1986). Detailed studies show that refugees' use of public assistance declines with time (Fass 1986; Montero and Dieppa 1982; Haines 1987), particularly as the refugees learn English (Strand 1979; Strand and Jones 1985). Rates also decrease when the refugees are sponsored by native groups rather than relatives (Bach and Carroll-Seguin 1986; Tran 1991), and is lower for smaller families (Rumbaut 1989a; Rumbaut and Weeks 1986). Nonetheless, Indochinese refugees remain an extremely poor population, and they have rates of public assistance significantly higher than natives and other immigrants (Jensen 1988; U.S. CCR 1988).

The refugees' poverty assumes an added significance due to the American welfare state's restrictive eligibility norms. According to the ORR: "Welfare dependency is probably the most commonly used measurement to assess the status of the domestic refugee resettlement program and the progress that refugees are making in becoming self-sufficient" (U.S. ORR 1988, p. 157). But the Indochinese have produced success stories. By 1984, the Vietnamese who arrived in 1975 had the same median income as the U.S. population (U.S. ORR 1987). On the tenth anniversary of the fall of Saigon, the American press seized the example of the 1975 wave as another instance of immigrant success in America (Doerner 1985; Greenberg 1985). A headline in the *Wall Street Journal* (Hume 1985) extolled that Vietnamese "early arrivals make it in entrepreneurial jobs; values that spell success: work, school, thrift, family," thus adding the Vietnamese to the myth that Asians are a "model minority." But federal officials use these gains to make invidious comparisons with those refugees who have not risen as quickly. When the 1975 refugee cohort attained income parity with natives, the ORR proclaimed: "Refugees as taxpayers are making a substantial contribution to the U.S. economy" (U.S. ORR 1987, p. 124).

A thorough study of economic achievement among Vietnamese and Laotian refugees found much evidence of progress (Caplan et al. 1989). Eighty percent of all households were below the poverty level their first year in the U.S., but only 30 percent after three and one-half years. By comparison, the poverty rate (at the time of the survey) was 12 percent among whites, 31 percent among Hispanics, and 36 percent among blacks. The survey also found that over 90 percent of all Indochinese households received cash assistance their first year in the U.S., although after three and one-half years only 45 percent continued to do so. Despite these signs that the Indochinese were not becoming an Asian underclass, their comparatively high rates of public assistance within the first several years swiftly diminished their symbolism as allied aliens.

Federal Officials Expect a Work Ethic

Government officials' phobia of refugees receiving welfare began during the Cuban migration. Cubans' receipt of public assistance rose sharply beginning in 1966 and peaked in 1973, thirteen years after the start of the migration (Taft et al. 1980). By 1975, the federal government had spent $1 billion on their resettlement, nearly one half being for cash assistance. As Congress fashioned the Indochinese program it had the Cuban experience in mind. When asked to justify why aid to Indochinese refugees who arrived in 1975 would end two years later one congressman remarked that "we hope they will be assimilated by that time" (U.S. HR 1975b, p. 14,346).

The class backgrounds of the first Indochinese refugees lulled the fears of many American officials. Like the first wave of the Cuban migration, many Vietnamese refugees who arrived in 1975 were professionals, high ranking military officers, and government officials, not "the rice paddy type" (U.S. S 1975a). The fact that a few of the refugees brought considerable wealth with them fueled the expectation that they might even be able "to pay their own way" without government aid (U.S. HR 1975a). One member of Congress sought to allay concerns that these refugees would become public charges by stating:

> we are talking about the most productive, industrious segment of the South Vietnamese and Cambodian populations, essentially their middle and upper classes. . . . A productive person is a productive person no matter in what society he or she finds oneself. There is no reason to believe that doctors, accountants, teachers, merchants, will not be as successful here as they were there (U.S. HR 1975b, p. 14,356).

But higher than expected rates of public assistance quickly changed such attitudes, indicating how restrictive eligibility norms had already begun to transform these political migrants into welfare clients. Only two years after the fall of Saigon, an immigration official hoped to induce Indochinese refugees in the U.S. to find work by making them wait several years to become permanent residents if they received public assistance (U.S. HR 1977a). Such attitudes became more pervasive when the next wave of Vietnamese refugees contained few elites. Congressman Danielson of California described this second wave as "illiterate in their own language," "unskilled and unemployed in their own economy," and "uncultured in their own culture" (U.S. HR 1979d, pp. 37,229—30). These thinly veiled racist comments received support from other members of the House, and raised fears that the underclass of Indochina would soon arrive on

American shores. In closing his argument for an amendment to increase federal funding to the states—the amendment passed—Danielson stated: "There is nothing wrong with these people, but they have got to be brought up from scratch, and I respectfully submit that that burden belongs to the U.S. Government." By 1979, Indochinese refugees continued to be admitted to the U.S. because they were allied aliens. But once they arrived, American attitudes toward welfare and work quickly eroded their historic symbolism.

As a result, welfare was one of the most contentious issues in the legislative struggle over the Refugee Act of 1980. One member of the House of Representatives opposed increasing federal aid because it "would be far more harmful to the United States if we allowed a refugee class of welfare recipients to develop" (U.S. HR 1979d, p. 37,232). Similarly, the Secretary of the Department of Health, Education, and Welfare argued that "if we take refugees into this country on the assumption that they are coming here to become Americans, my own opinion is that the faster we get them into the regular system of this country the better off we are all going to be" (U.S. HR 1979a, p. 230). Senators from California provided stark figures for the record: in 1979, 67 percent of the Indochinese in the state received cash assistance, and they stayed on the welfare rolls for 30 months compared to 22 months for natives. Senator Cranston warned that "unless job and language training programs are very successful, California and the Nation will have a substantial subclass of persons with increasing social problems" (U.S. S 1979b, p. 23,248).

A downturn in the economy, coupled with the arrival of refugees with fewer transferable jobs skills, dramatically increased rates of public assistance during the early 1980s. This development was beyond the control of the refugees, yet many congressmen and welfare officials across the country believed that the refugees had lost their work ethic. According to the director of the California Department of Social Services, refugees from the Third World found life on welfare very comfortable in contrast to an impoverished existence in their homelands:

> when these people get off the plane, they know where the welfare office is. They have the address. And they know what the benefits are. For a group of people whose average income was $62 a year for a family of four, now getting $601 a month, that can be very attractive (U.S. HR 1982a, p. 203).

Following a trip to California, the U.S. Coordinator for Refugee Affairs complained to the Congress "that the welfare system has helped to turn some of the most industrious, hard-working and talented refugees ever to come to this country into dependents" (U.S. HR 1982a, p. 9). Congressman Mazzoli opened hearings on the reauthorization of the Refugee Act by stating that Indochinese "refugees have come to view welfare as an entitlement and quickly abandoned their cultural work ethic" (U.S. HR 1982a, p. 4). Congressman Fish argued for reform of the resettlement program because refugees arriving "with a strong motivation to adjust rapidly to our society far too often fall victim to the enticements of the public welfare system" (U.S. HR 1982c, p. 3707).

The extent of refugees' use of public assistance also disturbed officials in the Office of Refugee Resettlement. The director of the ORR explained why he had decided to reduce refugees' eligibility for public assistance: "it came to our attention that refugees were arriving in this country with the expectation of 36 months of special benefits, and not only the expectation, but with the full intent to take advantage of it" (U.S. HR 1982a, p. 35). ORR subsequently initiated numerous projects to reduce the number of refugees receiving public assistance. The most ambitious effort was a project in California "designed to test whether the removal of refugee employment disincentives found in the AFDC program will result in more refugees becoming employed" (U.S. ORR 1987, p. 133). After two years, 6,000 refugee households were receiving less aid, 500 households had ended their aid because they found jobs, and 300 households had their aid cut off because they refused to cooperate with the project (U.S. ORR 1988).

By the mid-1980s, public assistance use even placed in jeopardy the refugees' admission to the U.S. A State Department panel evaluating the resettlement of the Indochinese concluded that "normal immigration procedures" were now appropriate (U.S. DS 1986). The panel made this recommendation in part because they believed many Indochinese families could provide the financial resources to new arrivals previously supplied by the resettlement program. During a congressional hearing, the Coordinator for Refugee Affairs reassured one representative that "I certainly share your belief that refugee [admission] numbers must be linked to the availability of domestic resettlement funds. . . . [Our] yearly consultations on refugee [admission] numbers will clearly state budgetary implications" (U.S. HR 1982a, p. 289). Although refugee advocates created a new form of social citizenship for Indochinese refugees, these rights and resources remain embedded in the American welfare state. As a result, federalist politics and anti-welfare attitudes ultimately negate the refugees historic relationship to the U.S.

Conclusion

As Indochinese refugees began arriving in 1975, refugee advocates used the welfare state to manage a migration caused by political and military defeat. The Senate and Executive Office created a new form of social citizenship by linking the refugees' status as allied aliens to a status in the social welfare system. Legislation in 1975—1976 established an assistance program solely for refugees from Vietnam, Laos, and Cambodia. Congress and the president reauthorized this assistance on three occasions as more refugees arrived. The Refugee Act of 1980 went even further, institutionalizing lenient eligibility criteria for public aid, as well as federal reimbursement to the states for 100 percent of refugees' cash and medial assistance costs for a specified period of time. Within five years of the fall of Saigon, arriving refugees had rights to resources different from those of immigrants and natives (see Table 3.4).

In one respect, the structure of the American welfare state augmented the aid provided to the refugees. Federalism distinguishes the American welfare state from its European counterpart; a few social welfare programs deemed most critical are national in scope, while most programs are primarily controlled by state governments. Usually, this dichotomy fragments new programs. But the historical context of the Indochinese migration—the novelty of allied aliens, absence of ethnic communities, and pervasive nativism—forced the state to centralize the resettlement program. National refugee advocates must assume the fiscal burden of refugee resettlement to assure that local welfare bureaus will treat as allied aliens the Indochinese refugees within their jurisdiction.

Table 3.4. Social Welfare Programs for Indochinese Refugees in United States.

Program	Date of Law	Type of Problem	Eligibility Criterion
Office of Refugee Resettlement*	1980		
Refugee Cash Assistance	1980	Low Income	Refugee
Refugee Medical Assistance	1980	Health	Refugee
Social Services	1975	English/Jobs	Refugee
Bureau for Refugee Programs**	1979		
Funds for Voluntary Agencies	1980	Casework	Refugee

* Department of Health and Human Services
** Department of State. The Bureau for Refugee Programs' primary function is providing assistance to refugees overseas and developing criteria for refugee admissions to the U.S.

Historical factors initiated the creation of the refugees' social citizenship, but the structure of the American welfare state determines its final form. Federalist politics make public assistance the most volatile issue in the resettlement program because federal funding eventually expires. Refugee advocates only established a temporary lull in this conflict, and clashes occur when funds are delayed or the reimbursement period shrinks. Each engagement between federal and state government over fiscal costs redefines the refugees' social citizenship.

The affect of federalism on the incorporation process is mild in comparison with a second feature of the American social welfare system: restrictive eligibility norms. Western European welfare systems generally assist the low income through the same programs that aid all other citizens. In the U.S., the social welfare system distinguishes the "deserving" from the "undeserving" poor, as evidenced by separate income support and medical coverage for the poor of working age. Indochinese refugees' moderate rate of welfare use during the late 1970s led congressmen and the staff of federal agencies to wonder if the refugees had become "public charges." When the rate more than doubled during the early 1980s, government officials called into question the refugees' work ethic. In fact, increasing use of public aid resulted from the arrival of refugees with little education and no transferable job skills during a recession. Although the American state created a special social welfare status for Indochinese refugees to promote their adaptation, the welfare stigma rapidly transformed the refugees from valued émigrés to burdensome welfare clients.

This eradication of the historical origins of the Indochinese migration parallels the previous finding on the effect of historical context on state incorporation. Nativism erodes the allied alien status of the refugees just as attitudes toward public aid reduce the refugees' political symbolism. But the welfare state not only displaces history and international events, it replaces them. Eligibility norms give the refugees a new identity, while federalism establishes their place in American politics. Yet the refugee advocates managing the incorporation of the Indochinese have concerns distinct from the social welfare system. As the refugees build ethnic communities, the interests of the American nation-state vie with those of the welfare state for control of the incorporation process.

4

Managing Ethnic Communities
in the Nation-State

Where the welfare state determines the type of social citizens international migrants become, the nation-state patterns their formation of ethnic communities. Nationality and the naturalization process may have once been the core of the western nation-state. Race and ethnic relations are more significant for the adaptation of contemporary immigrants. Yet the nation-state's interest in managing cultural pluralism is not isolated from the economic and fiscal interests of the welfare state. Whether migrants retain their mother tongue or rapidly learn the new language, whether they live with or far from compatriots, are issues that compete for the state's attention with the migrants' labor market performance and use of public assistance.

The American nation-state offers refugee managers two models for planning the incorporation of international migrants: one based on the experience of European immigrants, the other on that of African-Americans. At the local level, government officials and staff in nonprofit organizations encourage refugees to congregate and build ethnic institutions, believing that these practices were prerequisites for successful adaptation among European immigrants. However, at the national level a dispersal policy prevents new arrivals from settling in areas where large numbers of Indochinese already live. Concern that the refugees will prove costly to public aid bureaus leads refugee managers to sacrifice traditions in the American nation-state to meet the interests of the welfare state.

Patterns of inequality based on physical and cultural differences present French refugee managers with a different set of alternatives. Language, religion, and former colonial status are more important than race, and the struggle between the welfare state and the nation-state has a different outcome in France than it does in the U.S.

A Polarized Nation-State

The U.S. is a state that became a nation (Smith 1986). Territorial boundaries, a legal system, and a civil religion, rather than a core culture and ancestralism, are the constituents of the American nation-state. However, the American nation-state does not easily manage its cultural pluralism simply because it now has a universal conception of citizenship. According to Smith (1986, p. 150): "ethnic immigrants were offered citizenship and mobility within a single division of labor in return for assimilation into a common political culture and the shedding of old attachments and vernaculars." Evidence is mounting that European immigrants also attained mobility through the retention of ethnicity (Portes and Manning 1986; Morawska 1990). More importantly, African-Americans played a distinctive role in shaping the American nation-state, a role much different from the idealized experience of European immigrants: "So they accepted the offer of citizenship and mobility, but retained a 'primordial' ethnic attachment. In this way there arose the familiar modern phenomenon: the sundering of citizenship from solidarity" (Smith 1986, p. 151).

African-Americans never experienced this distinction and neither did the United States. American conceptions of liberty developed as property rights and the wealth produced from slavery were given priority over equal rights (Davis 1975; Morgan 1975). Black servitude was incorporated into the constitution in order to avoid sectional disputes and remained legal for eight decades after independence (Robinson 1971). Race had as much impact on American citizenship and national identity as did an ideology of civic rights (Jordan 1974). Moreover, the economic mobility of European immigrants came at the expense of blacks. White racism in the areas of work, education, and housing aided the descendants of Europeans and limited opportunities for the descendants of Africans (Lieberson 1980; Smith 1987).

The American nation-state is divided by the divergent histories of European-Americans and African-Americans. An immigrant legacy extols the trauma of uprooting, the growth of ethnic communities, and eventual assimilation. A minority heritage derived primarily from the experience of blacks reveals a caste-like situation and the need for political power to confront inequality. The socioeconomic problems experienced by blacks are increasingly related to their class background and ghetto isolation (Wilson 1980, 1987). Nonetheless, race continues to define the black experience in many noneconomic arenas (Fagin 1991). Blacks became increasingly segregated from whites during the 1980s due to racial discrimination (Massey 1990). Although ethnicity is now optional for the descendants of European immigrants (Waters 1990), race remains central to the lives of African-Americans. This history of race and ethnic relations leads to the conclusion that:

> The character of ethnicity has shifted over the last fifty years. It was once a primary axis of socioeconomic stratification and institutional segregation; it is now a symbol of cultural and political differentiation. However, for some minorities, especially blacks and Puerto Ricans, most of the barriers to achievement are still in place (Hirschman 1983, p. 416).

Asian-Americans fall between these white and black patterns. They arrived voluntarily as immigrants, but physical differences and economic exploitation transformed them into strangers (Takaki 1989). By attaining high levels of education, Asians are nearing income parity with whites (Hirschman and Wong 1984; Nee and Sanders 1985), although they continue to experience racism (U.S. CCR 1987). This paradoxical combination of intolerance and upward mobility has fueled the myth that Asian-Americans are a "model minority," exemplified by the Japanese who can emerge from internment and in two decades attain economic equality with whites.

In the case of the Indochinese, there is some evidence that refugee managers are influenced by the model minority stereotype. In 1975, the Small Business Administration "on its own initiative hired a group of Vietnamese and American business experts to give seminars in the camps on how refugees can apply for small business loans" (U.S. IATF 1976, p. 616). To encourage entrepreneurial pursuits among Indochinese refugees, the U.S. Office of Refugee Resettlement (hereafter ORR) funds sewing cooperatives for Hmong women and farming projects for the men (U.S. ORR 1984, 1985). In 1982, the ORR funded three Indochinese associations to provide management training to refugees seeking to open businesses (U.S. ORR 1983). The Vietnamese Chamber of Commerce in America, located in Westminster, California, was one of these associations. The Vietnamese population in the county numbers some 60,000, and the area is described by one Vietnamese association as "a thriving commercial environment considered to be the capital of the Indochinese community in the U.S." (National Association for Vietnamese American Education 1989, p. 44). These refugees hardly required the stimulation of federal funds to start businesses, and yet the ORR implemented such programs as it pursued its vision of Asian-Americans as entrepreneurs. But most policies made by refugee managers take neither the Asian-American or African-American experiences as models. Instead, they use the idealized experience of European immigrants.

Immigrant Legacy and Indochinese Communities

Indochinese refugees' initial experiences in the U.S. could have led refugee managers to conclude that they were becoming an ethnic minority. In 1979, the Justice Department's Community Relations Service reported five incidents involving Indochinese refugees and natives; the number of problems jumped to thirty-two in 1980 (Pompa 1980, 1981). Violence erupted between Vietnamese and native fishermen in Texas (Starr 1981) and California (Orbach and Beckwith 1982), but conflict occurred in other parts of the country as well. Surveys disclosed that Americans ranked Vietnamese among the lowest of the immigrant groups which have made contributions to the country (Public Opinion 1982). Whites ranked Vietnamese higher than blacks and Hispanics as a group *not* wanted for neighbors (Gallup Report 1989). Rumors that Indochinese refugees eat dogs are pervasive (Baer 1982; Mitchell 1987). Graffiti, assaults, and even bombings have plagued the refugees from California to Iowa to Massachusetts (U.S. CCR 1987).

The resettlement assistance for Indochinese refugees includes some programs first developed during the 1960s, thus allowing the refugees to benefit from the War on Poverty and the Civil Rights Movement (Hein 1991a). The ORR instructed voluntary agencies to arrange "staff development and training, including training Indochinese paraprofessionals and community volunteers" (U.S. ORR 1980, p. 28). Two thousand slots were reserved for refugees in Job Corps (U.S. ORR 1982). The ORR also obtained funds from the Office of Bilingual Education and Minority Language Affairs to help refugee children with limited English proficiency (U.S. ORR 1988). Refugee managers aided Indochinese businesses through a joint project with the Small Business Administration's 7(j) program, which provides managerial training and technical services "to socially and economically disadvantaged small businesses in order to overcome historic flaws in the free enterprise system" (U.S. Superintendent of Documents 1988, p. 789). The availability of this program even led one Indochinese association to conclude that "Indochinese and other refugee ethnic groups are considered minorities. Therefore, Indochinese owned businesses are eligible to receive [federal] financing" (IRAC 1984, p. 1).

But the ORR did not view the Indochinese as a new ethnic minority despite introducing them into programs first created for blacks and Hispanics. Through such programs the ORR hoped "to secure recognition for refugees as important clients of *mainstream* Federal agencies whose mission is to stimulate economic opportunities for special populations" (U.S. ORR 1985, p. 112, emphasis added). In short, the programs represented additional funding sources. Rather than learning from the experience of minorities in the American nation-state, refugee managers turn to the immigrant legacy to orient their incorporation of Indochinese refugees.

According to government officials and agency staff, the absence of preexisting ethnic communities has hindered Indochinese refugees' adjustment. A voluntary agency director describes what many in the resettlement program claim to be the historical role of an ethnic community for new arrivals:

> They were usually established people, native born Americans, or those who emigrated and became firmly adapted to our society. They brought with them opportunities to get involved, warm hearts, and lots of resources. They accepted the new persons and took them from a point of total dependence, right off the track or plane, to a point of successful independence. . . . What changed with the Indochinese influx was that there were large numbers of people coming all at once with great needs and no strongly established ethnic community (Friedline 1986, p. 45).

Between 1975 and 1980, the Vietnamese population increased from 18,000 to more than 300,000, and the number of Cambodians and Laotians rose dramatically as well. The missing migration from Indochina to the U.S. prior to 1975 established a guiding principle of the resettlement program: the Indochinese need help building ethnic communities. Several examples illustrate this policy of state-sponsored ethnicity. A Cambodian association in Arlington received federal funds to teach refugees how to read and write their *native* language as preparation for eventually learning English (U.S. ORR 1988). The only resettlement agency in Portland, Maine, listed "ethnic identity" and "refugee community development" as two of the federally funded services it supplied (U.S. ORR 1981, 1982). In Chicago, the Commission on Human Relations included "community organizing and development, cultural events" among its services for refugees (U.S. ORR 1983). Awareness of ethnic diversity is not surprising in Chicago, but even the Idaho state voluntary agency considered "the existence of an ethnic group as a support base" a necessary ingredient of successful refugee resettlement (U.S. ORR 1986). These isolated cases of managing the development of Indochinese communities are part of a larger policy that began with the use of the Asian-American community as a surrogate for the Vietnamese, Laotian, and Cambodian communities, which did not yet exist.

Asian-Americans as a Surrogate Community

Federal agencies obviously had refugees' ethnicity in mind when they distributed orientation literature entitled "We, the Asian Americans" to the first wave of Vietnamese. But organizations that would sponsor refugees out of the camps were of more immediate use than an ethnic identity. In 1975, the Interagency Task Force for Indochina Refugees funded Chinese-American associations in Los Angeles and New York City to resettle over 900 Vietnamese refugees of Chinese ancestry (U.S. IATF 1976). Relying on this ethnic community allowed 150 of the refugees to reunite with Chinese-Americans with the same last names and who were thus considered distant relatives. Refugee managers drew upon the immigrant legacy in the American nation-state within months of the arrival of the first Vietnamese refugees.

With the arrival of more refugees in the late 1970s and early 1980s, federal and state agencies increasingly turned to Asian-American organizations as they sought to link the refugees with an established ethnic community. In 1981, Asian-American associations accounted for 43 percent of all nonprofit associations in California which received funding to aid refugees. In the state of Washington, the Commission on Asian-American Affairs funded Indochinese mutual assistance associations (MAAs) to ensure "a long-term role for MAAs in assisting their people that is similar to the role currently played by Asian-American community groups which evolved in the past to assist Asian immigrants" (Berkeley Planning Associates 1982a, p. 63). Over time, Indochinese MAAs grew at the expense of the Asian-American associations, a direct result of state intervention in the adaptation process (see Tables 4.1 and 4.2).

The size of grants to the refugee organizations actually diminished as their numbers and geographic scope increased, suggesting that government policy aimed to promote the growth of MAAs, but merely purchase services from Asian-American associations. Indeed, most of the Asian-American associations specialize in a single service and provide the more professionalized adjustment services, such as mental and physical health care. Conversely, Indochinese MAAs tend to supply several services that are community based, such as English classes.

Funding policy also reveals that state governments showed great sensitivity to ethnic differences among Indochinese refugees. Spending declined for the Vietnamese and rose for Cambodian, Laotian, and Hmong associations as these latter groups increased in size. The arrival of ethnic Chinese refugees from Vietnam allowed Chinese-

Table 4.1. Distribution of Refugee Social Service Funds by the States to Asian-American Associations.

	1980	1981	1982
Number of Associations	17	13	11
% In California	53	38	45
Number of States	10	14	10
Funds Received			
% Under $50,000	18	15	18
% Over $250,000	12	8	18
Mean	$ 176,832	$ 111,550	$ 162,799
Total	$3,006,136	$1,450,152	$1,790,791
Services Provided (in %)			
English Instruction	6	5	25
Employment Related	41	53	44
Adjustment Related	53	42	31
Ethnicity (in %)			
Korean	12	8	9
Chinese	18	38	55
Asian	71	54	36

Source : U.S. ORR 1981, 1982, 1983.

American associations to become the leading Asian-American organizations working with Indochinese refugees. Mixed Indochinese MAAs increasingly received funds "to avoid creating disunity and disharmony among organizations" (Berkeley Planning Associates 1982b, p. 31). In 1982, the ORR developed a new policy to fund MAAs and to more explicitly manage the formation of Indochinese communities in accordance with the American immigrant legacy.

The Rise of Indochinese Associations

Federal support for Indochinese associations began in an advisory role and evolved into financial grants and contracts (Lewin et al. 1986). By 1976, the Refugee Task Force had already established an Indochinese Mutual Assistance Division in the belief that "historically, many ethnic groups have provided valued service through such community organizations" (U.S. DHEW 1978, p. 53). A year later, the Indochinese Refugee Program had staff to provide technical assistance to the estimated 140 Indochinese associations in the country. When the ORR began its formal policy of funding MAAs in 1980 it did so recognizing "the great potential and the historic

Table 4.2. Distribution of Refugee Social Service Funds by the States to Indochinese Refugee Mutual Assistance Associations.

	1980	1981	1982
Number of Associations	15	22	43
% In California	47	23	17
Number of States	10	26	42
Funds Received			
% Under $50,000	20	50	60
% Over $250,000	27	9	7
Mean	$ 227,974	$ 93,645	$ 80,199
Total	$3,419,609	$2,060,193	$3,448,558
Services Provided (in %)			
English Instruction	22	21	21
Employment Related	39	42	40
Adjustment Related	39	37	39
Ethnicity (in %)			
Vietnamese	47	23	21
Cambodian	0	9	12
Laotian	20	27	14
Hmong	0	5	14
Mixed	33	36	40

Source : U.S. ORR 1981, 1982, 1983.

appropriateness of refugees helping their newly arrived fellow countrymen" (U.S. ORR 1981, p. 13). That year, it distributed over $1 million to MAAs and 80 percent of these funds went to Indochinese associations.

In 1982, the ORR launched the MAA Incentive Grant Initiative to encourage local government to both fund MAAs and to allow these associations a greater role in the resettlement process. Under this policy, states receive money on the condition that they allocate a portion of their refugee social service budgets to MAAs rather than to traditional social service providers, such as voluntary agencies (Lewin et al. 1986). The first year, only fourteen states participated in the program. In 1984, the ORR began distributing the grants to states based on the size of their refugee population, rather than on a competitive basis as in the past; all but five states agreed to participate. Between 1982 and 1990, the ORR allocated over $22 million to state governments to promote the growth of refugee associations.

Refugee managers clearly evaluate the ideological interests of the American nation-state as they create refugee associations. But the interests of the welfare state compete with fulfillment of the immigrant legacy. A series of ORR sponsored seminars for refugee leaders began with the premise that: "It has long been recognized that self-help within the community is necessary for long-term adjustment and independence" (U.S. DHHS Region VII 1982, p. 5). However, a primary goal of the seminars was "increasing participants' self-sufficiency and reducing welfare dependency." The State Department's Coordinator for Refugee Affairs expressed how traditions in the American nation-state could serve the needs of the welfare state:

> Private nationality or ethnic group societies and associations are the classic self-help vehicle. If we are able to assist them with technical support and incentives—particularly those nascent societies, such as the Indochinese Mutual Assistance Associations, which represent new groups of refugees—we serve several objectives at the same time. We strengthen refugee self-respect, we reinforce the dignity of self-help, and we lower the public costs of the program (U.S. HR 1982a, pp. 9–10).

Ultimately, refugee managers place a higher priority on the price of refugee resettlement than on fulfilling the immigrant legacy by fostering Indochinese communities. Indeed, as the Indochinese began concentrating on the West and Gulf Coast, refugee managers implemented a dispersal policy to limit the development of refugee communities in areas of the country where their presence might prove costly to social welfare budgets.

Dispersing Refugees to Reduce Costs

American officials began the resettlement of the Indochinese confident that these refugees, unlike the Cubans in Florida, "would be scattered throughout the country to avoid any concentration" (U.S. HR 1975a, p. 17; also see U.S. HR 1977b, p. 68, 1979a, p. 238). A member of Congress went so far as to state that: "A principle long range aim of the resettlement program is to avoid a buildup of the refugees in any one area, largely in order to minimize their impact on specific labor markets" (U.S. HR 1975b, p. 14,340). Rather than an issue of assimilation, the American dispersal policy reflects the inherent conflict in the American welfare state between federal and state assistance. Congress insisted on unqualified federal funding of refugees' resettlement costs and widely publicized a statement by the director of the Interagency Task Force on Indochina Refugees:

Every effort will made to ensure that resettlement, to the extent possible, will not be concentrated in a few enclaves and will not result in economic or social service hardship. The Department of HEW ... will provide full reimbursement to State and local social service and health agencies for costs they may incur in providing income assistance, health maintenance, social services, and educational services to refugees who are in need of such assistance (U.S. HR 1975c, p. 3).

But Indochinese refugees had already established their settlement patterns by the time the last Vietnamese left the mainland reception camps in December of 1975 (see Table 4.3). Eight of the ten states in which the first wave settled continued to be the main sites into the 1990s. Florida and Oklahoma received comparatively large contingents of refugees in 1975 because of two military camps used as reception centers. But Massachusetts and Oregon replaced these states as refugees moved within the U.S. after initial placement (termed secondary migration). The tenacity of Indochinese settlement patterns is even more remarkable given that federal officials and voluntary agency staff have sought to locate refugees throughout the country since the arrival of the first Vietnamese.

In 1975, the IATF stipulated to the voluntary agencies that no more than 3,000 Vietnamese could be resettled in any one state, and the refugees were in fact relocated to all fifty states (Kelly 1977). However, when the last refugees left the mainland reception camps eleven states already had received more than the maximum. Together

Table 4.3. States with Ten Largest Indochinese Refugee Populations.*

1975	%	1980	%	1990	%
California	20.9	California	33.9	California	39.6
Texas	7.0	Texas	9.3	Texas	7.5
Pennsylvania	5.5	Washington	4.3	Washington	4.7
Florida	4.1	Pennsylvania	4.1	Minnesota	3.7
Washington	3.2	Illinois	3.5	New York	3.6
Minnesota	2.9	Virginia	3.2	Pennsylvania	3.2
New York	2.9	Louisiana	3.0	Massachusetts	3.1
Virginia	2.9	Minnesota	2.9	Illinois	3.1
Illinois	2.8	New York	2.6	Virginia	2.5
Oklahoma	2.8	Oregon	2.6	Oregon	2.2
Total	55.0		69.4		70.1

* Ranked by actual number of Indochinese refugees when percentages are equal.

Source : Kelly 1977; U.S. ORR 1981, 1991.

these states accounted for 58 percent of all the refugees resettled. Furthermore, the Vietnamese concentrated in key urban areas within each state. This residential pattern reflected the availability of sponsors, housing, and jobs, but also indicates that the federal government did not seek to disperse Vietnamese refugees at the city or neighborhood level. After 1975, secondary migration reinforced these patterns as the refugees moved to states with warmer climates, job opportunities, comparatively higher levels of public assistance, and large refugee communities (Desbarats 1985; Forbes 1985a).

By the early 1980s, sizable Indochinese communities had developed in certain areas of the country despite the dispersal policy. Yet federal officials viewed geographic concentration as a fiscal issue rather than a sign that refugees were resisting assimilation into the American nation-state. The Department of Health and Human Services stated that it was "concerned about the unequal geographic distribution of refugees, which has created serious strains on the capacity of some communities to respond to the needs of new arrivals, and about the number of refugees utilizing public cash assistance" (U.S. ORR 1982, p. 21). The voluntary agencies were also disturbed by the settlement patterns of the Indochinese, again for financial and public relations reasons. These agencies feared that secondary migration would undermine the support for refugees among segments of the public traditionally relied on as sponsors:

> If a refugee family leaves soon after arrival to join a relative or friend in another area, this disappointing experience can make sponsors unwilling to assist other refugee families or otherwise support refugee programs. Secondary migration, especially shortly after arrival, not only wastes funds expended by the private sector on the initial resettlement plan, but has an adverse effect on the community to which the refugee migrates where there can have been no planning for his resettlement (ACVA 1981a, p. 2).

Voluntary agencies make the initial placement of refugees but their services are partly funded by the State Department. In late 1981, the Department's Bureau for Refugee Programs formulated a new dispersal policy (U.S. ORR 1984). The Bureau requested that the voluntary agencies make a list of "impacted areas" in which further refugee resettlement was undesirable due to lack of jobs and affordable housing, long-term welfare dependency, and high rates of secondary migration by refugees already settled in the U.S. (ACVA 1982). In 1983, the ORR developed a formula to determine which counties were impacted, using the ratio of natives to refugees and the percentage of refugees receiving cash assistance as the key variables (U.S. Social Security Administration 1983). Significantly, it was primarily the refugees' effect on the welfare state that was at issue. Refugees "impacted" an area when their presence led to "a drain on community resources of sufficient magnitude to materially affect the quality of services to the general community" (U.S. DHHS 1983, p. 55,301). This dispersal policy meant that refugees without immediate relatives in the U.S. would be resettled away from large Indochinese communities (see Table 4.4).

The major impediment to this dispersal policy was that even by mid-1981, many Indochinese refugees were admitted to the U.S. as family reunion cases. A survey of sponsorship patterns among Indochinese refugees found 33 percent with close relatives already in the U.S., such as siblings, parents, and children; 34 percent with more distant relatives, such as cousins; 8 percent with friends; and only 25 percent with no contacts who could act as sponsors (U.S. GAO 1983). These strong kin ties meant that the dispersal policy could only be applied to about one-third of arriving refugees. The refugees' social networks proved stronger than the policies of the welfare state.

Despite the national dispersal policy, at the local level refugee managers support the formation of ethnic communities. Caseworkers in voluntary agencies, usually refugees themselves, use other refugees to

Table 4.4. Areas of the U.S. Restricted to Arriving Indochinese Refugees by 1982.

State	County	Principle City of Concern	Refugee Per Capita
California	San Diego	San Diego	159
California	Orange	Santa Anna	132
California	Los Angeles	Long Beach	217
California	Sacramento	Sacramento	171
California	San Francisco	San Francisco	53
California	Alameda	Oakland	216
California	San Joaquin	Stockton	129
California	Stanislaus	Modesto	NA
Illinois	Cook	Elgin	717
Minnesota	Ramsey	St. Paul	74
Oregon	Multnomah	Portland	70
Rhode Island	Providence	Providence	NA
Texas	All Counties on the Gulf Coast		NA
Virginia	Arlington	Arlington	62
Virginia	Fairfax	Arlington	987
U.S.	--	--	671

Source : ACVA 1982.

provide social services. In a city such as New York, which only developed Indochinese communities in the early 1980s, caseworkers actively construct residential concentrations. Placing clients in the same building allows older arrivals to socialize newer arrivals, lightening the tasks of caseworkers. One Indochinese caseworker reports: "I try to put all my clients together so that I can ask them to help each other out, even pick up new arrivals a the airport. It's easier for me that way" (Hein 1988, p. 470). Caseworkers also reduce the cross-cultural pressures of their job by using other refugees to deliver services. Another Indochinese caseworker stated: "I try to avoid saying anything that will make a client angry. I usually ask a friend or neighbor to tell him" (Hein 1988, p. 470). Of course, this strategy of using other refugees as quasi-caseworkers requires residential propinquity.

In a city like San Francisco, where refugees began concentrating as early as 1975, the ethnic community's supervision of newcomers is nearly total. Caseworkers' residual task for most new clients is simply negotiating a relatives helping role: "I call a sponsor and say you have relatives coming next month—you have to find them jobs, or register them with welfare, and housing. If the relative is in school they can help a lot, but if they work, one of us will have to find a friend to help" (Hein 1988, p. 470).

This support for ethnic communities at the neighborhood level is not only the result of the organization of social work in voluntary agencies. National level projects reveal that refugee managers actively construct refugee communities as they simultaneously attempt to meet the interests of the welfare state and the nation-state. For example, the Office of Refugee Resettlement installed 1,000 newly arrived Vietnamese in Phoenix and Tucson because of job and housing opportunities. But each city already had Vietnamese populations of about 1,500, which were expected to facilitate resettlement (Berkeley Planning Associates 1984). Projects for Cambodians and the Hmong provide a more detailed illustration of how the American state disperses refugees to reduce costs to the social welfare system and promotes refugee communities to fulfill the immigrant legacy.

The Khmer Cluster Project placed new arrivals in areas of the country that had not previously been resettlement sites but showed promise for successful adaptation. The ORR initiated the project by providing $700,000 to the Cambodian Association of America to coordinate the placement of some 8,000 Cambodians. Located in Long Beach, California, the largest settlement of Cambodians in the country, the association was charged with mustering the Cambodian community to assist in meeting the special needs of newly arrived Cambodian refugees. Goals include assisting in the resettlement of Cambodian refugees, developing community organizing skills, strengthening communications between the Cambodian community and existing service providers, strengthening the Cambodian communities' economic independence, and encouraging the integration of Cambodian communities into the mainstream of American life (U.S. ORR 1981, p. 11).

To implement this project a team of officials from the State Department, voluntary agencies, and the Cambodian association traveled to Thailand to select Cambodian refugees who had no relatives in the U.S., and thus would be unlikely to migrate after arrival. Ultimately groups of 300 to 1,000 Cambodians were resettled in Chicago, New York City, Houston, Dallas, Boston, Richmond, and six other cities. In each location the Cambodian association in Long Beach established an affiliated agency to supervise resettlement activities and provide "new arrivals with immediate evidence of an ethnic presence" (Granville Corporation 1982, p. 24). Efforts at community building went so far as to channel Cambodians of Chinese ancestry to Chinatowns in Boston and New York City. A year later, only 12 percent of the Cambodians resettled through the project had left these locations (IRAC 1982a). By selecting migrants overseas, matching them with American cities, and funding ethnic associations to provide them with services, the American state planned the formation of Cambodian communities across the country.

The Highland Lao Initiative was a more ambitious effort to manage the settlement patterns of Indochinese refugees. Secondary migration into the Central Valley of California had led to one-third of the Hmong population in the U.S. concentrating in and around the cities of Fresno, Merced, and Stockton (Olney 1986). Concerned over public assistance rates approaching 100 percent, the ORR hoped to attract Hmong in California to forty small Hmong communities in the South and Midwest, and to stem migration from these communities to the Central Valley. In 1983, the ORR spent $3 million in these Hmong communities to provide social services ranging from job placement and English language training, to farming projects and small business start-up money (U.S. ORR 1984). After one year, out-migration from many communities was greatly reduced and the Hmong population increased in some sites, particularly those in Wisconsin and Colorado (Coffey et al. 1985). Significantly, the project relied on refugee associations in over one-half of all sites to provide the social services that would anchor current residents and draw those from California. Like the project for Cambodian refugees, the funding of MAAs, and the deployment of Asian-American associations, the American state uses ethnic associations to manage the development of Indochinese communities.

State Creation of Ethnic Institutions

The American state's dual policy of dispersing refugees and funding their associations profoundly influences the institutional development of Indochinese communities. Dispersal means that the refugees are settled in numerous, small groups throughout the country. Although California, Texas, and Washington contain 52 percent of the Indochinese population, the remaining 48 percent are distributed among all the other states and only five states have fewer than 1,000 refugees (such as Alaska, where 100 Indochinese refugees live). Refugee associations that receive federal funding often become extensions of the state rather than representatives of their communities, particularly since they are funded to increase employment and reduce public assistance rates among refugees (Gold 1992; Indra 1987; Jenkins and Sauber 1988). Even American agencies that work with refugees tend to hire ethnically marginal individuals who can act as middlemen, rather than indigenous leaders (Hein 1988). Funding ethnic associations in the context of geographic dispersal allows state-sponsored organizations to become the dominant institutions in many refugee communities.

By 1980, Indochinese refugees had created almost 500 associations (Bui 1983) and the number grew to 800 by 1984 (Khoa and Bui 1985). This rapid growth parallels the arrival rates of the refugees but also the initiation of federal funding for Indochinese MAAs. Government support takes a range of forms: grants and contracts, start-up money which then can be used to attract other funding sources, or simply the circulation of "refugee dollars" from one agency to another (Lewin et al. 1986). A survey of MAAs found that only one in five received more than 10 percent of their income from funding sources outside of the resettlement program (Refugee Policy Group 1987). Reflecting this dependency on the state, a leading refugee association encouraged Indochinese MAAs to develop other funding sources because "self-help will . . . be especially critical as MAAs make the transition from initial resettlement to long-term community development" (IRAC 1986, p. 41). In fact, many MAAs consider their "membership" to be the number of clients served (Finnan and Cooperstein 1983). The result is a state-sponsored ethnic social welfare sector.

The ethnic affiliation of Indochinese associations matches the proportion of each ethnic group within the larger Indochinese population (see Table 4.5). However, highland Laotians (groups like the Hmong and Mien) have nearly twice as many. Approximately 50 percent of highland Laotians live in California, and another 34 percent live in the Midwest. Yet the number of highland Laotian associations is almost inversely related to their settlement pattern. California accounts for 20 percent of highland Laotian associations, while the Midwest contains 40 percent (Khoa and Bui 1985). This inverse relationship between population distribution and formation of associations resulted from the federal policy to attract refugees away from California by funding ethnic associations in other locales to provide social services.

Although most Indochinese ethnic groups create associations in proportion to their size, state incorporation influences the functions of these associations (see Table 4.6). More than one-half of Indochinese associations have a cultural function, but nearly one-quarter are the associations that receive at least some public funds to resettle other refugees. This state-sponsored social welfare sector is comparatively weak among the Vietnamese, and quite pronounced among Laotians, Hmong, Cambodians, and the mixed category.

The mixed associations test which goals Indochinese refugees will pursue once they overcome ethnic antipathies that developed in Southeast Asia. These associations overwhelmingly perform resettlement functions, suggesting that many originated because of

Table 4.5. Composition of Indochinese Population and Ethnic Affiliation of Indochinese Refugee Associations (in percent).

	Indochinese Population	Indochinese Associations
Vietnamese	64	53
Cambodian	16	14
Lowland Laotian	13	14
Highland Laotian	8	15
Mixed	--	4
Total	716,535	800

Source : Khoa and Bui 1985; Olney 1986; Refugee Reports 1988.

Table 4.6. Function and Ethnic Affiliation of Indochinese.Refugee Associations (in percent).

	All	Vietnamese	Cambodian	Lowland Laotian	Highland Laotian	Mixed
Cultural	55	60	53	63	39	29
Resettlement (MAA)	24	13	32	31	43	41
Special Interest	11	18	3	2	3	0
Political	7	7	12	4	2	21
Economic	4	2	0	1	14	9
Total	800	421	115	108	122	34

Source : Khoa and Bui 1985.

state incorporation. Of the twenty-two Indochinese associations funded by the ORR in 1980 (the first year of the new funding policy), six were mixed, seven were Vietnamese, four were Cambodian, three were Laotian, and one was Hmong (U.S. ORR 1981). Similarly, the state of Washington, which has the third largest Indochinese refugee population, has a policy of only funding coalitions of MAAs (Lewin et al. 1986). Participation in the incorporation process diverts resources and leadership from other organized activities.

The dispersal of Indochinese communities makes public funding of refugee associations even more significant. Cultural associations increase as a proportion of all associations as the size of the Indochinese population declines (see Table 4.7). Conversely, the proportion of special interest, economic, and political associations in refugee communities decreases as the size of their population declines. However, resettlement associations are most prevalent in states with medium sized Indochinese populations. Those refugee associations with ties to the welfare state even have greater weight in the states with the smallest Indochinese populations than they do in California.

Cultural and resettlement associations are likely to be present in all refugee communities. An association established to maintain a Buddhist temple or a Catholic church, and another to mediate refugees' relations with schools, employers, and welfare bureaus are institutional features of Vietnamese, Laotian, and Cambodian communities across the U.S. Conversely, special interest, political, and economic associations are disproportionately found in those areas of the country with large concentrations of refugees, such as the West

Table 4.7. Function of Indochinese Refugee Associations by Size of Indochinese Population (in percent).

State	Size	Function		
		Cultural	Resettlement	Other*
California	285,100	49	17	34
9 States	51,300-17,200	52	27	22
21 States	13,500-3,800	60	27	13
20 States and DC	Less than 3,800	62	23	15

* Economc, special interest, and political.

Note : For 800 Indochinese refugee associations in 1984.

Source : Khoa and Bui 1985; U.S. ORR 1985.

Coast. California accounts for only 23 percent of all cultural associations, and only 18 percent of all resettlement associations. However, it contains 45 percent of all special interest associations, 42 percent of all political associations, and 32 percent of all economic associations (Khoa and Bui 1985). State incorporation causes associations which receive public funding to become the dominant institutions in many refugee communities.

Conclusion

The American nation-state contains two, contrary traditions that profoundly shape the incorporation of international migrants. For European immigrants and their descendants, the importance of ethnicity had declined over time and assimilation is pervasive. For African-Americans, race continues to constrain social, political, and economic life even though class background often determines the range of their life chances.

This polarization between black and white paradigms presents the European immigrant legacy as the "only" choice for the incorporation of international migrants, since the African-American experience is fraught with unrelenting struggle and partial gains. It is thus not surprising that refugee managers pattern the incorporation of Indochinese refugees on an idealized model of European immigrant adaptation. For personnel in social welfare bureaucracies and nonprofit organizations, the African-American experience is a fate to be avoided rather than an alternative form of existence within the American nation-state.

Refugee managers' interpretation of the immigrant legacy is more novel than their choice of paradigms: ethnicity, not assimilation, is considered advantageous. They conceive the experience of European immigrants to be new arrivals entering an existing ethnic community and successfully adapting with the aid of established residents. The historical context of the Indochinese migration differs significantly from this representation: absence of ethnic communities prior to 1975 and rapid arrivals thereafter. Refugee managers believe these factors hinder the refugees' adjustment. As a result, the resettlement program supervises, in some cases even plans, the development of refugee communities. State intervention is most evident in the extensive public funding for Indochinese mutual assistance associations. These associations, which move refugees' from public assistance to the labor market, often become the dominant institutions in medium and small refugee communities, where insufficient numbers of refugees limit the creation of other types of associations. State incorporation shapes the refugees' integration into the nation-state just as it determines their acquisition of social citizenship through the welfare state.

In fact, refugees from Vietnam, Laos, and Cambodia need little assistance in forming ethnic communities. They quickly settled on the West and Gulf Coast, and by 1990 over 70 percent resided in ten states (compared to 45 percent for the total American population). Close kin ties among the refugees also promote the development of ethnic communities. Relatives or friends sponsored three-quarters of all new arrivals to the U.S. within ten years of the first wave of refugees in 1975. These flourishing communities would have fulfilled the immigrant legacy for refugee managers except that state, local, and municipal government became alarmed as refugees added to expenses for public aid, education, health, and other social welfare services. In response, federal officials and voluntary agency directors developed a dispersal policy to settle new arrivals away from "impacted" areas in California, Texas, and other states with large refugee communities. Ultimately, the state is more concerned with the costs of resettling Indochinese refugees than with managing their ethnicity.

This finding suggests the last component of the American mode of incorporation: the welfare state is predominant over the nation-state at the national level. Such a generalization is surprising for two reasons. First, there is a national structure to the American nation-state, and it is particularly pronounced when compared with the nation-state in a country like France. Second, the American welfare state is comparatively underdeveloped in contrast to its counterparts in Western Europe, which would seemingly inhibit it from playing a central role in the society.

Both observations assume that the nation-state and welfare state are institutionally independent. The Indochinese case suggests that there is a close relationship between historic patterns of race and ethnic relations and how the society collectively mitigates economic and life course hardships. Norms regulating ethnic pluralism are linked to other norms regulating the distribution of public resources. Tolerance, even encouragement, for local ethnic communities is predicated on members conforming to a national moral order represented by the social welfare system.

The migration of Indochinese refugees to the U.S. reveals three features of the American mode of incorporation. First, nativism supersedes other historical factors surrounding the Indochinese migration, particularly the refugees' identity as allied aliens. Second, state constructed social citizenship supplies the refugees with extensive resources, but the structure of the welfare state jeopardizes their new status and quickly stigmatizes them for receiving aid. Finally, the structure of the nation-state supports ethnic communities and institutions at the local level while allowing the interests of the welfare state to predominate at the national level. Variation in historical context, welfare state structure, and nation-state traditions lead to a very different form of incorporation for Indochinese refugees arriving in France.

PART TWO

Indochinese Refugees in France

5

Constants and Variables in the Indochinese Migration

The demographic characteristics of international migrants often explain a state's response to their migration. As a result, cross-national comparison of migrant adaptation usually must include the immigrants or refugees themselves as a cause of variation in modes of incorporation. This would be the case if the U.S. had ended the admission of Indochinese refugees following the arrival of the Vietnamese elite in 1975, and if France had only accepted destitute Chinese-Vietnamese boat people in 1979–1980. In such a scenario, class background, ethnicity, and other factors related to the refugees might explain the states' management of their adaptation.

Instead, French and American modes of incorporation result from the interaction of different historical contexts, welfare state structures, and nation-state traditions. Alternative causal factors are sufficiently similar in both cases to rule out the possibility that they played a role in determining state responses. These constants include the refugees' political identity, the timing and magnitude of their migration, and their ethnic and class background.

Political, Temporal, and Demographic Constants

Political Identity

Like the United States, France admits Indochinese refugees because they are allied aliens. French colonization of Indochina began with the capture of the southern portion of Vietnam during the 1850s, and the conquest continued for three decades. Cambodia came under French dominance during the 1860s, and Laos followed in the 1890s. France established the Union of Indochina in 1897, creating a single, colonial government for all three regions. Until World War One, Indochina was primarily of geopolitical value to the French Empire: a presence in the orient comparable to that of Hong Kong for the British. However, France sought to rebuild its war-shattered economy through exploitation of its colonies, and during the 1920s plantations, industries, and taxation increased dramatically. After defeat by Germany in 1940, France ceded the colonies to Japan, but then sought to return to power in 1945. French and Vietnamese troops fought against a predominately communist led national independence movement for nine years before conceding defeat in 1954. As Buttinger (1968, p. 101) concludes: "Who, in 1896, believed that the emancipation of French Indochina held the key to the solution of the perpetual crisis—administrative, military, and financial—that forced France, ever since Vietnam was fully conquered in 1883, to pay so heavy a price for it in blood, money, and political dissension?"

Indochinese refugees migrate to France because of this history. When the U.S. sought to "internationalize" the admission of South Vietnamese following the capture of Saigon, France was the only country to immediately step forward. Australia, Britain, Canada, and Germany only began significant resettlement operations in response to the Vietnamese boat people crisis in the late 1970s. A United Nations conference in Geneva on the plight of Indochinese refugees (in July of 1979) was required to gain the participation of countries which did not have historic ties to the peoples of Indochina.

The French response to the American appeal in 1975 stated: "Willing to accept Cambodians and Vietnamese who were civil servants of former French administration or who served in French forces during Second World War. Will consider applications from those with French academic qualifications or with special reasons to resettle in France" (U.S. HR 1976, p. 291). This ad hoc description of desired refugees soon became the formal admission criteria (JO II 1979), along with the ability to speak French (Le Monde 1975). Significantly, service to the empire and francophonism were the same requirements for Indochinese to become French citizens during the colonial period (Outre Mer 1937). According to the Minister of Foreign Affairs: "For reasons particular to her history, France adopts a benevolent attitude toward territorial asylum for persons from certain countries such as Laos, Cambodia, or Vietnam" (JO 1987, p. 830). The Indochinese comprise 70 percent of all refugees admitted to France between 1975 and 1990.

Timing and Magnitude

Despite the common political relationship between the people of Indochina and France and the U.S., resettling Indochinese refugees is primarily an American activity (see Table 5.1). The U.S. admitted more refugees in 1975 than France would by 1990 (see Table 5.2). Even on a per capita basis, the flow of Indochinese refugees to the U.S. greatly exceeds that to France.

Nonetheless, there are important similarities between the two migrations. First, both migrations began in 1975. This synchronization means that France and the U.S. developed policies for resettling the refugees independently of each other. Conversely, policy diffusion is evident in Japan, where the state compared American and Australian resettlement programs and then chose the latter (Koizumi 1991). Historical context and state structures are important determinants of state actions when states invent, rather than import, social policies.

Second, comparatively large numbers of refugees arrived when the French and American states formulated their policies to incorporate the Indochinese. In 1977, France received nearly five Indochinese refugees for every one migrating to the U.S. Between 1975 and 1979, France ranked second among the western resettlement countries. By the time other countries responded to the flow of boat people, France had already received 50,000 refugees, compared to 21,000 and 13,000 for Australia and Canada, respectively.

Finally, both countries admitted two-thirds of their total Indochinese refugee population by the early 1980s. These refugees comprised a similar proportion of all refugees admitted to France and the U.S. between 1975 and 1990. Thus the American and French states faced comparable tasks with respect to the timing and size of the Indochinese migration.

Table 5.1. Indochinese Refugee Populations in France and the United States, 1975-1990.

	France	United States
Total Number of Indochinese Refugees	126,100	978,715
% Vietnamese	34	64
% Cambodian	37	16
% Lowland Laotian	19	12
% Highland Laotian*	10	8
Percent of all Refugees Admitted to Country	70	73
Indochinese Refugee Per Capita	1:451	1:254

* Such as the Hmong; estimated for France.

Source: FTDA 1991; Refugee Reports 1990; U.S. Committee for Refugees 1991.

Table 5.2. Admission of Indochinese Refugees to France and the United States by Year, 1975-1990.

| Year | France | | United States | |
	Number	Cumulative Percent of Total	Number	Cumulative Percent of Total
1975	9,643	8	130,394	13
1976	12,136	17	14,466	15
1977	11,468	26	2,563	15
1978	12,402	36	20,397	17
1979	15,378	48	80,678	25
1980	12,001	58	166,727	42
1981	12,290	68	132,454	56
1982	9,207	75	72,155	63
1983	8,690	82	39,167	67
1984	5,175	86	52,000	73
1985	2,950	88	49,853	78
1986	2,764	90	45,391	82
1987	2,661	92	40,164	86
1988	2,644	95	35,015	90
1989	2,684	97	45,680	95
1990	4,007	100	51,611	100
Total	126,100		978,715	

Note : Figures include Amerasians and their relatives, as well as Vietnamese who arrive through the Orderly Departure Program.

Source : FTDA 1991; Refugee Reports 1989b, 1990; Regarde sur l'Acualité 1980a.

Ethnic and Class Composition

The Indochinese refugee population in the U.S. is primarily Vietnamese, with small proportions of Laotians and Cambodians. Conversely, the Indochinese refugee population in France is composed about equally of Vietnamese and Laotians, with a plurality of Cambodians. In addition, ethnic Chinese comprise approximately one-quarter of the Vietnamese population in the U.S., but a smaller proportion of the Vietnamese in France. Ethnic Chinese may account for 50 percent of Cambodians in France, but a much smaller proportion of Cambodians in the U.S.

These differences reflect the nature of French and American penetration of Indochina. French colonialism covered all three countries, although administrative centers were located in Hanoi and Saigon. Thus it is not surprising that the Indochinese refugee population in France is composed of roughly comparable proportions of Vietnamese, Sino-Vietnamese, Cambodians, Sino-Cambodians, highland Laotians, and lowland Laotians. American intervention to contain communism was primarily focused on South Vietnam, with forays into Cambodia and Laos. Again, it is predictable that the Indochinese refugee population in the U.S. would be largely Vietnamese. Thus French refugee policy is closer to the Israeli philosophy of "in-gathering exiles" than it is to the American tactic of using refugee admissions to recoup political losses or advance foreign policy goals. But both France and the U.S. have ethnically diverse populations of Indochinese refugees, although there is more diversity in the former than in the latter.

The class backgrounds of the arriving refugees follow a similar pattern (see Table 5.3). The use of different job and skill categories in France and the U.S. complicates the comparison. In addition, the application of occupational categories from an industrial economy to migrants from the Third World further reduces the utility of these data. Finally, the absence of data on the 10,000 Indochinese who

Table 5.3. Occupational Backgrounds of Indochinese Refugees in France and the United States, 1975-1983 (in percent).

France, 1976-1983	
Agriculture	11
Manual Worker	43
Skilled Worker	21
Commerce and Artisan	11
Managerial and Professional	6
Military	5
U.S., 1975-1983	
Farmer and Fisher	16
Laborer	2
Semi-Skilled	7
Skilled	13
Service Worker	6
Sales and Clerical	43
Managerial and Professional	13
*U.S., 1975**	
Farming, Fishing, and Forestry	6
Benchwork, Assembly, and Repair	4
Structural and Construction	7
Transportation and Miscellaneous	18
Service	8
Sales and Clerical	13
Medical	8
Managerial and Professional	26

* U.S Department of Labor job skills categories, not actual occupations.

Source : FTDA 1983a; Kelly 1977; U.S. ORR 1984.

arrived to France in 1975 (a wave of army officers and government officials) inflates the proportion of the refugees who are manual laborers. What can be concluded is that the Indochinese refugee populations in France and the U.S. are internally diverse rather than being composed of fundamentally different classes.

Because of these common attributes, the arrival of Indochinese refugees challenged policy makers in France and the U.S. in similar ways. In 1975, allied aliens from Indochina began arriving to the two western countries with the greatest historical ties to the region. Although France curtailed the migration in the mid-1980s, while the U.S. continued admissions into the 1990s, large numbers of Indochinese refugees arrived between 1975 and 1982, the period when the two states formulated their policies for managing the refugees' adaptation. Moreover, both refugee flows were quite heterogeneous: the migrants ranged from Saigon elites fluent in French and English to preliterate tribal minorities from the mountains of Laos. Thus differences between the French and American modes of state incorporation are far more likely to stem from variation in the historical context of the migration and the structure of the welfare state and the nation-state, than from the demographic characteristics of the refugees.

Historical Variation from
French Immigration History

The historical context of Indochinese refugees' arrival to France is in stark contrast to that for the U.S. Where political migrants from Vietnam, Laos, and Cambodia were America's first allied aliens, for France they were preceded by decades of migration that stemmed from failed foreign policy. France has a long history of asylum for political migrants. The Constitution of 1789 contained a phrase which has been reproduced in all subsequent constitutions: "All men persecuted for their actions in favor of liberty have the right to asylum in territories of the Republic." However, France received few displaced persons following World War Two and even fewer refugees fleeing new communist regimes in Eastern Europe (Marrus 1985). Instead, the flow of political migrants to France during the 1950s and 1960s was dominated by decolonization and the arrival of nearly 1.5 million repatriates (see Table 5.4).

The largest flow came from Algeria, and the French state went to unprecedented lengths to incorporate the *pieds noirs*. Formal assistance to citizens forced out of French colonies began in 1939, when the Ministry of Foreign Affairs created the Committee of Mutual Aid for French Repatriates. The Committee's powers increased

Table 5.4. Repatriates from Former French Colonies, 1954-1970.

Former Territory	Number	Percentage
Algeria	959,140	67.5
Morocco	239,659	16.9
Tunisia	175,546	12.4
Indochina	30,475	2.1
Subsaharan Africa	8,046	.6
Egypt*	7,354	.5
Total	1,420,220	100.0

* Egypt is not a former French colony. These repatriates are primarily French owners of cotton plantations.

Source : Papyle 1973.

during the 1950s as more migrants from former colonies arrived (de Vernejoul 1961). Legislation in December of 1961 vastly expanded social welfare programs for repatriates: finding employment and rehiring public employees; locating housing in a period when lodging was scarce; and indemnification for lost land, capital, and savings (JO 1964).

But even with French citizenship, the pieds noirs remained culturally distinct from the highly nuanced francophone mannerisms of the metropolis. Twenty-two years after the migration, a survey found that the French public thought the pieds noirs were less integrated into French society than were immigrants from Spain, Italy, Poland, and Portugal (Hannoun 1987). A pieds noirs rally in Nice marking the twenty-fifth anniversary of the migration drew a crowd of 300,000 (Noli 1987). The arrival of repatriates from North Africa was regarded by the French state, French civil society, and the repatriates themselves as a migration by an ethnically distinct populations who paid the price for failed French foreign policy.

The migration from Algeria also included a group of allied aliens called the *harkis*: Muslim troops under command of French officers. Between 1962 and 1964, 50,000 harkis and their dependents chose flight to France rather than remain in Algeria after independence (Documents Nord-Afriques 1965). By 1973, the harkis population, including the second-generation born in France, numbered 200,000 (Papyle 1973). Beginning in the late 1950s, France also began recruiting immigrant workers from former colonies. By 1975, one-third of all foreigners in the country were North Africans (Documentation

Française 1982), and extensive social welfare programs were implemented to provide housing, social services, and social control for these single, male immigrants (Hein 1991b). Decolonization, not East-West conflict, dominated twentieth century French history and the arrival of Indochinese refugees could only be a ripple in this larger flow of migrants uprooted by political change in North-South relations.

The second historical factor in the Indochinese migration to the U.S. and France is the development of Indochinese communities prior to 1975. Less than 20,000 Vietnamese resided in the U.S. when a communist government came to power in their homeland, but Indochinese migration to France was more than half a century old by the time refugees from Vietnam, Laos, and Cambodia began arriving. The earliest migrants were Vietnamese laborers recruited during World Wars One and Two to work in heavy industry and in military construction (Cross 1983; Horne 1985). In 1918, 2,500 Indochinese workers were "loaned" by the French government to the U.S. Army in what must have been the first contact between the American military and the Vietnamese (Khoa 1985). Students (McConnell 1989; Thompson 1952), Eurasian orphans (Tran 1964; Réach 1967), political exiles (Meunier 1974), and revolutionaries (Hemery 1975) also migrated, and by 1963 there were over 70,000 Vietnamese in France (National Institute of Statistics 1972). Between 1962 and the fall of Saigon in April of 1975, some 125,000 Vietnamese emigrated to France, although many also returned during this period. In 1974, the Cambodian population numbered about 6,000 and the Laotian population somewhat less, but 50 percent of both populations lived in the Paris region (Meunier 1974). These earlier migrations created an Indochinese, predominately Vietnamese, population numbering some 100,000 when the first wave of refugees arrived in 1975.

Public opinion is the final historical factor shaping the state's incorporation of Indochinese refugees in France and the U.S. The American public had distinctly negative reactions to the admission of Indochinese refugees, and many members of the U.S. House of Representatives shared their feelings. By contrast, French public opinion towards the refugees was highly favorable (see Table 5.5). In 1979, President Giscard d'Estaing went on national television to urge citizens to form sponsor groups. That year, private vessels commissioned by the French government began sailing rescue missions in the South China Sea, eventually saving over 10,000 boat people (Deloche and Thread 1987). Operations continued into the late 1980s. When a ship returned to its home port in Rouen with 229 Vietnamese, the refugees were greeted with flags, flowers, the Minister of Social

Affairs, and over $150,000 raised by the local populace to aid their resettlement (Bahaut-Meurant and Marie 1987). Even at the end of the 1980s, a study of adjustment among all refugees noted that the Indochinese benefit "from a very favorable image with the French population, which facilitates their access to employment, housing, and aid from volunteers" (Migrations Etudes 1989, p. 7).

Positive public opinion toward the refugees is especially noteworthy given the overwhelmingly negative attitudes toward other foreigners at the time. A 1974 survey found that 79 percent of respondents thought foreign workers took jobs from French citizens, and 65 percent believed that during a severe economic crisis foreigners should be laid-off first (Girard et al. 1974). Even though the policy of recruiting immigrant workers ended in 1974, a 1977 survey revealed that 61 percent of the public thought there were too many foreigners in France (Hannoun 1987). By 1983, 67 percent of the socialist electorate—the most liberal population in France on "the foreigner problem"—favored reducing the number of immigrant workers in the country (Jaffré 1986). Further analysis of the data in Table 5.5 indicates that even self-identified communists were willing to aid Indochinese refugees fleeing communist revolutions in their homelands. Altogether, only 32 percent of respondents answered "no" to all five

Table 5.5. French Public Opinion Towards Indochinese Refugees (in percent).

	Yes	No	Don't Know
Should aid to Southeast Asian refugees be an important subject for the French?	77	17	6
Do you agree with the idea that the European Economic Community should in the future except 1 refugee for every 1,000 inhabitants, thus 53,000 for France?	50	40	10
What are you personally ready to do for the refugees?			
Find a job:	40	54	6
Find housing:	47	47	6
Adopt a child:	19	77	4
Would you give about $20 a month for two years to help a refugee family?	21	73	6

Note : Survey of 1,000 French citizens.

Source : L'Express 1979.

questions on readiness to help the refugees. Thus more than two-thirds of the French public expressed willingness to aid Indochinese refugees and to honor the historical claims they could make upon France.

Political Variation from
the French Welfare State

The second set of factors shaping state incorporation of international migrants is the structure of the welfare state, particularly the role of the central government and the relationship between citizens and social welfare programs. In the U.S., social welfare policy and management of programs is divided between the central, state, and local government, a system called federalism. In France, the central government formulates policy but often allows interest groups and parapublic bureaucracies to manage the programs, a system called corporatism (Esping-Anderson 1990). Where American aid is designed to restrict citizens' access to social welfare programs, French eligibility norms are encompassing because they seek to include as many citizens as possible in public programs. Both differences dramatically affect how the French state creates social citizenship for Indochinese refugees.

Corporatist Politics

Class relations in France set the stage for corporatism because specialized programs developed prior to full centralization of the social welfare system. A tight labor market required employers to provide social security programs (Hatzfield 1971), both the working and middle class used private insurance (Ashford 1986), and shopkeepers and other nonsalaried, nonagricultural workers resisted integration into the national social security system into the 1950s (Fournier and Questiaux 1980). But it was the fragmentation of interest groups that ultimately required the separation of policy making and management (Rimlinger 1971). Splits between Catholic and communist unions, and the divergent interests of urban and rural areas, led to a patchwork of social welfare programs at the national level (Ashford 1982).

Political instability also contributed to the development of a corporatist welfare state. The first three decades of the twentieth century were critical years for the modern welfare state. But in France the Third Republic (1875–1940) was marked by political stalemates that effectively precluded the development of national democratic political institutions (Higley and Burton 1989). Frequent government turnovers during the Fourth Republic (1945-1958) further delayed development despite high levels of political mobilization and the presence of an industrial, urban labor force (Flora and Alber 1987). Between 1950 and 1975, France increased social transfer expenditures under center or center-right governments, while the trend in Western Europe went the other direction (Kohl 1987; Wilensky 1987).

Stephens (1979, p. 156) characterizes the political development of the French welfare state as a case of "corporate collectivism" because "public sector build up is carried out by socialists in coalition with Catholic or center parties, but then administered by conservative forces for a long period of time." Corporatism also describes the organization of the French welfare state: policy is formulated at the national level, but implemented through a collection of interest groups brought together by the state (Crozier 1964; Laroque 1984).

Encompassing Eligibility Norms

Although France had difficulty organizing a welfare state "the granting of social rights was hardly ever a seriously contested issue" (Esping-Anderson 1990, p. 27). Social welfare in France developed not as a response to paupers and urban misery, as in Britain and the U.S., but with the rise of republicanism and the national state (Ashford 1986). State intervention in the area of poor relief between 1871 and 1912 confirms that state spending hinged on the availability of resources rather than the severity of socioeconomic problems (Weiss 1983). After World War Two, the combination of economic surplus and social needs is a better predictor of social welfare expenditures in France than political mobilization (Hage and Hanneman 1980). Indeed, French social welfare expenditures are more closely tied to economic fluctuations than other European countries' expenditures are, and far more than expenditures in the U.S. (Kohl 1987). When the left came to power in 1981 for the first time in twenty-three years, its social welfare policies differed little from those of the right during the 1970s (Ross 1988). In France, the provision of social welfare is a firmly established responsibility of the state rather than the goal of a particular political party.

France lags behind Scandinavia in achieving a fully social democratic welfare state (Esping-Anderson 1990). Yet in contrast to the U.S., France seeks to include citizens in social welfare programs. By the late 1970s, 98 percent of the French population was receiving some form of social welfare payment (Fournier and Questiaux 1980). A survey found that the French public considers the hypothetical suppression of social security more serious than ending the right to vote or the ability to choose an employer (Laroque 1984). The family allowance program, which has no American counterpart, typifies this encompassing approach to social welfare.

In 1932, France became the first country in Western Europe to establish a national Family Allowance program. Approximately one-third of the French population benefits from the family allowance, slightly more than the number receiving social security (Fournier and Questiaux 1980). About 45 percent of family allowance funds are allocated without any eligibility requirements based on family income, but low-income families receive larger payments (Larroque 1984). The program also includes health and social services, often without income eligibility criteria (Documentation Française 1966). The family allowance epitomizes the approach to social welfare where "social assistance has been so fully freed from taint or stigma that it can be used wherever needed as a supplementary source of aid and not confined to any specific category of persons" (Marshall 1964, p. 316). This encompassing eligibility norm, coupled with a corporatist political system, explains much of the difference between the French and American forms of social citizenship created for Indochinese refugees.

Cultural Variation from the French Nation-State

Where the welfare state determines international migrants' access to public resources, the nation-state determines the development of ethnic communities. In the U.S., traditions of ethnic pluralism are split between an immigrant legacy from European-Americans and a minority heritage from African-Americans. The first tradition presents ethnicity as useful and eventually optional, while in the second tradition race leads to an inferior status in the society. This polarized pattern of race and ethnic relations contrasts with the concentric nation-state in France. Geography and language provide a cultural core in France, while religion and colonial history, not race, determine the acceptability of international migrants.

The Cultural Core: Geography and Language

The cultural core of the French nation-state developed as the state expanded markets and military control outwards from the Paris region (Braudel 1988). Present day France developed between the thirteenth and sixteenth centuries as Occitania, Brittany, Catalonia, and other independent domains fell to the French king by conquest or treaty. The tenuous relationship between the capital and the provinces continued for centuries, in part because of territorial disputes with neighboring countries. Nice, now the country's fifth largest city, only moved from Italian to French jurisdiction in 1860. Alsace, part of France since the mid-seventeenth century, became German territory between 1871 and 1918, and again during the Second World War. Although assimilation of the provinces to Parisian culture accelerated after the 1789 revolution (McNeil 1986), it only neared completion during the early twentieth century (Weber 1976). Renewed political mobilization by Basques, Bretons, Corsicans, and other regional ethnic groups during the 1970s reconfirmed that the French nation-state is composed of a cultural core and a periphery (Beer 1980).

Colonization in Africa and Asia between 1850 and 1900 augmented the formation of a cultural core. With an empire surpassed in size only by that of Great Britain, mainland France itself became the core of a francophonic world system. To justify imperialism, French foreign policy makers and intellectuals described it as a "civilizing mission" and referred to the colonies as "France over-seas" (Betts 1961). Colonialism helped define the French nation-state as surely as had expansion into Occitania six hundred years earlier. Regional ethnic groups, such as Bretons and Corsicans, tended to be over represented among *French* colonists in Indochina (Robequain 1944) and North Africa (Tafan 1986). French became the official language in the colonies, and France continued to seek a special relationship with francophonic countries after independence.

During the 1960s, 90 percent of French assistance to Vietnam went for language training, while other donor countries dispersed their aid among health, public works, and education (Sullivan 1978). A communist revolution changed nothing. In 1976–1977, France provided the equivalent of $124 million in financial aid to Vietnam, with French language instruction exceeding expenditures for all other public services (JO II 1979). This aid violated the American embargo on assistance to the new communist regime. But the French Ministry of Foreign Affairs justified the aid on the grounds that:

> The Vietnamese people were for too long part of France's destiny for us to abandon them when they are more and more isolated. . . . In addition, if we do not maintain a cultural presence, in less than a generation our language will cease to be taught, which will benefit Russian (the dominant power today), and English (after twenty years of American influence in the South). . . . Of all the western countries, France is the only one which can continue, by virtue of the past, to maintain such relations today (JO II 1979, p. 104).

Citizenship, Religion, and Colonial History

Colonialism eventually affected domestic race and ethnic relations as Asians and Africans migrated to France. Nearly 200,000 blacks, Muslims, and Asians were imported during World War One as France drained its colonies of labor to replace French workers sent to the front (Cross 1983). After World War Two, France again turned to colonies and former colonies for immigrant workers. By 1975, over one million North and Subsaharan Africans lived in France (Castles and Kosack 1985). Algerians, Moroccans, and Tunisians now account for more than one-third of all foreigners. Yet despite sustained immigration since the 1960s, French social scientists find little evidence that ethnic communities along the American model exist in France (Noiriel 1988; Schnapper 1991).

Citizenship is one means for the nation-state to assimilate foreigners, and, in comparison to Germany, France has relatively liberal naturalization criteria (Brubaker 1990). But, in contrast to the U.S., children born in France to immigrant parents retain their parents' nationality until they reach the age of eighteen. Acquisition of French citizenship is then automatic. In the late 1980s, a Commission on Nationality proposed that the second generation should have to request in writing to become citizens. According to the commission: France "is characterized . . . by a universal bill of rights and by a tradition of the nation-state where national unity resides in cultural unity" (Documentation Française 1988, p. 23).

The French nation-state's current inability to assimilate North Africans reveals the rings around its cultural core. The eminent historian Fernand Braudel (1990, pp. 214–215) describes the problem as "a clash of civilizations" because "Islam is more than a religion, it is a whole civilization full of vigor, an entire way of life." The French public shares this opinion. "Cohabitation" between the French and immigrants is made difficult not by differences in skin color or even language, but by immigrants' customs and religion (Acualités Migrations 1989). This view was tested in 1989 when a school administrator asked two Muslim teenage girls not to wear foulards. There refusal to remove their scarves caused a national debate over the separation of church and state, and the role of the French school as an agent of assimilation. By 66 percent to 26 percent, the French public disapproved of the Minister of Education's decision to allow the girls to remain in school (Acualités Migrations 1989).

Culture also is more important than race as a structural feature of the French nation-state. In 1969, 62 percent of the French, but only 20 percent of Americans, approved of marriage between blacks and whites (Dupin 1990). The hypothetical arrival of a North African family next-door elicits twice the opposition as would the arrival of a family of black Africans (Hannoun 1987). The survey found almost no objection to having black neighbors from the French overseas departments of Guadeloupe, Martinique and Réunion.

Nonetheless, the French nation-state is particularly sensitive to the geographic concentration of ethnic groups. The French public ranks drugs and delinquency as the most serious problems caused by immigrants. But combined, "ghetto of immigrants in community," "problems of cohabitation in neighborhood," and "problems of cohabitation in building" are about equal to these two problem areas. In fact, more evenly distributing immigrants receives the highest approval rating (76 percent) of nine measures to promote adjustment among immigrants. The next most popular solution (72 percent in favor) is rehabilitating undesirable neighborhoods where there are many immigrants (Hastings and Hastings 1991).

Added to this sensitivity to immigrants' religion and residential concentration is their link to colonial history. Approximately 45 percent of the foreign population in France are first and second generation immigrants from former colonies in Asia and Africa. Violent decolonization in North Africa, but a bloodless French departure below the Sahara, in part explains the different tolerance levels for North versus West and Central Africans (Belbahri 1987). Jean-Marie Le Pen, the leader of the far right National Front which proposes deporting immigrants, is a former paratrooper who saw action in Algeria, and many of his supporters are the pieds noirs (Mayer and Perrineau 1989). During the mid-1980s, a hate group responsible for a series of bombings against North African immigrants named itself after the French king who defeated an army of invading Moors in 732. Significantly, survey questions using the term "Arab" elicit more negative responses than those using the term "Muslim," suggesting a greater sensitivity to broad cultural differences (Hannoun 1987). Geography, language, religion, and history—in short, civilization—create a concentric nation-state in France.

Conclusion

The political, temporal, and demographic similarities between the Indochinese migrations to France and the U.S. after 1975 mean that the social characteristics of the refugees are unlikely to cause different modes of state incorporation. Of greater importance is the historical context of the migration. Migration to France due to military defeat and decolonization occurred for decades prior to the arrival of Indochinese refugees. Receiving allied aliens due to failed foreign policy was a novel experience for the American state. Indochinese communities existed in France before 1975, while they were absent from the U.S. until the refugees arrived. Positive opinion of Indochinese refugees among the French public is at odds with American nativism.

The refugees' social citizenship is determined by how these historical factors interact with the structure of the welfare state. Federalist politics in the U.S. contrasts with corporatism in France. Restrictive versus encompassing eligibility norms distinguish American and French approaches to the distribution of public resources, respectively. Historical factors also interact with the structure of the nation-state to determine the development of ethnic communities. Cultural differences and historical symbols influence migrants' passage into a concentric nation-state in France. Conversely, an immigrant legacy and a minority heritage lead to an uneasy coexistence in a racially divided nation-state in the U.S. The simultaneous arrival of Indochinese refugees to the U.S. and France reveals how this variation in historical context and state structures leads to different modes of incorporation for international migrants.

6

The French Mode of State Incorporation

Historical context makes each migration unique. Past events and the timing of the migration add elements to the adaptation process that will differ from one population of migrants to another. But at the macro-level, history itself is a variable because some societies are more influenced by the past than others. This cross-national variation in the importance of historical factors is well documented by the Indochinese refugee migration. Despite the immediacy of the Vietnam War, past events are notable for their absence in the American state's incorporation of the refugees. Conversely, the French mode of incorporation is quite historically determined even though France withdrew from Indochina in 1954.

Ultimately, it is the relationship between the welfare state and the nation-state that most determines a mode of state incorporation. States use their social welfare systems to define international migrants' rights to resources. Political models and norms for distributing public goods determine the type of social citizenship a social welfare system produces. Similarly, states draw upon traditions of race and ethnic relations as they manage migrants' cultural adjustment. The alignment of ethnicity, race, and religion in the nation-state determines the pattern of ethnic community formation. Variation in welfare state and nation-state structures causes differences in migrants' social citizenship and ethnic communities.

Distributing public goods and regulating cultural pluralism represent distinct state interests, and these interests compete for dominance at the national level. In the U.S., social welfare costs take priority over managing the development of ethnic communities. In France, preventing the creation of ethnic communities is more important than minimizing expenditures by the social welfare system.

Providing Social Citizenship

In the American mode of incorporation, a federalist welfare state encounters the country's first allied aliens resulting in greater centralization of aid than typically occurs in new programs. Pervasive nativism further pushes the central government to take full responsibility given the refugees' negative reception at the local level. Through the Indochinese Refugee Program and then the Office of Refugee Resettlement, the state channels resources to the Indochinese that they would otherwise not receive. Federal funding for initial resettlement aid and delegation of many resettlement tasks to nonprofit organizations frees the refugees from the control usually exercised by local public aid bureaus. But restrictive eligibility norms stigmatize the refugees and quickly transform them from allied aliens to welfare clients.

A very different form of social citizenship developed in France. Migration from former French colonies preceded the arrival of Indochinese refugees and the French state has a repertoire of programs at its disposal for incorporating international migrants. Although the state values these latest refugees, the corporatist political process channels them into preexisting programs which tend not to recognize "refugee" as a distinct type of client. However, encompassing eligibility norms mean that there are few negative labels attached to the recipients of aid. Yet the resettlement program exerts extensive control over the refugees because corporatism leads to the distribution of resettlement functions to numerous public and private organizations. Control is further heightened since positive public opinion toward the refugees encourages the state to utilize local sponsors whose distance from Paris allows them to mediate central government policy. Indochinese refugees arriving in France enter a form of social citizenship characterized by a moderate level of resources, a high degree of social control, but no stigma.

Frugal Resources

Unlike the U.S., France has signed the U.N. Convention Relative to the Status of Refugees and is obligated to provide to refugees the same social welfare benefits available to citizens. However, all the rights under the convention accrue after a migrant is certified a refugee, which is a lengthy process in France because migrants apply for the status after their arrival (Costa-Lascoux 1987). Some forms of social welfare are available to migrants waiting for a decision (Tiberghien 1985; de Wangen 1985). But with the arrival of Indochinese refugees the French state sought to assist an entire population of political migrants due to historical ties rather than because of a two decade old convention.

The corporatist political process immediately set to work when the first Vietnamese refugees arrived in the spring of 1975. The Ministry of Health sent a circular to each prefect (the French equivalent of governor) requesting that they locate vacant half-way houses in their department, assuring them that: "The financing will be supported entirely by the state from funds for the homeless. . . . The refugees will be eligible for all necessary forms of social assistance, particularly the family allocation" (MS 1975a, p. 2). A second circular reiterated that "there will be no thought of making communities receiving refugees bear the costs of their reinsertion. . . . Local initiatives will always be supported and supplemented through national solidarity" (MS 1975b, p. 3). The Ministries of Foreign Affairs and Health then organized a hurried meeting with the key organizations that historically worked with refugees, resulting in a Protocol on the Reception of Indochinese Refugees (FTDA 1975).

Reflecting on the meeting the director of one association described how the state used the social welfare system to manage the incorporation of Indochinese allied aliens:

> From that moment it became clear that the government would make a special effort to assure the successful reception of these refugees. This effort has not ceased to be confirmed. Today a collection of a dozen circulars coming from four ministries, without counting particular measures taken by other ministries, constitute the administrative arsenal launched by the government to facilitate the insertion of refugees from Indochina (FTDA 1976, p. 4).

By 1980, over 100,000 Indochinese refugees had arrived to France and the Cabinet reported: "Thanks to the financial effort of the State, which has provided $296 million, the insertion of the refugees in French society . . . is certain of being particularly successful" (Regards sur l'Actualité 1980b, p. 63). Clearly, corporatism shaped the refugee resettlement program: the state sets policy while interest groups and subnational government implement programs.

Setting the boundaries within which nonstate organizations pursue program implementation is the key task for the corporatist state. In the case of international migration, these "rules of the game" are migrants' status in the social welfare system. The French state subsumes refugees under broad social problems, rather than aiding them through the status "refugee," as the American state does (see Table 6.1). In some cases the refugees are simply made eligible for the same benefits as natives. The Ministry of the Interior provides residency cards which allow the refugees to obtain a family allocation and other basic forms of assistance (Ministère de l'Intérieur 1976). But most aid is provided by likening the refugees to known social problems rather than making "refugee" a domestic social problem. The Ministry of Labor made the refugees eligible for work permits and job training programs by listing Cambodians and Vietnamese with other special foreign populations, such as foreigners having served in the French military and Moroccans residing in France before independence (MT 1975; JO 1976a). Citing assistance to the pieds noirs, a decree authorizes the payment of unemployment insurance to refugees even when they lack sufficient work histories to qualify (JO 1984a).

The core of the French resettlement program is residence in a half-way house or *foyer d'hébergement*. Unless refugees immediately join relatives (termed the "individual solution") they will reside in a foyer and receive food, shelter, and social services for about six months. Immigrants from Algeria, Morocco, and Tunisia, all former French colonies, have lived in foyers since the late 1950s, and 60 percent of Indochinese refugees sent to foyers entered institutions also inhabited by immigrant workers (Hein 1991b). However, the state uses funds for the homeless to pay for refugees' residence in foyers, while immigrant workers pay for it themselves. Legislation added refugees to vagabonds, recently released prisoners, and

Table 6.1. Social Welfare Programs for Indochinese Refugees in France.

Program	Date of Law	Type of Probelm	Eligibility Criterion
Ministry of the Interior			
Residency Card	Prior to 1975	Foreigner	Nationality
Ministry of Social Affairs			
Residence in CPH	Prior to 1975	Homeless	Nationality and Refugee
Language Training	Prior to 1975	Foreigner	Residence in CPH
Insertion Allocation	After 1975	Unemployed	Refugee
Ministry of Labor			
Work Permit	Prior to 1975	Foreigner	Nationality
Job Training	Prior to 1975	Unemployed	Nationality and Refugee
Ministry of Foreign Affairs			
FILAID*	After 1975	Refugee	Nationality

* Cash grants for refugees with the individual solution.

other persons lacking lodging, and allowed foyers receiving refugees to obtain contracts with the state and become an official *centre provisoire d'hébergement* (CPH) or temporary settlement center (JO 1976b).

The CPH well illustrates how the central government sets policy on international migration, while interest groups, subnational government, and parapublic organizations provide aid to the migrants. This form of social citizenship results from the interaction of a corporatist social welfare system and a history of incorporating international migrants from former French colonies. In combination, these factors weaken the link between international and domestic policy in France. Certification as a "refugee" by the U.S. State Department translates into significant aid from the U.S. Department of Health and Human Services. But the connection between international migration and domestic aid is more tenuous between the French Ministry of Foreign Affairs and the Ministry of Social Affairs because their function is to define refugees' eligibility for other actors, rather than directly provide aid themselves.

The only assistance specifically for Indochinese refugees is cash grants averaging $300 from the Ministry of Foreign Affairs (Parais 1982). The Ministry of Social Affairs describes the consequences of refugees' lack of a special social welfare status: "once leaving the reception system the refugees have a tendency to fall into the traditional channels 'reserved' for immigrant workers. They become 'immigrant workers' with refugee status" (MAS 1985, p. 9). Assistance to Indochinese refugees is thus confined to their six month residence in a CPH, and refugees with the individual solution receive almost no assistance. According to the association which manages the CPH system: "As soon as the refugees have left a CPH, neither the associations nor FTDA are in any way responsible for their situation, which is the same as that of foreign workers in France. Only the refugees' permanent residence is better guaranteed because in no case will they be expelled to their country of origin" (FTDA 1981a, p. 2).

Estimates by the French government place the cost of resettling a refugee between $2,750 and $3,000 (JO 1983a; Regards sur l'Actualité 1980b). During the 1980s, the U.S. Office of Refugee Resettlement and the U.S. Bureau for Refugee Programs combined spent approximately $5,400 for each refugee resettled, excluding the cost of aiding refugees before they arrived to the U.S. Not only are per capita expenditures less in France, but the aid is almost entirely in-kind, such as shelter, food, and language classes. Conversely, about two-thirds of American resettlement costs are for cash public assistance, a resource which allows the refugees greater discretion over its use. In France, a history of migration from former colonies combines with a corporatist political process to diminish the resources refugees receive from their social citizenship.

Extensive Social Control

The French state funds the resettlement program and also sets general policy. But management of the program follows the corporatist structure of the larger social welfare system. An intricate division of labor multiplies the number of organizations working with refugees, while the American resettlement program conserves organizations. Policy regarding refugees in the U.S. is made through offices in the State Department and the Department of Health and Human Services. In France, each government bureaucracy manages a facet of the refugees' adaptation, such as residence permits, work authorization, and family allocation. As a result, refugee resettlement policy is comprised of "a collection of a dozen circulars coming from four ministries, without counting particular measures taken by other ministries" (FTDA 1976, p. 4). This division of labor extends to local government, the nonprofit sector, and even staff in CPHs. Allocating a single function to an organization increases social control over the refugees because they have no alternative source of services.

Each voluntary agency has a state contract to provide a single service, such as receiving refugees at the airport, opening CPHs, and aiding refugees who immediately join relatives (Gogler 1982; Quinsat 1984). In the U.S., a voluntary agency provides an array of resettlement services for the refugees it sponsors. The two most important associations in France are functional opposites. France Terre d'Asile gives CPH status to select foyers and then allocates refugees to them. The National Relief Committee (CNE in French) collects donations, job offers, and other resources in the private sector and dispenses them to refugees whose needs cannot be meet through the formal resettlement program.

There also are important political differences between the two associations. The CNE is composed of businessmen, government officials, and army officers (some having served in former colonies). These elites see in Indochinese refugees the vindication of colonialism, since human rights conditions under communist regimes are often as bad or worse than they were under the French administration. Conversely, FTDA originated in 1970 to promote the right of asylum following the deportation of hundreds of foreigners for their part in the strikes and demonstrations of the late 1960s. It developed into an important organization in 1973 with the arrival of Chilean refugees, who fled a right-wing coup. By organizing the work of voluntary associations according to corporatist principles, the French state includes in the resettlement program organizations that would not otherwise cooperate. The positive opinion of the refugees on both the left and the right requires the state to divide functions among the numerous groups seeking to aid Indochinese refugees.

The combination of corporatism and positive opinion also leads to a strong role for prefects, mayors, and other local officials. In its second circular to the prefects the Ministry of Health stated that assistance to Indochinese refugees "cannot be centralized. It must make use of multiple operations initiated locally which will be coordinated by your means" (MS 1975b, p. 3). Because of this policy, local government officials are gatekeepers to social welfare programs.

For example, in early 1981 a prefect stopped recognizing marriages among Southeast Asians that occurred in their homelands after communist governments came to power (FTDA 1981c). Since matrimony is a prerequisite for some forms of social assistance, this action curtailed the refugees' social citizenship. Local government officials also control the CPHs in their area. When FTDA sought to open a new CPH in the city of Chateauroux it learned that: "The mayor is strongly opposed to a new 'refugee' operation. . . . An aid to the mayor . . . would advise waiting for the outcome of the next municipal election" (FTDA 1983c, np). Mayors even take an interest in particular refugee families. An FTDA representative reported the fate of a Hmong family after it left a CPH near Dijon to stay with a relative in the nearby city of Brian. The relative would not house them and the family applied for public housing, whereupon: "The mayor of Brian, who had not been informed of their arrival either by the mayor of Dijon or by the CPH, refused to 'recognize' this family and they could not obtain housing, work, or social assistance" (FTDA 1984b, np). In the U.S., local government offices do not mediate the incorporation process. A federalist social welfare system allows the central government extensive control over the resettlement program because it pays the full costs for a period of time.

The American state also centralizes aid because of intense nativism at the local level. Positive opinion allows the French state to entrust the incorporation of the refugees to local sponsors. When 1,500 Indochinese refugees began arriving each month in the summer of 1981, the prefects received instructions to "coordinate the solidarity manifested by local communities, public and private organizations, the associations, and individuals supporting the refugees" (MSN 1981, p. 2).

The pervasiveness of local sponsor groups diversifies the

organizations resettling refugees in France. In the department of Ardèche, a Catholic association opened a center for Hmong refugees in an abandoned Carmelite convent (Gouverneur 1978). A description of the CPH at Douvaine provides a history of local social welfare: originally it was an orphanage, then a boarding school, and when Indochinese refugees arrived it also housed battered women and senior citizens (FTDA 1981f). Similarly, at the CPH in Laon, thirty Indochinese refugees share residence with unemployed youth, juvenile delinquents, and "women in distress" (FTDA 1983b). A survey of forty-eight CPHs found that in only two were the refugees the sole clients (FTDA 1981e). The most common CPH is an association for immigrants operating an immigrant foyer. But this type accounts for only 16 percent of all CPHs created between 1975 and 1979, suggesting the enormous diversity of the assistance, and thus social citizenship, provided to refugees (see Table 6.2.). In contrast to the use of local organizations to resettle refugees in France, in the U.S. thirteen national voluntary agencies sponsor refugees through branch offices in major cities (North et al. 1982).

The reliance on local rather than national sponsors in France encapsulates refugees within community relations, and consequently

Table 6.2. Organization of French Temporary Settlement Centers for Indochinese Refugees (in percent).

Type of Association Providing Services	Type of Institution Providing Housing			
	Immigrant Worker	Young Worker	Vaction House	Diverse
Immigrant Worker	16	7	2	0
Foyer Itself	10	11	5	2
Public Aid Bureau	2	0	1	2
Religious	0	2	1	3
Community	1	0	6	5
National	13	2	2	2
Refugee Reception Group	2	0	1	2

Note : For the 122 temporary settlement centers created between May of 1975 and July of 1979.

Source : Ajchenbaum et al. 1979.

gives sponsors greater control over the refugees' adjustment. Refugees in the U.S. have greater autonomy: their relationship with sponsoring organizations is more bureaucratic and these organizations are less dependent on local conditions for their operations. One consequence of refugees' dependence on community sponsors in France is that local conditions determine the extent of their social citizenship, for example, the closing of a CPH (see Table 6.3). Declining numbers of arriving refugee and the availability of jobs are the most frequent causes of closings. However, neither are very efficacious since they lead to closings only in combination with other causes. The administration of the CPH, the housing market, and the opinions of local officials, are more powerful causes in actually determining the fate of a CPH. On the whole, local rather than national conditions are more significant in shaping the resettlement of Indochinese refugees in France. Decentralizing incorporation to take advantage of positive public opinion increases local sponsors' control over the refugees by local sponsors, especially prefects and mayors. In the U.S., major changes in the resettlement program result from fiscal decisions at the national level, such as cuts in spending to balance the federal budget.

Because local officials control refugees' access to social welfare resources, many CPHs divide their social services by function. Separate staff help refugees get employment permits and a family allocation, while others work on housing and job training. A visit to one CPH disclosed that it had six different budgets for its staff as a result of local policy (FTDA 1984d). CPH staff explain that they specialize in a single service in order to have the expertise necessary to wrest benefits from a local government office. In the U.S., federal funds assure the supply of services, and refugees usually do not need

Table 6.3. Causes of Closing Among French Temporary Settlement Centers (in percent).

Type of Cause	All Causes	Only Cause
Decline in Refugee Admissions	34	32
Shortage of Jobs	26	38
Change in CPH	19	52
Local Government Objects	11	70
Shortage of Housing	6	80
Decision by National Agency	5	100

Note : For 93 causes for 71 temporary settlement centers closed between May of 1975 and July of 1979.

Source : Achjenbaum et al. 1979.

mediators in order to enter a language class or to apply for public assistance. In France, each stage of the incorporation process from the national to the local level is managed by a separate organization or caseworker. Corporatism and positive public opinion cause this functional division of labor, and it decreases refugees' autonomy.

Aid Without Stigma

In 1983, an Interministerial Delegate for Refugees was created to lobby government ministries on the right of asylum (MAS 1985). Yet within five years, the delegate's position was replaced by a Secretary for Humanitarian Action, who now handles problems related to poverty, unemployment, racism, and the adjustment problems of refugees (JO 1988). By expanding the jurisdiction of the post, the French state evidenced the encompassing eligibility norm in the social welfare system: social problems are linked to larger societal issues and thus should be solved collectively.

It might be argued that a moderate level of resources coupled with high social control explains why refugees in France are never accused of "welfare dependency" and "lack of self-sufficiency." However, these American stigmas fail to develop despite evidence that many refugees benefit from income support programs. The proportion of refugee households leaving CPHs without employment was low during the 1970s, but rose during the early 1980s. One survey found that 43 percent of single men and women, and 62 percent of heads of families, left CPHs either unemployed, with temporary jobs, or to enter training programs (FTDA 1982b). A meeting of CPH directors concluded: "The mass of families' income is assured by one person being employed, payments from unemployment insurance, and the family allocation" (FTDA 1982g, np).

Unemployment among refugees is a major concern of CPH staff, but the fact that the refugees rely on income support programs never becomes a stigma. There is heated debate when the refugees receive unemployment compensation while residing in a CPH, since technically the refugees are not in the labor force (FTDA 1982d, 1982f). Yet the encompassing eligibility norm in France leads to an acceptance of the refugees' use of social welfare programs, while the restrictive attitudes in the U.S. quickly stigmatize the very people the aid is designed to assist. To justify a reduction in the number of Indochinese admitted to France, the most disparaging remark the Ministry of Foreign Affairs could muster was that refugee admissions "must be measured against the cost of inserting a refugee into French society, which is evaluated at $2,755" (JO 1983a, np). American critics of the refugees immediately point to public assistance rates.

The absence of evaluations of moral worth based on use of public programs is especially evident in the core of the resettlement program: residence in a CPH. Staff in a Parisian transit center decide if arriving refugees require a stay in one of forty CPHs throughout France or if they can meet their needs with the aid of kin or French sponsors. It is highly revealing of the encompassing approach to social welfare that the term "collective solution" is applied to refugees lacking relatives in France but receiving state assistance, in this case funds for the homeless. Conversely, bypassing the CPHs to join relatives is called the "individual solution." Where American welfare state norms distinguish between public and private, norms in the French social welfare system use the dichotomy collective–individual. Refugees entering a state funded total institution are not thought of as abusing public resources, but ensuring their absorption by the society.

The principal concern of French refugee managers is the length of time refugees reside in a CPH. When the first Vietnamese refugees arrived in May of 1975, the Ministry of Health instructed the prefects:

> The public services of the department . . . must assure the most rapid social insertion possible for refugees housed in the centers. Their support in a collective settlement for more than a few months will transform them, little by little, and will mean the partial loss of the raison d'etre for the generous reception organized by France (MS 1975b, p. 3).

The proportion of refugees residing in CPHs past the six month limit increased substantially during the early 1980s, as more refugees arrived with broken families, fewer transferable job skills, and traumatic experiences of flight and persecution (Ajchenbaum 1983). The demographic change in the refugee flow occurred just as the French economy entered a recession, yet refugee managers often attributed increased dependence on the CPHs to the refugees themselves. Several CPH directors complained of the low "cultural and social level of the latest refugee arrivals," describing them as the "bottom of the barrel of the camps in Thailand" (FTDA 1984c, 1982c).

Clearly, French refugee managers evaluate refugees on their ability to adapt. But Indochinese refugees in France have never been considered a "welfare problem" even when many households rely on social welfare programs for their income. Instead, successful incorporation is measured by the refugees' assimilation into the French nation-state, rather than their cost to the welfare state.

Preventing Ethnic Communities

The American nation-state is dichotomous: ethnicity is approved of when modeled on the experience of European immigrants, while racial differences are penalized. Refugee managers pattern the Indochinese' cultural adjustment on this idealized immigrant legacy. The historical absence of Vietnamese, Laotian, and Cambodian communities leads refugee managers to direct the development of ethnic communities, particularly by funding Asian-American and Indochinese associations to provide sponsorship services. Yet the refugees are also dispersed to reduce resettlement costs, thus replacing cultural with fiscal norms at the national level. The incorporation of Indochinese refugees in the U.S. reveals that the welfare state is given a higher priority than the nation-state.

Refugees arriving in France have a very different experience constructing ethnic communities. The French nation-state is concentric because it contains a cultural core and rings composed of religion, historical symbols, and other components of a civilization. The assimilation of foreigners is a corner stone of this nation-state and dispersing arriving refugees occurs just as in the U.S. However, this policy primarily affects refugees who were peasants and laborers in their homelands. Preexisting Indochinese communities, largely in the Paris region, make social class the selection mechanism through which the state manages the assimilation of some refugees, while allowing others to plan their own adjustment. From officials in government bureaucracies to staff in CPHs, there is a consensus that preventing the development of ethnic communities is more important than minimizing costs to public treasuries.

The Effect of Class Background

French refugee managers are well aware of "the prior existence in France of numerous compatriots from former Indochina, sometimes installed for a very long time" (de Wangen 1980, p. 13). Indeed, FTDA established the individual solution for Indochinese refugees, when it had not existed for arriving Chilean refugees two years earlier, due to the presence of Vietnamese, Laotians, and Cambodians who migrated prior to 1975 (FTDA 1981b; de Wangen 1982). Refugee managers could have substantially reduced the costs of the resettlement program by utilizing established Indochinese as sponsors. Instead, they channeled two-thirds of the refugees into the CPHs, using the welfare state to ensure the assimilation of international migrants from former colonies.

The half-way houses which became CPH had an assimilationist function even before the arrival of Indochinese refugees. According to one circular, residence in a center

> permits the persons received to reflect on their situation, to identify and be able to master their lives. It also permits an apprenticeship in solidarity and in individual and collective responsibilities. Communally oriented action will finally enable them to be situated in the web of society (MS 1976, p. 5).

As Indochinese refugees began to enter these foyers, the Ministry of Health redefined "apprenticeship in solidarity" to include cultural adjustment. Through residence in a CPH, refugees would "be able to acquire, thanks to tested methods, a knowledge of the language and manners of our country" (MS 1979a, p. 1).

Such modest goals gave way to overtly assimilationist prescriptions as the arriving refugees' backgrounds increasingly reflected the mass of Cambodian, Laotian, and Vietnamese society, and less the francophonic elites who arrived following the events in April of 1975. According to the Ministry of Social Affairs: "The socio-cultural level of the refugees is weaker and weaker. The Southeast Asian refugees arriving on the quota are also 'economic' refugees who have not received an education" (MAS 1985, p. 8). The Ministry of Justice provided the most blatant denouncement of the cultural gulf separating these recent refugees from French civilization:

> Over the past several years France has experienced the arrival of very significant numbers of refugees, often from countries with languages, laws, and morals very different from ours. Their adaptation to our administrative system . . . is sometimes difficult because of their ignorance of our institutions, often of our language (JO 1984b, np).

The proportion of refugees sent to the CPHs matches the changing demographics of the migration. Nearly 11,000 Indochinese refugees arrived in France during the year following the fall of Saigon and Phnom Penh. Only 54 percent of this first wave of elites were sent to a CPH (FTDA 1976). But the proportion of refugees given this "collective solution" rose as farmers, fishermen, and unskilled laborers replaced government officials. By 1979, 65 percent of all Indochinese refugees had gone to a CPH (FTDA 1979) and for those arriving in 1980 and 1981 the rate was 70 percent (Ajchenbaum 1983). According to the Ministry of Health, if these latest refugees were allowed to bypass the centers they would "find themselves confronted by insurmountable difficulties, due to their ignorance of our language and our forms of existence" (MS 1980a, p. 1).

When François Mitterrand came to power in 1981, his socialist government changed admission criteria from past service to the empire and ability to speak French to having close relatives in France. But the proportion of refugees given the individual solution did not rise despite the growing pool of potential sponsors (FTDA 1987). The highest government bureau on international migrants stated unequivocally that "disadvantaged" Indochinese refugees should be sent to the CPHs (MSN 1982). In 1983, the Ministry of Foreign Affairs drastically reduced the admission of Indochinese refugees due to "the current possibilities for settlement and insertion of these refugees" (JO 1983b, np). Preexisting communities in a concentric nation-state can only be used by migrants from higher social classes.

The activities of sponsor groups also provides evidence that the French state is willing to pay for the assimilation of peasants and laborers even when an alternative exists. During the height of the boat people crisis in the summer of 1979, the agency coordinating private sponsorship received 9,500 offers of assistance from French associations and communities. However, 77 percent of the 5,600 Indochinese refugees admitted to France between July and September of that year went to a CPH (MS 1979b). Rather than providing refugees with individual solutions, the reception groups helped refugees leave a CPH early. Between 1975 and 1978, only 27 percent of all Indochinese refugees sent to the CPHs left in less than 90 days. With the advent of sponsor groups in 1979, 56 percent of the refugees left in under three months (Ajchenbaum 1981). Preserving cultural unity is such a high priority for French refugee managers that they are willing to increase the price of resettlement by sending refugees to the CPHs.

A survey of Indochinese refugees in the Paris region reinforces the conclusion that migrants' social class mediates assimilation in a concentric nation-state (Bonvin and Ponchaud 1981a, 1981b). Refugees who were farmers, soldiers, manual laborers, and servants in their home country are far more likely to have resided in a CPH (see Table 6.4). Conversely, office employees, artisans, shopkeepers, and professionals receive the individual solution. A stronger relationship exists for the refugees' level of education at the time of their arrival to France. Refugees with a university degree have a ratio of individual to collective solution of nearly three to one.

The most significant finding is that nearly three-quarters of the ethnic Chinese did not go to a CPH although they lacked a preexisting ethnic community. Conversely, the Vietnamese have less than half this rate even though many Vietnamese lived in France before 1975.

Table 6.4. Economic and Social Characteristics of Indochinese Refugees in France by Type of Resettlement (in percent).

Characteristic	Type of Resettlement	
	Individual	Collective
Occupation in Homeland		
Farmer and Soldier	18	72
Army Officer	21	79
Manual and Servant	27	63
Skilled Worker	46	54
Professional	54	46
Student	61	39
Commerce and Artisan	67	33
None	67	33
Office Employee	73	27
Education in Homeland		
None	42	58
Primary School	42	58
Junior High School	46	54
High School	59	41
University	73	27
Ethnicity		
Khmer	34	66
Vietnamese	37	63
Lowland Laotian	53	47
Chinese	73	27

Note : Survey of 405 heads of household in the Paris region.

Source : Bonvin 1987.

This pattern confirms the importance of class background. Only 16 percent of the ethnic Chinese refugees sent to the CPHS were farmers, fishermen, or manual labors in their homelands compared to 29 percent of the Vietnamese refugees. Clearly, French refugee managers want greater control over Indochinese peasants and workers than educated professionals. The French state allows westernized elites direct entry into the nation-state, while peasants and workers have their assimilation managed.

Dispersing Refugees to Preserve Cultural Unity

The function of Paris as the nation-state's cultural core explains in part the primacy of the dispersal policy in the French mode of incorporation. Paris has long been the center of the Vietnamese community in France, where students found educational opportunities and political activists achieved visibility (Khoa 1985). About half of the Cambodian and Laotian populations in France before 1975 also lived in the Paris region (Meunier 1974). Although refugee managers did utilize these preexisting communities as sponsors for elite refugees, they feared a "massive regrouping in the Paris region and above all in Paris" (de Wangen 1982, p. 7). The CNE, an association of businessmen and military officers, gives this justification for the dispersal policy: "When refugees are dispersed to all parts of France it permits them to more easily achieve insertion in the society" (Khoa 1985, p. 82). FTDA is an organization on the left, but it concurs on this issue with the view of its rival: the CPHs "are distributed to the greatest number of departments as possible in order to favor the insertion of the refugees" (FTDA 1979, p. 2). Preexisting communities in the core of the French nation-state heighten the assimilationist policies of refugee managers.

Between May of 1975 and June of 1979, 14 percent of all refugees with the collective solution went to CPHs in the Paris region; only 7 percent did so between the summer of 1979 and 1981, when poorer Indochinese began arriving in France (Ajchenbaum 1981, 1983). One result was increased migration to Paris among refugees released from CPHs elsewhere in France. From 1975 to 1979, CPHs outside of the Paris region lost only 3 percent of their refugees to the nation's core, but this proportion rose to 17 percent during 1980 and 1981. Paris is thought to be such a lure for the refugees that in the early 1980s some CPH directors proposed relocating the Parisian transit centers, which shelter refugees just off the plane, to the provinces "so as not to allow the refugees to be dazzled by the lights of the city" (FTDA 1981c, p. 2).

But the dispersal policy is extended to cities in the provinces and even neighborhoods within small towns, indicating that the value of cultural unity is pervasive rather than confined to the nation's core. Mayors and CPH staff are adamant that the refugees should not live near each other. To leave a CPH refugees must locate a dwelling and this is the most managed stage of their incorporation. The director of a CPH in a medium sized city confided during an interview:

> In the beginning when we began to get refugees the prefect asked me if when they left the foyer they would all live in the same area, if there would be a ghetto. We agreed that it would be better for their insertion to live in different parts of the city so that there wouldn't be any barriers between them and French society.

The proportion of foreigners already living in a town greatly influences local government's dispersal of Indochinese refugees. In 1983, the mayor of Mulhouse refused to allow more refugees to enter local CPHs because the proportion of foreigners in the city had reached 20 percent (FTDA 1983d). Another report describes in even more detail the importance of cultural unity even at the local level:

> Cerizay is a small village with a large factory that makes automotive bodies and which during the 1970s had recruited Portuguese workers in order to develop its activities. It built a foyer for young workers with 140 beds, but since 1979 its capacity has been reduced to 80. Currently, the factory's production is stagnant and there are more than 900 foreigners residing in Cerizay; its population is only 6,000. Due to this fact, there is a tacit agreement with the mayor that refugees not to be inserted in Cerizay itself (FTDA 1984a, np).

CPH staff and local officials prosecute the dispersal process down to the refugees' apartments. An assistant to the mayor of Amboise refused to create a special class for refugee children in the local school on the grounds that Indochinese refugees were already too concentrated in the low income housing projects (FTDA 1982a). In Bordeaux, the CPH is a collection of apartments in a housing project and the refugees are aided by a local sponsor group (Ajchenbaum et al. 1979). Although the seven apartments are dispersed throughout the complex and include refugees from Vietnam, Laos, and Cambodia, CPH staff were concerned that an "ethnic ghetto" might be forming. A staff member told an FTDA representative: "The fact that these lodgings are not grouped together promotes their contact with the other residents and therefore prepares them for insertion" (FTDA 1980a, np).

Not only does the French resettlement program prevent the development of ethnic communities, it uses the refugee migration to assist French communities, particularly towns in rural areas. France's demographic problems have historically influenced social welfare policy, such as the creation of the family allowance to increase fecundity. The admission of European immigrants during the nineteenth and early twentieth century was due to labor scarcity. Arriving Indochinese refugees provide a similar opportunity, albeit on a much smaller scale.

The policy of rural insertion developed under the theory that the refugees could be a demographic asset to France (Hassoun 1982). Government officials justified the policy on the grounds that rural areas could provide jobs suited for refugees unfamiliar with urban life

(MT 1981). The director of the CPH at Rodez boasted that the 200 Hmong who passed through the foyer were now employed in forestry work, an occupation he believed suited these former denizens of the Laotian highlands (FTDA 1981d). Boarding schools, retirement homes, and vacation complexes for workers' annual summer holiday (which take refugees on the off-season) received nearly one-fifth of all Indochinese refugees sent to CPHs between 1975 and 1979 (Ajchenbaum et al. 1979). These CPHs are predominately in small towns which have long experienced population losses to neighboring cities. Receiving refugees holds the promise of off-setting population declines.

The first CPH for Indochinese refugees opened for reasons that combined French patriotism with the need to halt the erosion of rural infrastructure. Operated by an association named for the commander of the French Army in Indochina during the early 1950s, the CPH at Bourneau is in a mountain community of some 600 residents and located on the grounds of a retirement home. One staff member described the importance of the arrival of sixty refugees: "the opening of the CPH allowed some of the employees at the retirement home to be kept on and prevented the closing of the public school" (Vallet 1980, p. 54). An FTDA representative reported in greater detail how Indochinese refugees could be used to mitigate the demographic crisis in rural France:

> The [director of the Porte-Leucate CPH] insisted that the national plan emphasize the insertion of refugees in rural areas. Of the 437 communes in [the department of] Aude, about 300 have less than 100 inhabitants! More than 100 agricultural workers depart each year and in certain places there is a virtual desertion. The local artisans (plumbers, painters, electricians, etc.) have practically disappeared and it is necessary to call upon artisans in neighboring towns. The schools close, the small shops as well. The insertion of the refugees can slow this cycle. And [the CPH director] observed that rural insertion does not mean making all the refugees agricultural workers, but artisans as well. He thinks that their adjustment would follow that of the Spanish [refugees] who were installed in the region forty years ago and are perfectly assimilated (FTDA 1981b, p. 2).

The most remarkable case of managing the Indochinese migration to buttress the nation-state is the creation of agricultural settlements in French Guiana (Comité Nationale d'Entraide 1981; Conoir 1986; Dupont-Gonin 1979). The project was organized by the National Support Committee, which counts former colonists among its supporters. Beginning in 1977, the association selected Hmong from the refugee camps in Thailand for their agricultural skills and transported them to the interior of this French Overseas Department north of Brazil. By 1986, 1,200 Hmong were living in Guiana producing fruits, vegetables, and rice. In an echo of justifications for colonialism during the nineteenth century, the Ministry of Health funded the National Support Committee on the grounds that:

> The installation of the Hmong in Guiana is a very positive element for the economy of this gravely underpopulated land . . . which imports 95 percent of its food. They are already producing a portion of the vegetable supply for the department and exporting to the Metropolis certain products which our country currently purchases from foreign sources (MS 1980b, np).

Ultimately, the French state failed to prevent the refugees from forming ethnic communities, as demonstrated by the thriving Chinatown in the thirteenth arrondissement of Paris (Guillon and Taboada-Leonetti 1986; Hamel 1982; White et al. 1987). Beginning in the late 1970s, arriving Chinese-Cambodian and Chinese-Vietnamese refugees took advantage of urban redevelopment to quickly populate the neighborhood. Using money from friends and relatives overseas, as well as indigenous techniques for capital formation, the refugees rapidly opened ethnic enterprises. An American politician would have lavished praise on the entrepreneurial spirit of the refugees and the valued taxes they generated. Yet the member of the National Assembly representing the area, a socialist, felt the neighborhood posed a threat to the French nation-state:

> The Chinese community installed in Paris finds itself confronted by a culture entirely different from hers but also ancient and also rich, which she cannot hope to dominate. Left to itself, this community will close in order to jealously guard its identity. It will constitute a ghetto which will live in communication only with other Chinatowns in Asia or America (JO 1985, p. 1525).

The French state is troubled not by ethnicity per se, but by the linking of a foreign culture to French territory. This "territory" may be only a few city blocks or a handful of apartments in a building. Yet for the French nation-state, an immigrant or refugee neighborhood is tantamount to a distinct nation, and thus is a threat to cultural unity. The fact that many of these international migrants are from former French colonies heightens this perceived threat to French civilization.

Conclusion

The American and French states create social citizenship and manage the formation of ethnic communities in distinct ways. In the U.S., the welfare state and the nature of social citizenship are prioritized at the national level. Conversely, the migrants' cultural adjustment and select traditions from the nation-state are predominate at the local level. In France, the assimilation of foreigners and preservation of cultural unity are given priority at both the national and local level. The interests of the French nation-state even extend into the micro-local level of neighborhoods and apartment buildings. These two modes of state incorporation result from variation in states structures, and how these structures interact with the historical context of international migration.

The welfare state is the raw material for creating social citizenship for international migrants. States select amounts of resources and degrees of rights that match migrants' status in the hierarchy of international migration. Vietnamese, Laotians, and Cambodians are valued allied aliens for both the French and American state. Yet Indochinese refugees arriving to the U.S. receive extensive resources in contrast to other migrants, experience only a moderate amount of social control compared to other recipients of public assistance, but are highly stigmatized by this aid (like all recipients). Refugees arriving to France encounter moderate resources, high social control, and no stigma.

The demographic similarities between the Indochinese refugee migrations to France and the U.S. mean that these forms of social citizenship result primarily from differences between the states, rather than from the social characteristics of the refugees. The most important differences are federalism and restrictive eligibility norms in the U.S. versus corporatism and encompassing eligibility norms in France.

Historical context augments these structural differences in the provision of social welfare, sometimes in unexpected directions. Nativism in the U.S. pushed national refugee advocates to centralize the resettlement program to a greater extent than other social welfare programs. Conversely, public support for the refugees in France decentralized the resettlement system as the state turned over responsibility to grass roots associations and sponsor groups. These patterns in the formation of social citizenship are reinforced by a history of migration to France due to North-South conflict, but East-West conflict in the case of the U.S. Indochinese refugees are not unique for the French Ministries of Foreign Affairs and Social Affairs. The arrival of allied aliens in 1975 due to a lost war was novel for the planners of American foreign and social policy. As a result, refugee managers in the U.S. invent new programs, while their counterparts in France rely on preexisting programs.

Where the welfare state determines access to public resources, the nation-state shapes the formation of ethnic communities. American refugee managers support the development of Vietnamese, Laotian, and Cambodian communities, believing that they are prerequisites for successful economic and social adjustment. However, they disperse the refugees nationally to limit the social welfare costs to states where large numbers of refugees already live. The French state also disperses arriving Indochinese refugees. But its goal is to prevent the formation of ethnic communities even when this policy increases government expenditures. Moreover, the French dispersal policy extends into cities, neighborhoods, and even housing projects, while the American policy is limited to the county level.

Again, the temporal and demographic similarities of the Indochinese refugee migration to France and the U.S. suggest that this variation results from different nation-state structures. An immigrant legacy and a minority heritage lead an uneasy coexistence in a racially divided nation-state in the U.S. International migrants can retain their ethnicity if its expression follows the idealized experience of European immigrants. A cultural core and an emphasis on differences between civilizations create a concentric nation-state in France. Assimilation of international migrants and cultural unity are the cornerstones of this nation-state.

Historical context amplifies these patterns of ethnic stratification. The absence of Vietnamese, Laotian, and Cambodian communities in the U.S. prior to 1975 accentuates the proclivity of refugee managers to model the refugees' incorporation on the immigrant legacy, rather than to emphasize that the Indochinese are a minority confronting racism. As a result, government agencies and nonprofit organizations support ethnic neighborhoods and institutions at the local level. Preexisting Indochinese communities in Paris heighten the assimilationist instinct of the French state, but also force refugee managers to allow some refugees to immediately join compatriots. Their selection mechanism is social class. Those refugees with Third World job skills and low levels of education are sent to temporary settlement centers throughout France where their assimilation is closely managed. Those who arrive already westernized can avoid most state controls.

The French and American modes of state incorporation clearly involve different relationships between history, the welfare state, and the nation-state. Chapter Nine uses this variation to develop some generalizations about state intervention in the adaptation process and the differences between France and the U.S. as host societies. Chapters Seven and Eight turn from the analysis of large organizations and historical events to the refugees themselves, for studies of states and international migrants must finally examine how modes of incorporation affect adaptation at the micro-level. A well developed branch of the literature addresses the economic gains or losses that migrants experience as a result of state intervention. A much less researched topic is the effect of state intervention on migrants' relationships to kin, friends, and community members. The following chapters explain why state incorporation challenges migrants' social networks and how variation in modes of incorporation lead to different challenges in the U.S. and France.

PART THREE

States and Migrants' Social Networks

7

Confronting a Social Conflict
in the United States

Like most Third World migrants in Western Europe and North America, Indochinese refugees arrive in France and the U.S. with nonwestern and preindustrial forms of self-help. In their homelands, Vietnamese, Laotians, and Cambodians rarely turned to government bureaucracies in time of need because the welfare state did not exist. Instead, social welfare is supplied through social networks: kin solve family problems through seniority and mediation; friends share information about jobs and prospective spouses; monks and shamans dispense mental and physical health care; neighbors and relatives pool savings and allocate the sum (Egawa and Tashima 1982; Hirayama and Hirayama 1988; Khoa and Vandeusen 1981; Moon and Tashima 1982). Indeed, the social welfare practices of Indochinese refugees are analogous to those of poor African-Americans who survive by exchanging income, goods, and services among kin (Stack 1974).

States use bureaucracies and formal organizations, not social networks, to provide social welfare. A Cambodian social worker eloquently depicts the resulting encounter between refugees' and the western welfare state:

In Cambodia we didn't have welfare or Social Security. We didn't have day-care centers or old-age homes or psychiatrists. We didn't need them. All we needed were our families and the monks. Most households had three generations living together. The grandparents' helped raise their grandchildren. The adults in the middle put food on the table. When there were problems and arguments the monks helped take care of them. . . . For generation after generation we followed our customs, until in 1975 the communists put an end to our way of life. We lost everything—our families, our monks, our villages, our land, all our possessions. Everything. When we came to the United States we couldn't put our old lives back together. We didn't even have the pieces (Ngor 1987, p. 433).

How refugees reconstruct their lives with the aid of their social networks is determined by the structure of the welfare state and nation-state, and the relationship between these two institutions. The American welfare state treats international migrants as individuals and expects them to conform to norms minimizing use of public resources. Conversely, the American nation-state supports the formation of ethnic communities at the local level, thus nourishing migrants' social networks. The American mode of incorporation challenges Indochinese refugees' social networks because the state simultaneously individualizes migrants through the welfare state and communalizes them through the nation-state. The result is conflict between refugees' social networks, which pursue collective adaptation, and local refugee mangers who treat refugees as individuals or households, not as members of extended kin groups or an ethnic community. Collective or individual use of public assistance is the most contentious element of the incorporation process at the micro-level.

Local Refugee Managers and Access to Welfare

Financial difficulties are high among the problems reported by Indochinese refugees in the U.S. (Dunning 1989; Strand and Jones 1985; Wolf 1981). State incorporation provides one way of meeting this need: public assistance. Of the 714,000 Indochinese refugees who arrived between 1975 and 1984, 72 percent received cash public assistance during their first year, but only 39 percent received it after three years (U.S. ORR 1985). Other surveys show that about 80 percent of Indochinese refugees receive cash public assistance their first year and that the proportion drops to about 25 percent after three years (U.S. ORR 1983, 1984). One study of Vietnamese and Laotian refugees noted substantial economic progress, but also found that "only 2 percent of the households in our sample [of 1,384] had managed to climb out of poverty after six months or less on cash assistance and without benefit of specialized refugee programs and services" (Caplan et al. 1989, p. 215). Although long-run aid is the exception, Indochinese refugees' household subsistence is temporarily tied to the welfare state. One survey of Vietnamese refugees found that 83 percent knew of services that would help them apply for welfare (Dunning 1989).

Like natives, to obtain aid refugees must convince "street-level bureaucrats" that they qualify and deserve assistance (Lipsky 1980).

But a unique feature of refugees' social citizenship is their ability to have nonprofit organizations, rather than public aid bureaus, make many of the decisions regarding their eligibility for public assistance. These organizations are usually the voluntary agencies which receive a grant of about $500 from the Bureau for Refugee Programs in the State Department for each refugee resettled. Native directors and Indochinese caseworkers thus become intermediaries between the refugees and the social welfare resources provided by the American state (Gold 1992; Hein 1988; Ledgerwood 1990; Mortland and Ledgerwood 1987).

The voluntary agencies employ many dedicated staff who spend long hours aiding refugees with seemingly insurmountable problems (Rose 1983, 1986). Historically, these private organizations relied on their own funds to support refugees. But since 1975, refugees' new ties to the welfare state inexorably draw these agencies into the public aid system (Wright 1981).

Local refugee managers' resistance to refugees receiving public aid stems from this organizational history of self-reliance. The International Rescue Committee, founded in 1933, states that its "goal for resettling refugees in the United States is to bring about their absorption into the economic and social fabric of American life by providing housing, educational support, employment and language services, counseling and medical services" (U.S. ORR 1983, p. 59). Most voluntary agencies share this goal of promoting rapid adaptation with little or no reliance on public assistance. World Relief helps "refugees toward creating productive lives and experiencing successful resettlement" (U.S. ORR 1983, p. 69). For the U.S. Catholic Conference the "aim is to bring refugees quickly to dignity and self-sufficiency in their new country through employment" (U.S. ORR 1983, p. 68).

Religious values can contribute to this aversion to public assistance. A Protestant voluntary agency describes its emphasis on the work ethic: "Refugee resettlement is regarded by the LIRS and the Lutheran network as a moral commitment, a voluntary effort carried out by concerned congregations and others to help refugees become self-sustaining, contributing community members as quickly as possible" (U.S. ORR 1983, p. 61). Inevitably, agencies also draw upon the restrictive eligibility norms in the welfare state. An agency in San Francisco provides a "What is Welfare?" document to caseworkers for use with clients. The document reveals how the agency attempts to stigmatize welfare for refugees:

> Welfare is not a solution to your financial needs. Welfare does not give you freedom to do everything you want to do. There are many

restrictions and conditions put on people who take welfare. People care
about you when they give you advice on how to get off welfare. People
are not caring about your future when they advise you how to stay on
welfare, or how to abuse welfare. Your attitude towards welfare and
working is very important to your successful future in America.

Local refugee managers control access to welfare and their
prevailing sentiment is that refugees should be discouraged from
receiving it. As a result, conflict is inherent to refugee resettlement in
the U.S. Refugees' social networks intervene in this struggle between
clients and caseworkers over the goals of the incorporation process.
Membership in communal and kin networks leads refugees to make
collective assessments of and decisions about resources like income
support. However, the social welfare system expects refugees to act as
individuals. Indochinese refugees resist state incorporation by placing
welfare in the context of the ethnic community and the extended
family.

Family and Kin Ties

Vietnamese, Laotians, Hmong, and Cambodians do not have
precisely the same types of families, and their kinships systems and
marriage customs are quite different (Center for Applied Linguistics
1981; Chhim et al. 1989; Vandeusen et al. 1981). Yet in contrast to the
family form presumed by the American social welfare system, the
"Indochinese" family is larger and often includes extended kin, such as
parents living with married children, or a sibling living with a
married brother or sister (Haines 1982). Among contemporary Asian
migrants, unmarried Vietnamese over eighteen years old are among
the most likely to live with a relative who is not their parent and are
the least likely to live alone (Kanjanapan 1989). Upgrading cousins to
the status of siblings, or close family friends to the status of cousins—
what anthropologists term fictive kinship—is another practice
distinguishing Southeast Asian from American families. Migration
further extends the range of Vietnamese, Laotian, and Cambodian
families. Even after resettlement in the U.S., refugees maintain close
contact with relatives who live in other parts of the U.S., in other
resettlement countries, in countries of first asylum such as Thailand,
and in their homelands. In the context of this diaspora, social welfare
decisions by an individual or household can have repercussions for
family members elsewhere.

Indochinese receive public assistance because they are poor, but
their relationship with the welfare state is complicated because they

are also refugees. New members periodically arrive to the U.S., changing the equilibrium of the families they join, and their status as international migrants remains ambiguous for the public aid system. During an interview, a Vietnamese caseworker recounted a case that illustrates how public assistance becomes enmeshed in the reconstruction of refugee families:

> I had a case of a Vietnamese woman who arrived as an immigrant. Her father had signed a statement that she would come here as an immigrant and could not get welfare for two years. When she got to San Francisco her family refused to support her because she was pregnant. I told her to apply for AFDC because she already had two children, but her I–94 [visa] said she was an immigrant and AFDC refused. She applied for General Assistance but was refused because of her family's income. She couldn't even get food stamps because her family had two cars. There was a hearing at the Department of Social Services after she gave birth and she finally got some assistance.

Because many Indochinese families are extended, the decision to work or receive welfare is often made for the group by senior family members. A caseworker I interviewed in San Francisco discussed how gender roles shaped one family's decision to apply for public assistance. A cousin sponsoring her extended Chinese-Vietnamese family of twelve met with the caseworker several days before the family's arrival. She agreed to help some of her relatives find jobs in Chinatown, where she worked as a secretary. When the family arrived the caseworker explained the importance of work, especially for the single brothers and sisters. The caseworker also pointed out that they could take English classes at night while working during the day. The cousin said she would talk these plans over with her family during the week and then return to the agency. A week later, the cousin and her relatives returned, but she sat quietly while the uncle explained the family's position and asserted his patriarchal role as the eldest male. They had discussed the issue of work and welfare, the uncle reported, and believed that it would be appropriate for them all to temporarily receive welfare so that they could improve their English. As this case indicates, state incorporation treats refugees as individuals, but they respond as members of social networks like the extended family.

The confrontation between Indochinese families and the American social welfare system also occurs because their kin ties are fluid while the system expects permanency. Caseworkers report that many refugee couples married in the Southeast Asian refugee camps: the single men to improve their chances for resettlement (families are given preference) and single women to gain protection against other men. These marriages often end in divorce in the U.S., and fathers may be eager to keep a child in order to retain public assistance benefits. A public aid worker in California reports: "One of my Vietnamese supervisors was so upset when she found out what her staff were finding with some new cases. Young Vietnamese men marrying Vietnamese women with kids so they can become 'step-parents,' then go to college with AFDC support" (Finnan and Cooperstein 1983, p. 160).

Such actions might be explained simply as cheating, but they are actually part of a complex interaction between the American welfare state and refugees' conceptions of kinship. Southeast Asian families are highly structured, but also very fluid, and relatives can detach themselves from large kin groups and form their own households. In an oral history one Vietnamese refugee describes splitting his extended family of sixteen into three households. He realized that American sponsors were willing to help only nuclear families (Santoli 1988). Some Indochinese refugees may attach themselves to households to which they are unrelated by blood. In an autobiographical essay a Cambodian refugee recounts how from 1974 to 1979 he changed households four times as illness and revolution deprived him of living relatives (Khath 1989). Most refugees have this ability to create fictive kin bonds: cousins can become "brothers," and in-laws can become "cousins." But fictive kinship leads to confrontation with the American public aid system. A study of Cambodian refugees describes the case of a thirty-two year old widow, a fourteen year old "brother," and how the older refugee eventually lost her welfare benefits: "Within ten days after arrival, this case had been registered for AFDC and Food Stamps. . . . About a month after arrival, it became known that the fourteen year old was not really the brother of this refugee, as he had claimed to be in order to get into this country" (Berkeley Planning Associates 1984, np).

Aid from the resettlement program takes on an added significance because it becomes linked to refugees' kinship ties that extend outside of the U.S. Many Indochinese in the U.S. feel compelled to send money to relatives in the refugee camps or their homelands. An employed Vietnamese refugee describes this pressure to aid kin overseas: "I'm able to make enough money to send three hundred dollars a month to my parents in Vietnam. . . . I work fourteen hours a day, seven days a week to feed my parents as well as myself. If I didn't send the money every month, they would starve to death" (Kalergis 1989, np). About 60 percent of Indochinese refugees in Thai camps receive money from relatives in the west, with an average of three or four remittances a year totaling almost $400 (Institute for Asian Studies 1988). Given the demands of kinship, refugees will share their income with relatives even if the source of these funds is welfare rather than employment.

Public assistance becomes far more than "income support" when refugees seek to sponsor relatives to the U.S. Many voluntary agencies do not allow refugees to apply for the admission of family members if the sponsor is receiving public assistance. This policy can influence a refugees' choice about working or receiving aid. A study of refugees' migration patterns in the U.S. illustrates the effect of the policy on a Vietnamese family: "The members of this household visited California with another family, but decided to return to Arizona because the woman realizes that she will be eligible for family reunification only if she is employed, and she is anxious to be reunited with her husband [still living in Vietnam]" (Berkeley Planning Associates 1984, np). Similarly, a Cambodian refugee reports in an oral history that she operates a doughnut shop open, despite going into debt, in order to have the financial resources to meet the immigration requirements that will allow her to sponsor a cousin (Santoli 1988).

Voluntary agencies vary in how strictly they adhere to this policy. But kinship, employment, and welfare are inextricably linked in the American mode of incorporation because the welfare state evaluates refugees as individuals while refugees' social networks involve collective ties. The following note from a director to a caseworker concerns whether or not the voluntary agency should help a single mother on AFDC sponsor a relative:

> [She] is not working and wouldn't promise to help find work for her relative so [another voluntary agency] refused to take her case. The American Council of Voluntary Agencies in New York offered it to us. Would you contact her and see what her situation is and tell her if we take her case we will expect him to try to work and that she will try to help him.

Refugees who have achieved a degree of economic security may still consider the resettlement program a resource they can turn to when relatives arrive from overseas. A case file describes a caseworker's meeting with the owner of a Vietnamese restaurant in San Francisco soon after three relatives arrived:

> [She] stressed that her business has been running very slowly these days. She thinks she can't support three of them. She asked me for financial support. I explained to her that since her relatives decided to

go on welfare we will just help to pay the rent deposit, buy some furniture, and give them pocket money, and she will assist them with other needs until they receive their welfare grant.

A refugee in the U.S. can even be pressured by family members still overseas to make sure they will get the money they know is available to refugees resettled in America. One case file contained this letter written by a refugee to the agency which sponsored him and was about to sponsor some of his relatives:

> Please accept my apologies for this letter regarding my relatives in Thailand and Philippines camps. I would like to know your agency's policy about how much you provide refugees for each person when they come to the United States. In the case of my sister's family of three, how much will you help?

The American mode of incorporation entails such a powerful conflict between public assistance and refugees' membership in kin networks that refugees in the U.S. must evaluate whether the kin requesting their aid are sufficiently close to warrant a confrontation with an agency over work and welfare. A caseworker wrote in her case file: "I told [Vietnamese refugee in the U.S.] to get a job first, then he could sponsor this family." Three weeks later, the caseworker logged this entry: "He decided he cannot take care of these people who are not his immediate family." State incorporation jeopardizes refugees' kinship bonds and this dilemma is illustrated in greater detail by the following case.

During the third visit to his caseworker (a native woman named Joan), a Cambodian man (Dara) mentioned that he might be leaving New York City. He explained through a Cambodian caseworker that he had received a letter from his "sister" (actually his cousin) in Louisiana asking him to join her family. Since Dara was successfully resettled Joan was reluctant to see him risk a new start. Dara already spoke some English, had found himself a part-time job, lived in a building slated for a federal improvement program, and had completed the paperwork for the numerous public bureaucracies that refugees must pass through.

Joan pointed out that "this is the United States and you're free to go where you want," but that welfare and food stamps were less in Louisiana and that the voluntary agency had already spent close to $2,000 in resettling his family in the U.S. At one point Dara tried to explain more clearly to Joan why he had to move: "My sister's family asked me first and also helped me in the [Thai refugee] camps. If I don't go there I'll have a bad name with my family." Life in the camps is austere at best and aid from kin is not quickly forgotten. His caseworker again stressed that he was free to leave but that she would not help him make arrangements. Later she confided to me: "The client's culture can often work against us as a type of counter-culture." Eventually, another Cambodian caseworker convinced Dara that it would be best if he stayed in New York and Dara did not join his relatives in Louisiana. In this case, the welfare state's ability to individualize international migrants proved stronger than the inertia of refugees' kin networks.

Ethnic Community and Survival Strategies

War and flight fragment many refugee families, and they compensate for this loss by attaching greater importance to relations with compatriots (Gold 1989; Haines et al. 1981). Refugees in the U.S. are more likely to ask community members for help than they were in their homeland, particularly for financial problems (Dunning 1989; Moon and Tashima 1982). Employment is another area where the ethnic community shapes the adaptation of refugees: members exchange job referrals, share transportation costs, provide child care, and collectively define what is a "good" job (Finnan 1981; Finnan and Cooperstein 1983). In 1975, only 5 percent of employed Vietnamese refugees had found their current job through Vietnamese friends, while 37 percent had relied on American sponsors (Montero 1979a). Ten years later, after Indochinese communities developed, 30 percent of employed Indochinese refugees had located their job through friends, 15 percent through voluntary agencies, and only 10 percent through sponsors (Forbes 1985b). A San Diego survey found that 27 percent of Indochinese in the U.S. less than four years worked mostly with other Southeast Asian refugees (Rumbaut 1989a). The ethnic community is an especially important source of information about employment for those refugees with limited English proficiency (Bach and Carroll-Seguin 1986).

The importance of the ethnic community for solving refugees' financial and employment problems indicates how the Indochinese respond collectively to the hardships of economic adjustment. Public assistance is an important, albeit temporary, phase of refugees' economic adjustment in which the ethnic community also plays a significant role. Ethnic communities not only provide information to members about jobs, they also circulate rumors, gossip, and survival strategies. Some of these strategies involve public assistance, thus pitting the welfare state's individualized conception of aid against the collective conception developed by refugees' ethnic networks. The fact that the American nation-state supports the building of refugee communities at the local level only exacerbates this conflict.

The development of an oral tradition of survival strategies began before the refugees reached the U.S. Prior to resettlement, Indochinese refugees usually experience years of uncertainty in meeting basic human needs. Not only have they moved several times within their homelands and throughout Southeast Asia in search of asylum, but they have found themselves under a succession of regimes in which the supply of resources varied tremendously. In a decade, Cambodians experienced five regimes, each with its own rules determining economic life and household subsistence: relative prosperity under Prince Sihanouk until 1970; hardships under the military dictatorship of General Lon Nol until 1975; genocide under the Khmer Rouge until 1979; famine under the Vietnamese until the early 1980s; and finally scarcity in the refugee camps in Thailand until they resettle in the west. A Vietnamese women describes how a history of economic scarcity and political uncertainty shaped her survival strategies:

> We Vietnamese have grown up and lived in a period of continuous war for over a century, ever since the French came to our country. I, too, was uprooted and forced to move many times because of war. That's why I and many others never had long-range plans. We lived day by day. One government after another rose and fell, with no continuity (Freeman 1989, p. 392).

American nation-building projects in the 1950s and relief for civilians displaced by war during the 1960s introduced western aid to Indochinese subsistence patterns for the first time (Wiesner 1988). But during the 1970s, the creation of refugee camps in Thailand for Laotians, Vietnamese boat people, and especially Cambodians led to a sustained relationship between western relief agencies and the refugees' survival strategies (Mason and Brown 1983; Shawcross 1984). One Cambodian refugee explains how the availability of United Nations' food supplies determined her flight from Cambodia to Thailand: "Aid from foreign countries seemed to come in waves, so we had to consider carefully the international situation in order to time our escape attempt" (Criddle and Mam 1987, p. 264). Another Cambodian refugee describes how parents benefited from their children while in the Thai refugee camps:

> The orphanage got the best rations. . . . Parents sent their children to live there, partly for the food and partly in the hope that they would be

adopted. Once the child was in the States, the parents hoped to stage a dramatic and touching reunion. I reckoned about forty percent of the orphans fell into this category. . . . One day there was a check up and [the woman who ran the orphanage] came rushing round the camp, begging for children so that she could make up the numbers (May 1986, p. 271).

As these anecdotes suggest, Indochinese refugees respond to changing economic and political conditions by developing short-run subsistence strategies. Refugees continue to use these survival strategies in the U.S. even though their socioeconomic conditions have improved. Unlike immigrants who plan their adaptation before arriving, few Indochinese refugees arrive expecting to improve their education, locate a good job, or open a small business (Velasco et al. 1983). A survey of Indochinese refugees in Thai camps found that over 60 percent could not name an occupation they expected to work at should they be resettled in the west; the most frequent choice was mechanic, but this job was cited by only 10 percent of the refugees (Institute for Asian Studies 1988). Instead of selecting options like education or employment on the basis of long range goals formulated in their homeland, refugees use their survival strategies. In this context, income support programs become the latest resource at refugees disposal to meet their needs. An American sponsor perceived this interpretation of public assistance while helping a Hmong family complete a thirty-six page form to determine if they were eligible for public assistance:

The difficulties of verification are extreme for a family that fled its village on foot, crossed the mountains in a trek that few survived, and spent five years in a resettlement camp before traveling nine thousand miles to a new home. Their aim was survival, not the preservation of records—which they would not be able to read anyway (Tillema 1981, p. 39).

A Vietnamese caseworker I interviewed described in his own words how public assistance entered his clients' survival strategies: "Refugees are like any other people in a strange land. They use welfare for self-protection and to get a time to relax, to learn, to prepare." A caseworker who arrived in 1978, before public assistance became a permanent feature of community survival strategies, reveals how his thinking might have been shaped had he arrived in the 1980s, when public assistance became an accepted source of income among refugees:

I took a job as soon as I got here. I saw [native] people looking for food in trash cans and I thought: "This is their country and language, what will happen to me?" I went to a job counselor right away because the surroundings forced me to work. But it's good I didn't know about welfare.

The Indochinese caseworkers I interviewed agreed that refugees first learned about public assistance from other refugees in the Southeast Asian camps who received letters from relatives already in the U.S. These camps provide refugees with the first milieu in which to reestablish contact with compatriots following their flight. A caseworker in New York City gives a vivid example of how ethnic networks create survival strategies involving aid from the resettlement program.

Shortly after arriving, the leading members of an extended Chinese-Vietnamese family told this caseworker that they knew she was going to spend a sum of money on their case for furniture, rent, clothing, and other immediate needs, and that all would be better off if she gave them the whole sum then. Like many refugees, the caseworker reported, this family learned about resettlement practices in the refugee camps in Thailand, where knowledge of public assistance payments and the aid provided by each voluntary agency is common. The family declined the apartment in the Bronx already rented by the caseworker, and even refused the job interviews she had lined up for them. The leading family members stated that they wanted to live and work in Chinatown. Sometime later, she discovered that they had taken some gold with them when they fled Vietnam, and then used this capital to open a Chinese restaurant supply store in Chinatown. In this case, the folk wisdom of the ethnic network coupled with economic opportunities in New York's Chinese enclave presented refugees with a collective mode of adaptation. The resettlement program expected the refugees to adapt as a single household.

Refugees' socialization to ethnic community norms regarding public assistance continues in the U.S. Upon arrival, most refugees are immediately placed by their caseworkers or relatives in buildings where other refugees live. Older arrivals develop a folklore about public assistance and transmit advice to new arrivals. A Chinese-Cambodian caseworker illustrates the existence of this folk wisdom with an incident common to local refugee managers: "We have a lot of fights with clients. For example, one client said he would go to work but then other refugees told him not to. They told him that since he had a large family he could get welfare. So he avoided coming to see me." A Vietnamese caseworker with similar experiences concludes: "To say that clients are 'not highly motivated to work' is a label. Clients have fixed ideas in their minds and are out of touch with the reality of the social welfare system. They get these ideas from informal channels: relatives and friends in the United States." Community formation is thus an underlying cause of why refugees incorporate public assistance into their collective survival strategies.

A second cause is that the failures of the American social welfare system provide good reason for refugees to pool their knowledge of public assistance. The director of a social service consortium in Orange County, California, notes that "the system fails to be consistent and credible, [and] the refugee learns to rely on the 'bamboo grapevine' for direction and to get ahead through manipulation of the 'loopholes' in the system" (U.S. HR 1982a, p. 228). Restrictive eligibility norms further contribute to this confrontation between refugee managers and refugee communities.

Refugees' primary defense in this struggle is to use their social networks to develop a collective interpretation of state assistance, including detailed knowledge of how the welfare system works. During an interview, one caseworker pointed to a file and said: "I have a client here and I told him to call his worker at welfare since he finished screening and now has to do intake. You know its very hard to get in touch with workers at the welfare department. But he didn't do that. He said his sister told him to wait until after I filled out his forms." To retain control over the incorporation process, local refugee managers try to convince clients that the voluntary agency is a more reliable source of aid than the ethnic community. One Cambodian caseworker reports how she counteracts the ethnic network's transmission of survival strategies to her clients:

> Friends and relatives tell them one thing and we tell them another. So I say to them: "What will happen when your friends and relatives forget you, who will look after you? You don't know English. How will you get a job? If you want someone to look after you then you have to come here." That's how I make them believe me.

Alone, the restrictive eligibility norms and the individualizing approach of the social welfare system would be sufficient to bring local refugee managers into conflict with refugees' social networks. The American nation-state's support for ethnic community formation exacerbates this conflict. At the local level, voluntary agencies support community formation through residential clustering (Hein 1988), and by encouraging respected community members to become involved in the community's social welfare (what social workers term "the theory of natural community helpers"). One American social worker in California reports how she encouraged a Cambodian caseworker to "ask some already well-settled compatriots to introduce [other refugees] to American customs and help them find others from their home towns and villages" (Collins 1983, p. 61).

However, agencies cannot control the information that circulates through the networks they help reconstitute. When San Francisco initiated a mandatory employment program for all arriving refugees in 1984, Indochinese caseworkers discovered that relatives and neighbors informed newcomers about benefits under the previous resettlement program. The following dialogue took place during a weekly staff meeting at a voluntary agency:

> *Chinese-Cambodian Caseworker*: My new clients say "What about the other [refugees] who don't have to go to work? They've been here three years and I've been here three weeks." *Native, White Director*: Tell them they came at a different time and now there are different rules and its those people who are home with welfare that is the reason.

As the above dialogue suggests, ethnic communities enable refugees to make collective rather than individual claims for public aid. In Arlington, Virginia, the increasing strength of the Vietnamese community lead to more militant demands for better jobs or more public assistance. The Indochinese population in the state numbered only 3,700 at the end of 1975; the community had grown to 9,200 by the beginning of 1980. During this period, refugees' class backgrounds shifted from government officials to peasants, mechanics, and street vendors. Agencies were at a loss to explain refugees' higher expectations for jobs and benefits, since they were no longer resettling former elites. The director of one agency in the state describes the evolution of refugees' attitudes toward work and welfare as the strength of the ethnic community increased:

> Over the past three years we have observed some attitudinal and behavioral changes among refugees around the "public support" system. Three or even two years ago, accepting welfare was seen as an embarrassment, a livelihood to be accepted only as a last resort until employment could be found. Today we are experiencing adult enrollees who refuse employment opportunities and hold out for, in staff judgment and experience, unrealistically high starting salaries and opportunities (U.S. HR 1979b, p. 114).

The ethnic community plays such a central role in mediating refugees' conceptions of work and welfare that resettlement agencies require community support to conduct their operations. In Houston, a

Cambodian employment program recruited clients by going "out into the community two or three nights a week, knocking on doors in the neighborhoods that had the heaviest concentration of Cambodian residents. They also held meetings hosted by 'village leaders' at each of the apartment building complexes to familiarize the residents with their services" (Cichon and Semons 1986, p. 11). In Chicago, a Cambodian mutual assistance association also used the ethnic community in its efforts to move refugees into the labor force. The association found good paying jobs for a handful of easy-to-place refugees, believing that "as the spirit in the community becomes more job-oriented and less welfare-oriented, more people will follow suit and take jobs" (Cichon et al. 1986, p. 16).

A study of job placement programs in Kansas City, Minneapolis, Providence, and San Diego found a similar relationship between the Hmong community and refugee managers (Gimbert and Semons 1988). Unlike other ethnic groups, the Hmong often consider programs helpful even if they do not obtain a job. Rather than the economic outcome of the service, the Hmong evaluate resettlement agencies by their relationship to the Hmong community. In one city, Hmong reported dissatisfaction with an agency which had a good record of placing clients in jobs, but also had a history of conflict with local Hmong leaders.

A tragic example of the community shaping refugees' interaction with public assistance occurred in Portland, Oregon. In 1981, the federal government delayed funding to state governments for resettlement services, including public assistance. Resettlement agencies sent letters to their clients advising them that all expenditures would be suspended on a given date. Oregon had a large Hmong population, an ethnic group whose religion includes a belief in the ability of spirits of the dead to communicate with powerful entities, and animal sacrifices in religious rituals. Shortly after receiving a notice that his public assistance would be terminated, a sixty-two year old Hmong man told his family "he was going to commit suicide because he would be a sacrifice to the community and then the government would do something" (Pullen 1986, p. 51). He hung himself two days later. The director of Portland's refugee bureau reports that "the money had come the Friday night before, but I'll never convince the Hmong community that Mr. Vu's sacrifice was not the thing that brought the money back" (Pullen 1986, p. 51). Few refugees engage in such extreme forms of resistance. But the ethnic community allows the Indochinese to define their adaptation as a collective endeavor while the welfare state pursues their incorporation as individuals.

Conclusion

At the micro-level, American incorporation is a series of encounters between refugees and representatives of the welfare state who seek to minimize their use of public assistance. Refugees can avoid contact with the welfare state by working, but most use state resources in the early stages of their adaptation. The refugees, like other international migrants from the Third World, bring with them indigenous forms of social welfare supplied through social networks. State incorporation thus is a confrontation between two social welfare systems: one comprised of bureaucracies that consider clients to be individuals, the other composed of social networks that treat members as part of a group. The welfare state individualizes refugees even as they experience adaptation as extended families and ethnic communities.

These communal and kin networks are not alternatives to state resources since refugees can receive assistance from public sources as well as through their social networks. Yet extended families require refugees to evaluate state resources with respect to the needs of a wide range of kin, some of whom may not even reside in the U.S. Similarly, the ethnic community promotes the inclusion of state resources in refugees' repertoire of survival strategies: short-run subsistence techniques developed under conditions of scarcity in Southeast Asia. Kin and ethnic networks collectivize the incorporation process and allow refugees to resist refugee managers. This conflict is exacerbated by the relationship between the American nation-state and welfare state. The former supports the development of ethnic communities, and thus social networks; the latter expects residents to use public resources as individuals and conform to restrictive eligibility norms. In France, variation in the structure of the nation-state and welfare state leads to a very different challenge to Indochinese refugees' social networks.

8

Evaluating a
Social Contract in France

In contrast to the institutional contradictions in the American mode of incorporation, the relationship between the welfare-state and nation state is highly synchronized in France. First, the French nation-state predominates over the welfare state at the national *and* the local level. Second, both institutions treat residents and clients (respectively) as members of national collectives. Conversely, the American welfare state treats clients as individuals, while the American nation-state treats residents as members of ethnic communities. This variation in state structures in France and the U.S. explains why international migrants' social networks conflict with the American mode of incorporation, but confront a social contract in France.

In the U.S., Indochinese refugees' kin and communal ties resist incorporation by collectively evaluating public assistance and bureaucratic encounters. There is an inherent conflict between refugees' social networks and the host society institutions which manage their adaptation. The French welfare state is more compatible with migrants' social networks. Both native and migrant social welfare systems emphasize groups, although the French welfare state is oriented to a republic, and migrants are oriented to the extended family and the ethnic community. As a result, the French mode of incorporation presents refugees' with a social contract, offering resources in exchange for assimilation into the host society.

In France, the state attempts to displace refugees' social networks by sending them to *foyers d'hébergements*, or lodging hostels. Some refugees have strong ties to kin and community, and their networks provide resources far superior to those the state offers. These refugees have distinctly negative views of the foyers. But refugees' with fragmented families and few social contacts allow host society institutions to substitute for the social networks they lack. The French state's ability to assimilate international migrants is greatly determined by the strength of migrants' social networks.

Local Refugee Managers and Residence in a Total Institution

Total institutions are "forcing houses for changing persons" that are both residential communities and formal organizations (Goffman 1961, p. 12). An average foyer accommodates about ninety refugees at one time, although eight of the approximately forty foyers in France can shelter 150 refugees or more. During the 1970s, 33 percent of all Indochinese refugees entering the foyers left within four months and only 15 percent were still there after six months (Ajchenbaum 1981). By 1981, changes in the demographic characteristics of arriving refugees led only 18 percent of them to leave in less than four months, while 28 percent stayed past six months (Ajchenbaum 1983). Foyers are clearly total institutions, and the dimensions of their completeness indicates how the French state uses host society institutions to replace migrants' social networks.

Refugees living in a foyer receive French classes, basic health care, assistance in applying for work and residence permits, and help finding a job and housing. But like all total institutions, a foyer massively intrudes into the lives of residents. For example, foyer staff control refugees income from the family allowance by giving them a daily sum. Most foyers divert some of this money into an account with a local bank or voluntary agency. Some even keep the funds in the foyer. Approximately 30 percent of foyers give the money directly to the refugees, 65 percent hold it but allow refugees access to it when needed, while 5 percent give the sum to the refugees only when they leave (Ajchenbaum et al. 1979).

Refugees also contribute to the maintenance of the building and grounds. A visit to one foyer disclosed that "the refugees take care of cleaning the property and [the director] believes that this is part of their adaptation to French life" (FTDA 1982h, p. 2). At another foyer "a woman from the reception association regularly visits each family to guide them in housework and daily purchases" (FTDA 1983e, p. 2). The foyer in Limoges (the largest in France) places refugees into "villages," half of a floor occupied by refugees of the same nationality (FTDA 1981c). Each village has a "chief" who acts as interpreter, distributes cooking equipment and food, and supervises refugees' maintenance of the foyer.

Regulating food is the most intrusive feature of a foyer because refugees prefer to prepare food for themselves. About 60 percent of foyers purchase food for refugees and dispense it at collective meals (Ajchenbaum et al. 1979). The annual report of the foyer in Limoges listed one of its problems as: "the difficulty of getting refugees to accept a diet different from that in their homelands" (GATREM Indochine 1980, p. 3A). After visiting another foyer where this issue arose, a representative from the association which manages the foyer system reported: "Debate took place on the eternal dilemma: collective or individual meals. . . . The least harmful solution seems to be that of progressive individual meals, accompanied by training in French life and French budgets" (FTDA 1982e, p. 2).

These details of foyer life appear pedantic, but since World War One, the French state has used collective habitations to initiate international migrants into the society (Noiriel 1988). Polish immigrant workers were quarantined during the 1920s; in the 1930s, Spaniards fleeing the collapse of Republican Spain were interned. Eurasians arriving from Indochina, and Muslim troops migrating from North Africa, entered camps in the 1950s and 1960s, respectively. Many Algerian immigrant workers still live in foyers constructed prior to the ending of labor immigration in 1974. For international migrants, residence in a total institution means separation from their natural sources of social welfare during the adaptation process: kin and communal networks.

In the case of Indochinese refugees, staff in a Parisian transit center decide if a newly arrived refugee will join kin or reside for six months in a foyer. Since 1975, approximately two-thirds of arriving Indochinese refugees have been sent to one of these total institutions. During an interview, one staff member stated that proximity to kin is an important consideration when selecting where to send refugees. However, her discussion of other criteria clearly reveals that refugee managers believe international migrants' adjustment is better managed by host society institutions than by social networks:

> The relatives of a refugee are usually unable to help a new arrival because they don't have the resources or just arrived themselves. So we have to decide which foyer is best for the refugees. First and foremost, near relatives and friends in France. Single men to the provinces and away from cities where they could get into trouble. Large families to the provinces, and the handicapped to cities with specialists in their ailment. Those with job skills, for example an engineer, to cities; conversely, peasants to the country. The availability of places in a foyer matters too.

Foyer staff whom I interviewed in a city in western France

("Beauville," a fictitious name) provided even more detailed information on the state's incorporation of Indochinese refugees at the micro-level. The director of the foyer explains why the state uses host society institutions to closely manage the adaptation of international migrants:

> The collective solution is a regrouping of specific populations. There's a French mentality about collective settlements of the disabled. But of course it's also easier to control people when they are in one place. Collective solutions are used when there is a risk to integration going badly. For example, the camps for the harkis [in the 1960s].

Another staff member went even further in describing the assimilationist function of the foyer. He plans refugees' job searches and language instruction. During an interview, he made reference to *formation*, a French term for occupational or educational training that also connotes socialization:

> Many refugees need a *preformation* before they are ready for *formation*. We need to rid them of beliefs they have acquired, such as that one knows French after two weeks in a French course in a Thai refugee camp; everything is done by machines in France; and so on. Some think if they work in a factory for two weeks they will get a permanent job. We have to orient them to our technical culture. We have to prepare the ground and fix any problems that could come up later. Unfortunately, it is individuals who have to change because the social environment doesn't, or only a little. If you plant an orange tree in [western France] you can only prepare the soil. The climate will determine the rest, and so this orange tree will have to adapt.

A Vietnamese social worker in the foyer provides an invaluable perspective of these institutions. She arrived to France as an immigrant (that is, before the refugee migration began in 1975) and also received social work training in the U.S. According to this woman, the assimilationist function of the foyer stems from the structure of the French nation-state:

> In France, there is a very tight culture and one has to have a place in it. It's not like in the United States were there are ethnic communities. When one is outside French society one experiences marginality. If you guard your identity as a foreigner you will be outside. The French use terms like "readaptation" or "reinsertion" for services to bring people back in. Like the foyer. The foyer is an apprenticeship in communal life where one can carry some responsibility oneself before leaving. It's an apprenticeship in autonomy.

In their own words, these refugee managers describe how a total institution presents Indochinese refugees with a social contract: receiving resources in exchange for assimilation, and accepting a host society institution in place of kin and communal networks. The latter is facilitated by the fact that some foyers are directed by husband and wife teams (Ajchenbaum et al. 1979; FTDA 1980b, 1982c). The foyer in Troyes allows refugees, like errant children, to return if their first attempt at outside living fails. One report by the association that manages the foyer system notes that "the small centers facilitate the creation of a somewhat familial atmosphere" (FTDA 1981e, p. 3). Yet the social contract is more than a metaphor for the French mode of incorporation. During their first few days in France, refugees are asked to sign a document which reads in part:

> We also declare that we have no financial resources and neither sponsor nor family in France capable of helping us. We ask to be financially supported, for a limited period of time, in the provincial reception center which FTDA will offer us. We promise to respect the house rules and the organization of the center. . . . We certify that we have been informed that any false declaration on our part or any nonobservance of the commitments made above will immediately result in the forfeiting of our place in any reception center.

Whether or not refugees' friends and kin have sufficient resources to aid them is the key clause in this passage, and that decision is made by refugee managers. As might be expected, many refugees hope they will not be sent to a foyer. Yet others speak of the foyers with great attachment, and during the early 1980s refugee managers increasingly encountered refugees reluctant to leave. The strength of refugees' ties to family, friends, and compatriots determines if they are willing to exchange their social networks for state resources.

Strong Networks Reject the Social Contract

Through participant observation I obtained detailed information on members of a Khmer (ethnic Cambodian) kin network who all exhibited a strong aversion to the foyers. This network consists of eight households totaling thirty-five individuals: sixteen are parents, one is a grandparent, and eighteen are children of which all but three are minors (see Table 8.1). Two sisters, and the sisters' two male cousins (who are considered brothers according to Khmer kinship

Table 8.1. Members of a Strong Khmer Network in the Western Suburbs of Paris: Family Composition, Date of Arrival, and Relationship to Central Informant.

Central Informant	Primary Relatives	Secondary Relatives	Tertiary Relatives
Older Sister Husband Three Children 1983	Younger Sister Husband Three Children 1981	Blood Uncle Wife No Children 1976	Fictive Kin Uncle Wife Three Children 1982
	Older Cousin Wife Mother-In-Law Three Children 1980	Brother-In-Law Wife One Child 1983	Brother-In-Law's Aunt* Husband Three Children 1984
	Younger Cousin Wife Two Children 1981		

* Lives 200 miles away.

customs), constitute the core of the network. The network is supplemented by four other households: an uncle by blood, a fictive kin uncle, a brother-in-law, and the brother-in-law's aunt.

All the men and most of the women attended high school in Cambodia and could speak some French before they arrived in France. Two brothers also learned English and were employed as English teachers in a refugee camp in Thailand. This moderate level of education placed members of the network at about the top-third of Khmer society in terms of social status. All of them lived during the period when the Khmer Rouge controlled Cambodia and sought to eliminate this strata: knowledge of French or English was grounds for execution (for personal accounts of the Cambodian Holocaust see May 1986; Ngor 1987; Syzmusiak 1986; Yathay 1987). When I contacted this network during 1987–1988, all but one of the households lived in the western suburbs of Paris.

"The Foyers Are Only for Peasants"

The blood uncle fled from Cambodia to Thailand after only a few months under the Khmer Rouge. Like most refugees, he wanted to migrate to the U.S., but he also applied to the French embassy and was accepted by France first. He arrived in France in 1976 and stayed in a foyer for two months. When we discussed the value of his residence in the foyer he stated:

> The foyers are only for peasants who have large families and don't speak French. A foyer first teaches the language and then a skill. If a refugee speaks some French like myself and my relatives, they don't need to go to a foyer. Life in them is hard. I left as soon as I could to look for work and housing myself.

This description exaggerates the type of refugees sent to the foyers. But it is revealing that the over representation of the least westernized refugees in these institutions (a result of state policy) stigmatizes the foyer for refugees from or aspiring to enter the middle-class. The above passage also suggests that some refugees prefer to manage their own adaptation rather than rely on state programs.

The brother-in-law and his family had been sponsored by a French reception group in a Parisian suburb and thus avoided residence in a foyer. I asked the brother-in-law if he felt less prepared to adapt to French society because he had not received language instruction and job training. He replied:

> I wanted a job and a place to live quickly, so the center wasn't necessary. In the center they will have you work in a bakery or as a security guard, and then pay you a little. But then they will force you, I mean encourage you, to take that job. You can refuse but the next time they will ask you again.

I later discovered why the brother-in-law held this negative view of the foyer. His self-sufficiency skills are so great that he actually earned enough money to buy a car by crafting and selling gold jewelry. He learned this skill from a friend while living in a Thai refugee camp, where he purchased the tools and materials necessary to manufacture jewelry before coming to France. He regularly sends the finished pieces to his sister and mother who live in Long Beach, California. Long Beach is the home of the largest Cambodian community outside of Southeast Asia—numbering some 20,000—and his relatives sell this Cambodian-style jewelry and then send the money back to France.

The brother-in-law's views suggest a second reason why some refugees dislike the foyer: the fact that they are total institutions. Indochinese refugees who escaped from their countries after communist governments came to power in 1975 frequently use these despotic regimes to measure the political character of institutions they encounter in the West. Living in a foyer is the closest experience Indochinese refugees have to life under Asian communist regimes. The older sister's husband once commented: " Six months is a long time to stay in a foyer. The mayor of the town decides how much money and help to give the refugees. A Communist or a National Front mayor will not give a lot."

Closely linked with the totalitarian qualities of the foyer are immediate economic issues for refugee households. While other Indochinese refugees experienced food shortages, Cambodians who lived under the Khmer Rouge endured several years of starvation. Individuals competed for subsistence, sometimes by trying to eat out of a communal bowl faster than one's neighbors, at other times by theft. Food remains a highly charged symbol of past trauma. According to the older sister:

> The most important thing about a foyer is whether one has to eat in the cafeteria or if they give you money to cook for yourself. Refugees in the [Parisian] transit center know ahead of time which foyers allow them to cook and which give them food. There's a bulletin board in the transit center which lists which foyer refugees will go to. Each time new names are put up everyone rushes to find out where they will go. They hope they will not be sent to a foyer which uses a cafeteria.

Individuals in this kin network hold unmistakably negative attitudes toward the resources provided by the French state to promote their adaptation. These views are explained by the functions of this kin network for its members. Sponsoring relatives to France and economic self-sufficiency are incompatible with residence in a total institution.

Men Create and Women Reproduce the Network

There is a pronounced sexual division of labor in the creation and maintenance of this kin network. Adult males were primarily responsible for transplanting the network in France between 1976 and 1984. The men visited association and government offices to complete sponsorship papers for the families still in Southeast Asia. Refugee managers examined the language ability and socioeconomic position of the males in deciding not to send these families to the foyers. Once the network was in place, the women took responsibility for its daily reproduction.

Wives nourish kin ties by forging the interpersonal links that keep members in contact. The husbands do not perform this function for a variety of reasons. One adopted a western religion proselytized in the Thai refugee camps and now dedicates most of his free time to studying its books and attending its meetings. Another husband compulsively gambles on horse races, loses, and is self-absorbed; a third has a drinking problem. But regardless of these individual character traits, employment largely precludes the husbands from performing the activities that maintain the network. All the adult males work at irregular hours: nights, weekends, when they are called on, or six days a week. Most work as manual laborers and are frequently too tired to communicate with relatives.

Conversely, wives share employers and work at home, and so can easily contact kin. The fact that the Cambodian community is residentially dispersed means that the children in this network do not meet other Cambodians at school. If parents want them to socialize with ethnic peers it must be with cousins, and these dates are arranged by the women as part of their child rearing responsibilities. In addition, most social occasions center around food and it is again the women who supply traditional Khmer cooking. This kin network allows most of its members to avoid residence in a foyer and also enables them to have a degree of self-sufficiency from the social welfare supplied by the state. However, the men were responsible for the short-run task of recreating the network, while the women undertake the long-run function of maintaining kin ties.

When the Network Failed

The blood uncle was the first member of this network to arrive, and upon leaving the foyer he immediately set about sponsoring another household. Other households arrived in Thailand, contacted members already in France, and were eventually admitted to France on the basis of having close relatives already there and probably because most adult males already spoke some French. Moreover, each family was aided by sponsor groups organized by a national association, local Catholic churches, or the mayor of a town. Thus by 1983, seven households in this network were living in the Parisian suburbs and only the first household to arrive had passed through a foyer.

However, when the eighth and last household arrived in 1984, refugee managers sent it to a foyer. The brother-in-law tried to become the sponsor for his aunt's family by requesting that the association which had sponsored him now find a reception group for his relatives. He reported that his request was denied by the association on the grounds and that there were too many refugees in the Paris region. The brother-in-law explained the association's decision, revealing a keen understanding of the primacy of the nation-state in the French mode of incorporation:

The French government has a policy of dispersing the refugees. It doesn't want them to live in the same area. I wanted that family to come here but the problem was housing. We couldn't find an apartment without the help of the association, so they were sent to a foyer. Now they live near the foyer in Nancy. That's more than 300 kilometers from here.

This setback did not deter the aunt's family from trying to move near their relatives. However, the lack of housing in the Paris region meant that they could not simply arrive and rent an apartment without a voucher from an employer or a resettlement association. Nonetheless, the aunt's son did move in with the brother-in-law's family shortly after leaving the foyer. He lived with them for almost a year while working in Paris before an accident forced him to return to his parents' home. Two years later, there were still hopes that the aunt's family might move to Paris. The husband visited his wife's nephew and discussed plans for opening a small grocery store. The uncle needed the active participation of his French-speaking nephew to handle the paper work involved in opening an enterprise. The nephew decided he was not ready to start a business and that ended all plans for his aunt's family moving to Paris.

This incident is a case where the network could not be reconstituted, primarily because of the state's dispersal policy. It also points to one of the network's central functions for its members: the formation of cooperative adaptive strategies. As households in this network took up residence in the suburbs of Paris, members developed economic ties. The most important ties are mutual aid with piecework among women and an indigenous savings system.

Women in the Informal Ethnic Economy

All the adult women in this network own sewing machines and produce finished clothing on a piece-rate system from precut pieces of cloth distributed to them by other refugees. The younger sister estimated that about one-half of the Cambodian women she knew in the Paris region sewed at home. This work is legal, provided that workers' register the sewing machine and pay a tariff at the time of its purchase. However, the ratio of the piece-rate price to the retail price for a pair of pants is approximately 1:30.

The two distributors in this network are Chinese-Cambodian refugees. One of them knew several of these households because they lived near each other in a Thai refugee camp. After migrating to France and settling in the suburbs of Paris, it was expected that he would recruit workers among people he already knew. The second

Chinese-Cambodian distributor obtained six female workers from the first distributor after marrying his sister. With this group of workers the new in-law went into business. He explained how he became a middleman in the clothing industry: "I saw a sign for a contractor with ten to eighteen workers to make clothes. It was in a Jewish store. Many Jews in Paris work with clothes. I have only six workers, and that's not a lot. Some contractors have twenty."

One of the workers he received was the older sister's sister-in-law. Even though the two women produce clothes for different contractors, they still maintain cooperative ties. Once, the contractor gave one of the women a new style of clothing to sew and only verbal instructions rather than a model to follow. The new style proved difficult to reproduce simply from memory. When the contractor returned to pick up the finished clothes, each article was deficient. This woman gave her relative half of the deficient clothes to resew for her so that she would not fall behind in meeting the production schedule.

The brother-in-law (the most assimilated member of the network) once tested the resiliency of these economic ties: he tried to prevent his wife from continuing to sew. She was the least assimilated member of the network (she spoke French poorly and disliked French food). This unlikely couple had been coerced into marriage during the Khmer Rouge regime. Since arriving to France, the husband had tried to persuade his wife to enroll in a French class. However, his wife felt uncomfortable in class and often skipped school citing the piecework as demanding all of her spare time. Finally, the husband forbid her to sew clothes at home. The events which followed this decision demonstrate that the network can prevent members from weakening its strong ties.

The initial repercussion of the ban was felt by the older sister because the two often called upon each other for help when they were behind schedule. The older sister now began lagging in her own work and she frequently telephoned her sister-in-law asking for help. This situation went on for almost one year before the inertia of the kin network finally succeeded in forcing the husband to accept the fact that his wife would do piecework at home. This change was caused by a combination of factors: the needs of the kin network, the tenacity of the contractor, and the assimilationist policy of the French state.

During this period, the woman had been attending French classes. At some point she became acquainted with a Cambodian man and he began calling her at home, hanging up if the husband answered. This flirtation—a serious breach of Khmer married life—was prompted by a peculiar feature of the French resettlement program: government certification of refugees' marriages and their children's paternity. The Office for the Protection of Refugees and Stateless Persons had recently informed the husband and wife that their marriage was not recognized by the French government because it had been performed under the Khmer Rouge regime without the couple's consent. Despite the best efforts by the couple and the birth of a daughter, the marriage had always been in jeopardy. State intervention tilted the odds against them.

With the multiple liabilities of going to school now apparent to the woman—lack of income and contact with other men—she was eager to begin sewing. During one of the older sister's routine phone calls for assistance the woman agreed that the contractor could come by with an order of clothes. The contractor was also eager to regain his former employee. He had mocked her effort to assimilate during their last meeting when he learned she was going back to school: "What are you trying to do, get a certificate?" The piecework system depends on trust between worker and contractor. Payments are made to workers on a monthly basis, while they deliver clothes on a weekly basis. On the other hand, employers may buy sewing machines for workers and then wait for repayment, which entails the risk that a worker will switch to another employer or not repay the loan. Since the woman was a former employee with a good record, and had purchased the sewing machine on her own, the contractor quickly moved to bring her back into his piecework network. Despite the fact that the woman lived about forty-five minutes from his home, the contractor came by with the highest priced piecework available: children's pants at $1.50 each.

As it became apparent to the husband that his wife would soon stop taking French classes, he activated the one network to which he had access: the staff of the resettlement association which sponsored his family. He called the woman who directed his sponsor group and asked her to keep his wife in school. He apparently valued assimilation for his wife so highly that he was willing to risk a potential affair. In turn, the director located a French woman who lived near the couple and was willing to volunteer to "help refugees." The volunteer visited the woman several times, was treated coldly on each occasion, and the French class was full by the time she agreed to register. The contractor came by with the clothes several days latter and the husband watched in futility as his wife began piecework again. Three networks interacted over the problem of weakening kin ties. The Chinese-Cambodian contractors and the Cambodian women who did the piecework overpowered an assimilated individual and his network of refugee managers.

Indigenous Savings System

Members of this network pool money through a savings system they used in Cambodia. Each household periodically acquires the whole sum, a practice they term a *tontine* (cf. Light [1972] on the rotating credit associations among Chinese and Japanese immigrants in the U.S.). The basic principle of the tontine is that each member regularly contributes a predetermined sum of money. A member can collect the sum of all money contributed at their discretion. If there are twelve members, the tontine can be organized so that participants contribute funds every month, and each month one member has the option of claiming the total sum. Those members who forfeit their turn and allow another member to take the sum are paid interest by the member who claimed the sum in their place. If a member forfeits a turn two times in a row, s/he will be paid interest by the entire group, with higher interest paid by members who took the sum earlier and lower interest by members who took the sum later. Interest rates are usually established by secret bids, with the highest bid winning.

Six of the seven households in the Parisian suburbs participate in the tontine and each pays about $150 a month. The older sister reports that she and her relatives practiced (she used the French verb *jouer*, to play) the tontine in Cambodia for as long as she can remember, and that up to thirty people had taken part. In her opinion:

> The tontine is better than a bank because there is no fixed interest and you can get the money when you need it. I don't take my share very often. I save it for an emergency. Maybe one of my children will get sick or my husband will lose his job. Other people use the money to buy a car or a television. My husband doesn't play because he has a regular job, but I only sew at home so I play.

As participation in the tontine and the informal economy indicate, indigenous social welfare among members of this kin network is of more utility than resources supplied by the state in exchange for assimilation. Residence in a foyer would damage this network because of the duration of the stay, but more importantly due to the dispersal of members throughout the country. The ability of these Cambodians to provide their own social, occupational, and financial support promotes their self-sufficiency from French society and the institutions the French state uses to incorporate international migrants.

Weak Networks Accept the Social Contract

Not all refugees reject the foyers, and many express attachment to one. To understand what leads some refugees to value a total institution, I interviewed foyer staff and Cambodian refugees in a city in western France called Beauville (a fictitious name). One Khmer woman, a widow, had particularly positive responses to her stay in the foyer. As I traced the network of kin around this woman it became apparent that all of them held the foyer in high regard. They also had weak relationships with family members and friends due to the hardships of migration, the state's dispersal policy, and their position in the life cycle. In sharp contrast to the Cambodians in suburban Paris, those in western France formed a network on the basis of their deficiencies rather than their strengths.

The network in Beauville is composed of four kin groups, although many members formed their own households after arrival (see Table 8.2). Altogether, this network of twenty-four individuals contains nine parents and fifteen children and grandchildren, although only eight

Table 8.2. Members of a Fragmented Khmer Network in a City in Western France: Family Composition, Date of Arrival, and Relationship to Central Informant.

Central Informant	Primary Relatives	Secondary Relatives
Widow One Child 1982	Sister Husband One Child 1984	Sister's First Daughter Marries** 1984
		Sister's First Son Marries** 1986
Widow's Son Leaves Home in 1987*	Cousin Husband Son and Daughter-In-Law Two Grandchildren 1985	Sister's Second Daughter Arrives* Husband Three Children 1986
		Sister's Husband Forces Second Son to Leave Home in 1987
		Distant In-Law Husband Daughter One Grandson 1975

*Lives 60 miles away.
** Lives 260 miles away.

of the children are minors. Even though these Cambodians belong to a network, they are unable to provide the social welfare they most need, and the foyer assumes a major role in their lives.

The Foyer as Substitute Community

The distant in-law's household was the first of the network to arrive in Beauville. This family managed to flee during the early months of the Khmer Rouge regime. After escaping, the family became lost in the jungle for two weeks. The husband had been a gun runner for bandits on the Thai-Cambodian border, and the family fortunately met one of the bands the husband had supplied. The bandits helped the family with the dangerous border crossing, even carrying the husband in a sling when he became incapacitated from lack of opium for his addiction. The husband had used what little opium he had to drug his grandson so that the infant's cries would not reveal their departure to Khmer Rouge guards. They were among the original Cambodian families sent to Beauville in 1975.

The distant in-law described her six months in the foyer as enjoyable. She recounted how the refugees received meal tickets to use at a local cafeteria and the humorous scenes which transpired as groups of Cambodians encountered French cuisine for the first time. Neither she or her husband, the distant in-law reported, wanted to leave the foyer. At the time, there were few Cambodians living in the town while there were ten Cambodian families living in the foyer. Because it was easier to form friendship networks inside the foyer than when living outside, refugees like this woman responded positively to life in a foyer.

In 1980, the woman's son-in-law made a difficult decision. He informed his wife, pregnant at the time, that he was returning to Thailand to join one of the noncommunist Khmer guerrilla groups seeking to drive the Vietnamese army from Cambodia. (The Vietnamese invasion started in December of 1978, and ended four years of genocide under the the Khmer Rouge, but led to a new communist government handpicked by Vietnam). When I spoke with this family in 1988, the husband was still engaged in the struggle to free Cambodia. However, the man's wife and parents-in-law considered his enlistment abandonment rather than patriotism, and reported that they would refuse to take him back should he return. This and other incidents involving members of the kin network revealed the weakness of their personal ties.

Foyer Staff as Substitute Kin

The widow and her two young boys were sent to Beauville in 1982 not realizing that her relatives lived there. She is one of the most

active participants in Cambodian events in the town, such as atten-
dance at the local temple, dancing at ceremonies, and participation in
the departmental Cambodian association. In addition, she has
extensive knowledge of herbal medicine and traditional cooking. The
widow's strong organizational and cultural affiliations initially
suggested that she would not become attached to the foyer. However,
she had stayed in the foyer longer than any other refugee. When I
later discovered that as a child she had been given by her parents to
an infertile female relative, I knew the widow had long developed
the skill of meeting her social welfare needs by attaching herself to
other people's networks to replace those she lacked.

I asked the widow about life in the foyer and she spoke in Khmer
to a son who translated into French. Her use of the French term
handicapé suggested that she had adopted language of the French
social welfare system as part of her social identity. She reported with
great emotion how foyer staff had helped her and the response of the
directors (the Le Bons, a fictitious name) when she left:

> I stayed in the foyer for almost two years because my children were in
> school. We had to save money before we could move out. I have two
> children and no husband—I'm handicapped—and it was difficult. The
> foyer helped a lot with all the papers and finding this apartment. When
> I moved out Mr. and Mrs. Le Bon cried.

The foyer eventually obtained a rare, full-time factory job for the
oldest son. However, the job was in a city sixty miles away and the son
left his mother's home. He now shares an apartment with a
Frenchman, has a French girlfriend, and his mother complains that he
only visits once a month. As the widow's family grafted itself to a
social welfare institution which had departmental wide connections,
household members became dispersed and some members assimilated
more quickly than others. But despite this negative effect for the
family, the widow still holds the foyer in high regard. I asked her
why the foyer would be so helpful several years after her family
moved into their own apartment. She responded by using a kinship
metaphor to describe the role of the foyer director and his wife: "Mr.
and Mrs. Le Bon help all the Cambodians here. They are like the
parents of the Cambodians in Beauville."

The bond between this Khmer woman and the foyer staff suggests
how refugees with weak networks avail themselves of a host society
institution's paternalism. Lacking close ties to relatives, such refugees
use the institutional completeness of the foyer as a surrogate for the
bonds kin would provide. However, dependence on a social welfare
institution further weakens ties among family members.

The Problem of Fictitious Kin

The widow was reunited with her cousin by chance when the two unexpectedly met on a street in Beauville. How this fortuitous reunion occurred, and the role played by the French state, again illustrates that weak networks lead migrants to evaluate positively host society institutions seeking their assimilation.

During an interview at the French embassy in Thailand, the husband in the family told an official that he had a relative somewhere in France. It was 1985 and refugees in the Thai camps realized that with every passing year western countries were admitting fewer refugees. The husband resorted to fiction to improve the family's chances for resettlement.

The cousin's family was subsequently admitted to France. When officials at FTDA (the association which channels refugees to the foyers) conducted an interview, they learned that the relative did not exist. By chance, the FTDA officials sent the family to Beauville, but the family's file still listed them as having a relative. Local refugee managers found them a French sponsor group, presuming that the presence of this relative meant that the family did not need the full range of assistance provided by the foyer. In addition, the husband had worked as a chauffeur for Cambodian government officials prior to 1975 and spoke some French.

When the French sponsors discovered that there was no relative they felt that their contract to help the cousin and her family had been violated. They placed them in an apartment with another Cambodian family, but then ended all contact. In reporting how these events transpired the cousin concluded: "We weren't lucky [like other refugees]. It would have been better if we had stayed in the foyer." Lacking kin in France, the cousin surmised that the foyer was best for refugees like herself.

The cousin's husband proved to be the strongest member of this kin network: he had greater status and more community contacts than other relatives. Through study, work, and savings, many Indochinese refugees in the West achieve a higher class status than they had in their home country. But cultural mobility also occurs, and this process is well illustrated by the cousin's husband. By regularly participating in temple activities while in Cambodia, he had learned the Buddhist prayers and chants used in weddings and baptisms. Although far from well trained in Buddhism, once in western France his skills were in great demand because few other refugees could recite these ceremonial incantations. When the one Cambodian monk in the city moved to Paris claiming that community donations provided insufficient support, this former government chauffeur became one of the leading religious figures for Cambodians in the area.

The husbands' religious background led him to a profound insight into the relationship between France and the Cambodian people. Following a family meal, I asked him to comment on the irony of Cambodians migrating to France when it was Frenchmen who first went to Cambodia. His reply (interrupted by the widow) related the Buddhist conception of sin ("do good get good, do bad get bad") to the resettlement of Cambodians in France:

> *Cousin's Husband*: The French were in Cambodia for eighty-seven years.
>
> *Widow*: They came to be our bosses. They built roads and bridges. They built the market in [my home town of] Battambang. The Cambodians were kind of silly. For money we used to use gold and silver as big as this [pointing to a baguette]. The French came and gave the Cambodians paper money and the Cambodians thought it was great because it was so light. But then the French took the gold and silver.
>
> *Cousin's Husband*: Now they have to take us in and feed us. The French sinned and now they have to take care of us.

From this man's perspective, France clearly has an obligation to aid Cambodian refugees. State assistance, like the foyer, is partial compensation for past colonization. Yet this positive evaluation of the foyer is linked to membership in a weak kin network. The upward cultural mobility of the cousin's family shifted the center of the network away from the widow. The network became weaker as a result because the cousin had only indirect bonds to the sister's adult children and almost no link to the distant in-law's family.

The Problem of Disappearing Kin

Additional evidence of the bonding process between members of this network and the foyer was provided when the widow was joined by her sister's family. This family arrived in France in 1984 and was sent to a foyer about 200 miles from Beauville. The arriving sister knew the widow lived in western France and requested that FTDA officials send the family there but was denied. The sister reported that an FTDA official explained that their relationship could not be verified because the two sisters did not share the same last name.

Khmer naming customs are quite distinct from those in Europe and North America, and refugee managers tend to use western norms to evaluate relations among kin. Cambodian parents sometimes choose a grandparent's personal name for a newborn child's family name. The fact that Khmer personal names are often gender neutral, signifying plants, animals, days in the Buddhist calender, or abstract qualities like lucky, avoids the problem of giving children names of the opposite sex. This unique naming practice results from the comparatively large number of children, and especially nieces and nephews, that Cambodian parents have. With four, five, or six offspring common, preserving the family name for another generation is not difficult, especially since women do not change their last name after marriage. Instead, parents may honor a grandparent by using his or her personal name for a child's family name. Although infrequent, it is possible for siblings to have different family names but share the same parents. This is the situation of the widow and her sister, and the French state's imposed interpretation of Khmer kinship ties initially inhibited the recreation of their kin network.

The sister's family stayed in the foyer for seven months until a daughter found a job and they rented an apartment. Soon after, the daughter married and moved out, forcing the family to find a cheaper apartment now that they were deprived of a wage earner. Then a son married and moved to his in-law's house, again making it impossible for the remaining members to pay the rent on their current apartment. The second marriage occurred in 1986 and the parents and two sons then joined the wife's sister.

The sister explains that she and her family moved to Beauville because the widow lived there. Yet the widow was initially located there because of the foyer and remained in the town because of her close ties to this institution. As marriages weakened the kin ties within the sister's family, they gravitated toward a household bonded to a foyer. Strong ties between one kin member and a host society institution lead to chain migration on the part of a family whose own network was dissolving.

The arriving household stayed in the widow's apartment until the departmental Cambodian association obtained an apartment for them in the same low-income housing project. Then the foyer initiated the paperwork to obtain social security for the sister and her husband, who were in their early fifties. Foyer staff were also instrumental in obtaining several apprenticeships for the son, and were continuously looking for a permanent job for him. The widow's close ties to both the foyer and the Cambodian association were crucial for the sister's household obtaining help. However, the other son could not find employment and eventually moved out after heated disputes with his father over his work ethic. He now lives with a French girlfriend, further distancing himself from the family.

In 1986, a daughter and her family arrived in France and were sent to Beauville because her parents lived there. After residing in the foyer for one year, staff found the family an apartment in a town sixty miles away. But for the next four months, the daughter lived with her parents in Beauville during the week in order to continue French classes in the foyer (courses were not offered in her town). The foyer also found a job for her husband sewing clothes in a textile factory. In Cambodia, the husband was a teacher and his income and social status made him a prominent member of the kin network. Although he accepted the factory job, both husband and wife bitterly object to a male head of household doing what they perceive as women's work. The husband is a shy man to begin with and the stigma of his new job further erodes his status in the kin network. Yet when I asked the couple if their stay in the foyer was useful they recited the usual litany of benefits: the family allocation and language courses, obtaining residence and refugee cards. Families joining the network in Beauville did obtain assistance from the foyer, but the effect of this aid was to weaken rather than strengthen the personal ties among members.

Conclusion

The French mode of state incorporation is a social contract in which international migrants are offered resources in exchange for assimilation. To use these resources, refugees must loosen, if not break, ties with their kin and communal networks. Host society institutions like the foyers attempt to replace the functions of the extended family and ethnic community. Some Indochinese refugees accept this contract because the collective approach to social welfare in France is similar to the communal aid provided by kin and ethnic networks. Other refugees find state assistance entirely incompatible with the aid provided through their social networks.

Indochinese refugees who are members of weak social networks are more likely to accept the social contract offered by the French state than those who belong to strong networks. A fragmented kin network in the city of Beauville in western France holds the local foyer in high regard and greatly values the resources it provides. One woman even called the directors of the foyer the "parents of the Cambodians in Beauville," indicating how some refugees allow host society institutions to substitute for the social networks they lack. The comparatively weak ties in the network result in part from members' position in the life cycle: adult children are forming families of their own; senior members are not in the labor force; conflicts between parents and maturing children are common. State incorporation also erodes this network. National refugee managers in Paris dispersed members to different regions because few heads of household had the class background necessary to meet the degree of westernization required for bypassing the formal resettlement program. Once in this program, local refugee managers in Beauville resettled refugees from the foyer in adjacent cities and located jobs throughout the department, thus requiring geographic mobility of members who want housing and employment. A network ill equipped to provide social welfare to members avails itself of a host society institution, in the process further fragmenting ties among kin.

Conversely, refugees with strong networks attain a degree of social welfare self-sufficiency that allows them to reject host society institutions that seek to replace their bonds with kin and community. In the suburbs of Paris, a strong network finds little value in the formal resettlement program because it threatens their goals upon arriving to France: to reunite kin and then pursue collective adaptation through an indigenous savings system and employment in the ethnic informal economy. Members must avoid state incorporation to maximize the social welfare provided through their network. The strong ties in the Parisian network result in part from members' position in the life cycle: the adults are employed and the children have not yet begun to form families of their own. The higher social status of the males in this network, particularly their ability to speak French before arriving to France, coupled with the working-class incomes of their kin sponsors, enabled six of the eight families to avoid residence in a foyer. Position in the life cycle initially determines the strength of migrants' social networks. State intervention poses a different threat.

9

Conclusion: History, States, and Migrants' Social Networks

Indochinese refugees usually apply to several resettlement countries for admission. Very different experiences await these migrants depending on which host state eventually grants them entry. To a great extent, the adaptation of international migrants is determined by class background, gender, and labor market conditions. Yet the adaptation process also is shaped by migrants' relationship to the host state, particularly the historical context of the migration, the organization of the social welfare system, and the prevailing pattern of race and ethnic relations.

Deciphering this combination of causal factors reveals a mode of state incorporation: a national model guiding how a state manages the entry of international migrants into host society institutions. Modes of state incorporation explain many of the macro-level differences in the adaptation of international migrants in host societies around the world. They also have effects at the micro-level. Each type of state intervention poses a distinct challenge to migrants' relationships to kin, friends, and the ethnic community. A host society is ultimately measured by the constraints it places on migrants' membership in social networks.

The Relative Importance of History

The timing of the Indochinese migration created different environments for the French and American states. Allied aliens arriving due to military defeat are unique for the U.S., but fit neatly within the pattern of migration to France due to decolonization. Laotian, Cambodian, and especially Vietnamese communities existed in France before the refugees arrived, but were absent from the U.S. Only the top echelons of the American elite value the refugees for their political identity, while nativism is prevalent among the American public and many politicians. In France, the refugees find unanimous support because of their historical ties to the nation.

Not only is there variation in particular historical factors for the two host states, but the impact of history also differs. The past is comparatively less important for the American state's incorporation of the refugees. Despite decades of migration to the U.S. due to East-West conflict, the arrival of Indochinese refugees caught the planners of American foreign and social policy off guard. Military defeat in a hot-war was a novel experience for the American state. Even the incorporation of Cuban refugees did not provide a model for managing the adaptation of Indochinese refugees. In fact, congressmen and federal bureaucrats viewed the Cuban resettlement program as an example not to be followed.

In addition, nativism eroded Indochinese refugees' political symbolism with remarkable swiftness. International migration to the U.S. accelerated during the 1970s and 1980s, and the American public and many members of the House of Representatives viewed refugees from Vietnam, Laos, and Cambodia as simply additional newcomers rather than allied aliens. These attitudes were not primarily caused by bitterness over a lost war or even worsening economic conditions. Instead, negative responses to the refugees stemmed from traditional xenophobia and racism.

Finally, Indochinese communities did not exist in the U.S. prior to 1975. Despite America's extensive military and political intervention in mainland Southeast Asia since the 1950s, France remained the economic and cultural pole for Vietnamese, Laotians, and Cambodians considering international migration. For the American response to arriving Indochinese refugees, history mattered more for its absence than for its presence.

This ability to disassociate past from present, international from domestic events, is truly astonishing in the case of Indochinese refugees. American troops withdrew only two years prior to their migration, while military and financial assistance ceased only with the collapse of pro-American governments in the spring of 1975. Yet Indochinese refugees' encounter with American amnesia is far from unique. African-Americans find that whites do not consider slavery relevant to contemporary racial inequality. The conquest of the southwest during the 1800s is a definitive event for Chicanos in the region, but not for Anglos. Nineteenth century treaties guaranteeing ecological and political rights are prized by Native Americans yet considered outdated by the descendants of European immigrants who settled the frontier. Japanese-Americans interned during World War

Two waited more than four decades for the American government to recognize its violation of the constitution. The incorporation of Indochinese refugees reveals in detail how historical events of significance for ethnic minorities are expunged from the American memory.

History is more important for the French mode of incorporation. The refugees assumed their place among migration flows to France due to North-South conflict. On the one hand, the independence of French colonies in the 1950s and 1960s lead to repatriations on a large scale, particularly the pieds noirs from Algeria. France even received thousands of Muslim troops who had fought for the metropolis and now found their lives in jeopardy. On the other hand, during the 1960s, France turned to its former North African colonies for labor. The state expected the migration of these immigrant workers to be temporary. But it developed social welfare programs for Algerians, Moroccans, and Tunisians, particularly the *foyers* or lodging hostels. One year after halting labor immigration, the French state used these social welfare institutions to resettle Indochinese refugees.

The French public and politicians also recognize the refugees' historical symbolism as allied aliens despite the fact that four decades have passed since the decolonization of Indochina. One-fifth of the public claims they would donate $500 over two years. Even the communist portion of the electorate is willing to aid refugees fleeing communist revolutions in former French colonies. Although nativism against foreigners rose during the 1970s and 1980s, France makes an exception for refugees from Vietnam, Laos, and Cambodia.

Lastly, history matters because Indochinese have been living in France since the 1920s, and they migrated to France, rather than the U.S., until 1975. Despite wars for independence in the early 1950s, colonization established strong ties between France and the peoples of Indochina. Communist containment, the American form of intervention, proved comparatively ineffective in creating a bond between American society and Vietnamese, Laotians, and Cambodians.

The passage of time may have allowed the French to polish colonialism, removing the memory of forced labor, high taxes, and pacifications campaigns. Conversely, the recency of the Vietnam War might have made Americans numb to historical realities. But historical symbols are shaping the incorporation of other international migrants in France. Much of the French public continues to associate North Africans, particularly Algerians, with a bloody struggle for independence that led France to the brink of civil war. French public opinion surveys still ask respondents if they believe torture is justified if it will save lives, a reference to army atrocities in

Algeria. North African children are taught about the victory of Charles Martel over an invading Muslim army in the 700s. Political instability in the Middle East and North Africa rejuvenates tensions that in fact existed well before the colonial era. Human rights violations in former African and Asian colonies, even genocide in the case of Cambodia, allow invidious comparisons between the politics of current regimes and those of the French administration. What ever the validity of such contrasts, France uses history to appraise international migration in a way that the U.S. does not.

The Ascendancy of the Welfare State
in the United States

Variation in the importance of history for the French and American modes of incorporation is paralleled by different relationships between the welfare state and the nation-state. Determining international migrants' access to public resources dominates the American mode of incorporation at the national level. The interests of the nation-state remain local. In the case of Indochinese refugees, historical factors heighten the state's interest in social citizenship rather than ethnic community formation. The novelty of arriving allied aliens requires refugee advocates to develop new resettlement policies since existing social welfare programs cannot provide the necessary aid. Extensive nativism limits the availability of local sponsors, forcing refugee managers to centralize the resettlement program at the national level. Yet the structure of the American welfare state and nation-state ultimately determines the relationship between social citizenship and ethnic community formation.

The welfare state is the central institution managing the refugees' adaptation because social citizenship for international migrants is inherently problematic for the American social welfare system. The type of temporary, remedial assistance required by underskilled workers who need job training is scarce even for natives. Nor does the system contain a flexible form of cash assistance for intact families suddenly deprived of income or for individuals with little work history. The income support and social services refugees receive compensate for deficiencies in the national system. Reflecting on the problem of aiding Indochinese refugees, the Department of Health and Human Services concluded that "the long-range solution depends on a substantial reform of the welfare system."

Federalism further hinders the development of social citizenship for international migrants. The admission of immigrants and refugees is a national decision, but social welfare assistance is predominately local. National and state government conflict over the extent of federal obligations to fund programs for migrants. Each confrontation redefines the rights and resources available to immigrants and refugees, placing their social citizenship in permanent jeopardy. Like the absence of remedial aid, federalism is incompatible with international migration, and thus requires the constant reshaping of social citizenship by the welfare state.

Restrictive eligibility norms are a second cause of the welfare state's centrality in the American mode of incorporation. Rates of public assistance use among Indochinese refugees increased during the early 1980s. These refugees had lower levels of education and fewer transferable job skills than earlier cohorts, and also arrived during a severe recession. Yet federal officials and voluntary agency staff quickly charged the refugees with losing their work ethic and lacking self-sufficiency, expecting the refugees to take underpaid jobs that often did not provide health insurance. The American state and public use the consumption of public resources to evaluate the progress of international migrants. This diffusion of norms from the social welfare system to other host society institutions augments the centrality of the welfare state in the incorporation of international migrants. As a result, many issues regarding migrants' social class are refracted through the social welfare system, while in France it is the nation-state that mediates class background.

The rapidity with which the welfare state transforms Indochinese refugees from political migrants to welfare clients is surprising given their unambiguous historical symbolism. But the American social welfare system has long shaped immigration policy. A national public aid program did not exist until the 1930s, but in 1917 immigrants could be barred from the U.S. if they were "likely to become a public charge," a measure meant to limit the admission of Southern and Eastern Europeans. In the years leading up to World War Two, this policy obstructed the entry of European Jews fleeing fascist governments.

Sustained international migration since the liberalization of immigration laws in 1965 has meant an even more prominent role for the welfare state. Status in the social welfare system has become a key variable for arriving migrants as the state creates combinations of rights for migrants who are neither foreigners nor citizens. Some migrants arrive to the U.S. as immigrants, but receive refugee assistance, such as Amerasians from Vietnam and their relatives. Other migrants enter as a refugees, but have no special status in the social welfare system, such as privately sponsored Cubans. An even more contorted relationship between international migration and the welfare state developed from the Immigration Reform and Control Act of 1986. To obtain permanent residence, Mexicans immigrants residing illegally in the U.S. had to pass an English and civics test (normally a requirement for full citizenship), and agree to limitations on their future use of public assistance.

While the American welfare state constructs and reconstructs social citizenship at the national level, the American nation-state directs race and ethnic relations at the city and neighborhood level. Refugee managers encourage Indochinese refugees to form residential clusters and create ethnic associations, believing that ethnic communities facilitate the adaptation process. Some projects select refugees overseas for settlement in areas of the country with job opportunities and low public assistance benefits. One scheme actually channeled Cambodians and Vietnamese of Chinese ancestry to American cities with large Chinatowns. Mutual assistance associations which cooperate in the incorporation process receive extensive public funding, and they often become the dominant institutions within refugee communities.

The absence of Indochinese communities in 1975, and rapid arrivals over the next ten years, fostered a belief among refugee managers that these political migrants faced an unusual historical handicap. But the importance of ethnic communities for the American mode of incorporation results from a complex relationship between the welfare state and the nation-state, not historical context. Although refugee managers support ethnicity, rather than immediate assimilation, this position is predicated on the belief that stable communities are a prerequisite for economic and social adaptation. As the policy of dispersing refugees among the states indicates, ethnicity is valued not for its own sake, but because it is thought to increase self-sufficiency and diminish reliance on the social welfare system. Pluralism at the local level presumes the ascendancy of the welfare state at the national level.

The value placed on the ethnic community in the American mode of incorporation also results from a racially polarized nation-state. American traditions of race and ethnic relations are split between an immigrant legacy and a minority heritage. Refugee managers' depict the European immigrant experience as migrants joining a community and being assisted by established residents to assimilate over time. This idealized portrayal is artificially contrasted with the formation of a racial caste and political mobilization based on racial solidarity, a tradition embodied by African-Americans. The American state's tolerance, even encouragement, for ethnic communities modeled on the experience of European-Americans requires a less acceptable alternative.

This selective use of nation-state traditions suggests that contemporary immigration from the Third World to the U.S. is marginalizing African-Americans. Most of these migrants from Asia, Latin America, and the Caribbean will themselves encounter racism. Many will also experience economic inequality like that of native blacks. But despite the increasing proportion of ethnic minorities in the American population (16.5 percent in 1970, 24.4 percent in 1990), the Indochinese case indicates how the structure of the American nation-state reinforces the European tradition. State intervention among new immigrant populations is offsetting the demographic weight of ethnic minorities by channeling the expression of ethnicity.

The Predominance of the Nation-State in France

Where the American mode of state incorporation prioritizes the welfare state, the French mode of incorporation pursues the interests of the nation-state. Constructing social citizenship for immigrants and refugees is not the state's central preoccupation. Instead, French refugee managers strive to assimilate foreigners and preserve cultural unity. As in the U.S., historical factors augment this trend. In the case of Indochinese refugees, positive public opinion allows the state to rely on local rather than national sponsors. Prior incorporation of migrants from former colonies further minimizes the need to elaborate Indochinese refugees' access to public resources. But it is the organization of the social welfare system and patterns of race and ethnic relations that ultimately propel the nation-state to its position of dominance.

The French welfare state did not become the front line institution managing the incorporation of Indochinese refugees because international migration poses fewer problems for the corporatist, as opposed to federalist, social welfare system. Corporatism confines policy setting to the central government, but program administration to interest groups and parapublic organizations. The link between immigration and social welfare policy is determined by the central government. The French state channels international migrants into preexisting statuses in the social welfare system, rather than making "refugee" a new social problem, as in the United States. Indochinese refugees join divorced women without work histories to receive unemployment payments, recently released prisoners to enter half-way houses, and foreigners who fought for France to obtain job training. Once the central government converts refugees into such domestic statuses, nonstate organizations gain control of their access to public resources.

The corporatist system also provides a place for competing groups, further diminishing the complexity of providing social citizenship to international migrants. To resettle Indochinese refugees, the state funds an organization of former colonists and army officers as well as an organization originally formed to prevent the expulsion of foreigners engaged in leftist activities. Each organization has a different function in the resettlement program and provides different services to the refugees. Participation in program implementation by affected parties ensures support for social policies.

Encompassing eligibility norms ultimately prevent international migrants' access to public resources from dominating the French mode of incorporation. The social welfare system seeks to include, rather than exclude, participants. The state uses total institutions to process Indochinese refugees into France. In these temporary settlement centers, often termed *foyers*, the refugees receive shelter, food, and social services for about six months. The French state's remarkable description of residence in a foyer as "an apprenticeship in solidarity" well illustrates the encompassing eligibility norm. One of the state's expected functions is to create a republic through the expenditure of public resources. Thus refugee managers show little revulsion when refugees initially rely for income on unemployment insurance and the family allowance. This absence of stigma for the recipients of aid minimizes the importance of social citizenship for the French state.

Yet the French welfare state, like all western social welfare systems, is currently being tested by the forces of international migration. NonEuropean immigrant families, which tend to be larger than native families, receive proportionately more family and housing allocations than do French citizens. In the mid-1980s, the city of Paris enacted two laws to exclude foreign families from a type of family allocation. Both laws were eventually annulled by the national government. Despite conflict over resources, the host society still prioritizes the interests of the nation-state.

In France, having Indochinese refugees achieve "insertion" means limiting their residential concentration. The fear that refugees will form "ethnic ghettos" begins with their concentration in the Paris region. Despite a dispersal policy, a Chinese-Cambodian and Chinese-Vietnamese enclave developed in Paris, and the neighborhood's representative in the National Assembly views it as a threat to French civilization. Cambodian, Laotian, and especially Vietnamese populations living in the Paris region before the refugees arrived heightened the French state's fears over residential concentration. Yet local government officials in other French cities are equally adamant that the refugees not form ethnic communities and they disperse the refugees among neighborhoods. Refugee managers even express concern when several refugee families live on the same floor in a public housing complex. Irascible shopkeepers can be expected to correct refugees' speech; only the state and its refugee managers can shape residential patterns. This drive to prevent the formation of ethnic communities results from the structure of the French nation-state.

Where the American nation-state is founded on the distinction between race and ethnicity, the French nation-state is based on geography, language, religion, historical symbols, and other attributes of civilization. The polarization of the American nation-state is distinct from the concentric nation-state in France, with its cultural core in Paris and opportunities for assimilation based on culture and colonial history. Cultural unity is a key value for the French nation-state. It will increase costs to the social welfare system in order to manage the assimilation of Indochinese refugees at the national, local, and even the micro-local level of the housing project.

A hidden feature of the concentric nation-state is the importance of social class. International migrants who arrive already westernized experience much less state intervention than their compatriots who have Third World job skills and low levels of education. Indochinese refugees with university degrees and professional job skills are rarely sent to the foyers where staff closely monitor residents' language training, job search, and choice of housing. Conversely, refugees who were agricultural labors are usually given this "collective solution." Class is also important for state incorporation in the U.S., but it impacts adaptation through the social welfare system, not through race and ethnic relations. For the American state, migrants' class backgrounds are potential costs to health, social service, and especially public assistance programs. For the French state, social class is linked with migrants' ability to assimilate.

Muslim, black African, and Asian populations are an increasing proportion of French society as a result of immigration and higher fertility rates. Indochinese refugees have formed an ethnic community in the thirteenth arrondissement of Paris. Sustained immigration of ethnic Chinese, and the area's economic viability due to the formation of ethnic enterprises, will sustain this Chinatown past the first generation. North African immigrants pose an even greater challenge to the French nation-state, particularly with the advent of a second generation during the 1980s. Intense nativism and xenophobia toward Algerians is inhibiting the function of such traditional mechanisms of assimilation as unions, churches, and schools. French scholars observe that these institutions have declined as forces of solidarity for the French population as well. They do not note that there has been no corresponding decline in the value placed on cultural unity.

The Indochinese case suggests that direct state intervention is compensating for the malaise afflicting many French social institutions. Current state efforts to more closely regulate the naturalization process and define French citizenship provide only the most obvious examples. But with the erosion of the nation-state's traditional foundations, the state also is intervening at the local level, as evidenced by the creation of refugee managers in foyers. The incorporation of Indochinese refugees indicates that the French state will bear costs to the welfare state rather than become like the American nation-state, where ethnic communities and racial segregation are integral features of the society.

Conflicts or Contracts with Migrants' Social Networks

State incorporation brings together two social welfare systems since the international migrants have their own methods for solving social problems. Vietnamese, Laotians, and Cambodians come from societies without welfare states and their social welfare repertoires are composed of kin and ethnic networks rather than government bureaucracies. Indochinese refugees, like other international migrants from the Third World, have a collective approach to adaptation. Depending on which host society they enter, immigrants and refugees meet distinct challenges to their social networks

In the American mode of incorporation, refugees are expected to use state resources as individuals or households, not as members of an extended kin group or an ethnic community. Refugees' resist the social welfare system's individualization of the adaptation process and turn to their kin and ethnic networks for a collective response. Use of state resources is an element of their collective adaptation, and the result is a constant conflict between refugees and refugee managers.

In France, refugees' social networks confront a social contract. The French mode of incorporation seeks to replace refugees' social networks with host society institutions. In exchange for state resources, refugees must accept dispersal and weakened ties to kin and community, thus promoting their assimilation. Refugees in social networks with limited ability to supply members with social welfare look favorably upon this social contract. Those who are members of strong networks reject state resources, relying instead on indigenous saving systems and work in the ethnic informal economy.

The structure of the welfare state and nation-state in the host society determines if international migrants encounter a social conflict or a social contract. The American state promotes social welfare individualism at the national level and ethnic solidarity at the local level. The French state preserves cultural unity at all levels and uses social welfare programs to increase social solidarity. Where the American state seeks to prevent refugees from becoming dependent on host society institutions, the French state hopes to replace refugees' social networks with host society institutions. Thus, in the U.S., refugees' collective approach to adaptation meets support from the nation-state but resistance from the welfare state. Conflict is inherent for international migrants in the U.S. because one institution supports migrants' networks, while the other recognizes only individuals.

Refugees' traditions of self-help through kin and communal networks are a threat to both institutions in France. For the French nation-state, preservation of social networks inhibits assimilation, while the welfare state is designed to promote French, not Indochinese, solidarity. International migrants confront a social contract in France because the welfare state uses the same collective approach to social welfare as migrants' networks, while the nation-state seeks to replace migrants membership in kin and especially ethnic networks with membership in French society.

Measuring Host Societies

In some host societies, history shapes the present, and international events cross national borders to influence domestic events. In others, the past has little importance and only the most significant global developments receive recognition. Cross-national variation in the effects of history explain some of the differences among states' intervention in the adaptation of international migrants. When historical context is diminished, the state becomes more central to the adaptation process. Nonstate, particularly local organizations, become prominent as the importance of historical context increases.

A second salient dimension of a host society is the balance between social citizenship and race and ethnic relations. State interests may emphasize the politics of distributing public resources or regulating cultural pluralism. In addition, these interests may be pursued at the national or local level, or both levels. Cross-national variation in the relationship between the welfare state and the nation-state explains another portion of the differences among states' actions to manage the entry of international migrants into host society institutions. The more the interests of the welfare state are predominate at the national level, the more state actions regarding social citizenship affect other areas of state intervention. When the interests of the nation-state are predominate at the national level, state actions have fewer repercussions for other state actions.

A final measure of a host society is its response to migrants' kin and ethnic networks. At one extreme, the host society may completely deracinate migrants, while at the other extreme it might develop and coopt their networks. There are more moderate outcomes. In some host societies, migrants enter conflicts with host society institutions and their social networks are sources of resistance. In others, migrants must decide whether or not to accept a social contract that requires them to relinquish membership in social networks for membership in host society institutions. Position in the life cycle, migration histories, and other internal factors establish the initial strengths and weaknesses of migrants' social networks. But the relationship between the welfare state and the nation-state accounts for the type of challenge a host society poses to these networks. The greater the dominance of the welfare state, the greater the conflict between between migrants' social networks and host society institutions. Conversely, the greater the dominance of the nation-state, the more migrants' relationships with host society institutions resemble a social contract.

The migration of Indochinese refugees to the U.S. and France reveals different types of host societies. The American experience involves historical amnesia, a polarized culture, and contradictory institutions. Historical events are profoundly relevant and yet ignored. Ethnic communities are encouraged provided they promote integration rather than separatism. Support for pluralism at the local level is predicated on individual conformity to national norms governing the distribution of public resources. In such a society, conflict is inherent, almost routine, for international migrants because the demands of the host society are incompatible with each other and the functioning of kin and ethnic networks.

The French response to Indochinese refugees reveals a host society with historical consciousness, a concentric culture, and synchronized institutions. History not only matters, its importance is exaggerated. State interests converge in assimilating foreigners and promoting social solidarity through public programs, although preserving cultural unity is predominant. The common position of host society institutions presents international migrants with a social contract, one which requires forfeiting ties to social networks in exchange for entry into host society institutions. How states manage the incorporation of international migrants reveals as much about the host society as it does about the adaptation of the migrants in the long-run.

Bibliography

Books, Journal Articles, and
Nongovernmental Agency Reports (other than FTDA)

Journal articles are identified by issue number or month, followed by page numbers. Year of publication is sufficient to identify volume. Newsletters and many non-American journals not use volume numbers.

Acualités Migrations. 1989. "Immigrés: L'Inquête qui Dérange." *Acualités Migrations* 302:18–20.

Ajchenbaum, Yves. 1983. *Les Populations Originaires d'Asie du Sud Est Accueillies en France au Sein des Centres Provisoires d'Hébergerement, 1980–1981*. Paris: France Terre d'Asile.

_____ . 1981. *Les Populations Originaires d'Asie du Sud Est Accueillies en France au Sein des Centres Provisoires d'Hébergerement, 1975–1979*. Paris: France Terre d'Asile.

Ajchenbaum, Yves, Geneviève Chandlier, Jean-Pierre Hassoun, and Françoise Ponchaud. 1979. *Le Dispositif d'Accueil des Réfugiés du Sud-Est Asiatique: Les Centres Provisoires d'Hébergement au 1er Juillet 1979 et Leurs Incidences sur l'Insertion des Réfugiés*.Paris: ADRES et FORS.

Amenta, Edwin, and Bruce G. Carruthers. 1988. "The Formative Years of U.S. Social Spending Policies: Theories of the Welfare State and the American States During the Great Depression." *American Sociological Review* 5:661–78.

American Council of Voluntary Agencies. 1982. "Impacted Areas." Letter sent to the U.S. Department of Health and Human Services, November 24, 1982. New York: American Council of Voluntary Agencies.

_____ . 1981a. "United States Coordinator's Consultation Document: Refugee Placement." Letter to the Office of the U.S. Coordinator for Refugees, July 16, 1981. New York: American Council of Voluntary Agencies.

_____ . 1981b. Voluntary Agency Placement Policies: Impacted Areas and Areas of Special Concern. New York: American Council of Voluntary Agencies.

Anderson, Perry. 1974. *Lineages of the Absolutist State*. London: NLB.

Ashford, Douglas. 1986. *The Emergence of the Welfare States*. New York: Basil Blackwell.

_____ . 1982. *Policy and Politics in France: Living with Uncertainty*. Philadelphia: Temple University Press.

Bach, Robert L., 1988. "State Intervention in Southeast Asian Refugee Resettlement in the United States." *Journal of Refugee Studies* 1:38–56.

——. 1978. "Mexican Immigration and the American State." 1978 *International Migration Review* 4:536–58

Bach, Robert L. and Rita Carroll-Seguin. 1986. "Labor Force Participation, Household Composition and Sponsorship among Southeast Asian Refugees." *International Migration Review* 2:381–404.

Baer, Florence E. 1982. "'Give Me...your Huddled Masses': Anti-Vietnamese Refugee Lore and the Image of the Limited Good." *Western Folklore* October:275–91.

Bahout-Meurant, Arielle, and Alain Marie. 1987. "Rouen Terre d'Asile pour 229 Boat People." *Le Quotidien de Médecin* July 29.

Bailey, Samuel L. 1990. "Cross-Cultural Comparison and the Writing of Migration History: Some Thoughts on How to Study Italians in the New World." Pp. 241–53 in *Immigration Reconsidered: History, Sociology, and Politics*, edited by Virginia Yans-McLaughlin. New York: Oxford University Press.

Bailyn, Bernard. 1986. *The Peopling of British North America*. New York: Knopf.

Barnet, Richard. 1983. *The Alliance: America, Europe and Japan, Makers of the Postwar World*. New York: Simon and Schuster.

Beer, William R. 1980. *The Unexpected Rebellion: Ethnic Activism in Contemporary France*. New York: New York University Press.

Belbahri, Abdelkader. 1982. *Immigration et Situations Postcoloniales: Le Cas des Maghrébins en France*. Paris: L'Harmattan.

Bendix, Reinhard. 1978. *Kings or People: Power and the Mandate to Rule*. Berkeley: University of California Press.

Berkeley Planning Associates. 1984. *An Evaluation of the Favorable Alternative Sites Project: Final Report*. Berkeley: Berkeley Planning Associates.

——. 1982a. *Study of the State Administration of the Refugee Resettlement Program*. Berkeley: Berkeley Planning Associates.

——. 1982b. *The Adminstration of the Refugee Resettlement Program in the State of Washington*. Berkeley: Berkeley Planning Associates.

Betts, Raymond F. 1961. *Assimilation and Association in French Colonial Theory*, 1890–1914. New York: Columbia University Press.

Binder, David. 1975. "Ford Seeks Rise in Refugee Entry." New York Times May 3:1

Blaufarb, Douglas. 1977. *The Counterinsurgency Era*. New York: Free Press.

Bonvin, François., 1987. "Personal Communication." M. Bonvin provided the author with the raw data for the following two articles.

Bonvin, François and François Ponchaud. 1981a. "Insertion Sociale des Réfugiés du Sud-Est Asiatique (I)." *Recherche Sociale* 78: Special issue.

——. 1981b. "Insertion Sociale des Réfugiés du Sud-Est Asiatique (II)." *Recherche Sociale* 79: Special issue.

Boswell, Thomas D., and James R. Curtis. 1984. *The Cuban-American Experience: Culture, Images, and Perspectives*. Totowa: Rowman and Allanheld.

Boyd, Monica. 1989. "Family and Personal Networks in International Migration." *International Migration Review* 3:638-70.

Braudel, Fernand. 1990. *The Identity of Frace: Volume Two*. New York: Harper Collins.

_____. 1988. *The Identity of France, Volume One*. New York: Harper and Row.

Brubaker, William R. 1990. "Immigration, Citizenship, and the Nation-State in France and Germany: A Comparative Historical Analysis." *International Sociology* 4:379–407.

_____. 1989. "Membership without Citizenship: The Economic and Social Rights of Noncitizens." Pp. 145–62 in *Immigration and the Politics of Citizenship in Europe and North America*, edited by William R. Brubaker. Lanham: University Press of America.

Bui, Dianna. 1983. "The Indochinese Mutual Assistance Associations." Pp. 167–80 in *Bridging Cultures: Southeast Asian Refugees in America*, edited by Asian American Community Health Training Center. Los Angeles: Asian American Community Health Training Center.

Butler, David. 1985. *The Fall of Saigon: Scenes From the Sudden End of a Long War*. New York: Simon and Schuster.

Buttinger, Joseph. 1968. *Vietnam: A Political History*. New York: Praeger.

Canadian EIC. 1986. "The Canadian Approach to the Settlement and Adaptation of Refugees." *Migration News* 2:14–25.

Caplan, Nathan, John K. Whitmore, and Marcella H. Choy. 1989. *The Boat People and Achievement in America: A Study of Family Life, Hard Work, and Cultural Values*. Ann Arbor: Michigan University Press.

Castles, Stephen. 1984. *Here for Good: Western Europe's New Ethnic Minorities*. London: Pluto Press.

Castles, Stephen, and Godula Kosack. 1985. *Immigrant Workers and Class Structure in Western Europe*. Oxford: Oxford University Press.

Center for Applied Linguistics. 1981. *The Peoples and Cultures of Cambodia, Laos, and Vietnam*. Washington, DC: Center for Applied Linguistics.

Chan, Sucheng. 1991. *Asian Americans: An Interpretive History*. Boston: Twayne Publishers.

_____. 1990. "European and Asian Immigration into the United States in Comparative Perspective, 1820s to 1920s." Pp. 37–75 in *Immigration Reconsidered: History, Sociology, and Politics*, edited by Virginia Yans-McLaughlin. New York: Oxford University Press.

Chantovich, Supang, and E. Bruce Reynolds (eds.). 1988. *Indochinese Refugees: Asylum and Resettlement*. Bangkok: Institute of Asian Studies, Chulalongkorn University.

Charlton, Roger, Lawrence T. Farley, and Ronald Kaye. 1988. "Indentifying the Mainsprings of U.S. Refugee and Asylum Policy." *Journal of Refugee Studies* 3/4:237–59.

Chhim, Sun-Him, Khamchong Luangpraseut, and Huynh Dinh Te. 1989. *Introduction to Cambodian Culture; Laos Culturally Speaking; Introduction to Vietnamese Culture*. San Diego: Multifunctional Service Center, San Diego State University.

Cichon, Donald J., and Maryann Semons. 1986. *Evaluation of the Refugee Targeted Assistance Grants Program: Volume II, Cross-Site Analysis of Programs and Issues in Serving Hard-to-Place Clients*. Washington, DC: U.S. Office of Refugee Resettlement.

Cichon, Donald J., Maryann Semons, and Cynthia J. Gimbert. 1986. *Evaluation of the Refugee Targeted Assistance Grants Program: Volume I, Site Portrayls*. Washington, DC: U.S. Office of Refugee Resettlement.

Coffey, Zimmerman, and Associates. 1985. *An Evaluation of the Highland Lao Initiative*. Washington, DC:Coffey, Zimmerman and Associates.

Collins, Alice. 1983. "Rebuilding Refugee Networks." Pp. 53-66 in *Rediscovering Self-Help: Its Role in Social Care*, edited by Diane Pancoast, Paul Parker, and Charles Froland. Beverly Hills: Sage.

Comité Nationale d'Entraide. 1981. *Les Réfugiés Hmong en Guyane*. Paris: Comité Nationale d'Entraide.

Congressional Quarterly. 1981. *Congressional Roll Call 1980: A Chronology and Analysis of Votes in the House and Sentate, 96th Congress, Second Session*. Washington, DC: Congressional Quarterly.

_____. 1980. *Congressional Roll Call 1979: A Chronology and Analysis of Votes in the House and Sentate, 96th Congress, First Session*. Washington, DC: Congressional Quarterly.

_____. 1977. *Congressional Roll Call 1976: A Chronology an Analysis of Votes in the House and Sentate, 94th Congress, Second Session*. Washington, DC: Congressional Quarterly.

_____. 1976. *Congressional Roll Call 1975: A Chronology and Analysis of Votes in the House and Sentate, 94th Congress, First Session*. Washington, DC: Congressional Quarterly.

Conoir, Yvan. 1986. "Comité Nationale d'Entraide Franco-Vietnamien, Cambodgien, Laotien." *Refugees* 31:41-2.

Copeland, Ronald. 1983. "The Cuban Boatlift of 1980: Strategies in Federal Crisis Management." *Annals of the American Academy of Political and Social Science* 467:138-50.

Cornut-Gentile, François. 1986. "La Paroles aux Immigrés." Pp.109-18 in *Opinion Publique*, edited by SOFRES. Paris: Callimard.

Costa-Lascoux, Jacqueline. 1987. "L'Insertion Sociale des R'éfugiés et Demandeurs d'Asile en Europe." *Revue Européenne des Migration Internationales* 3:151-68.

Criddle, Joan D., and Teeda B. Mam. 1987. *To Destroy You Is No Loss: The Odyssey of a Cambodian Family*. New York: Atlantic Monthly Press.

Cross, Gary S. 1983. *Immigrant Workers in Industrial France: The Making of a New Laboring Class*. Philadelphia: Temple University Press.

_____. 1980. "The Politics of Immigration in France During the Era of the World War I." *French Historical Studies* 4:610–32.

Crozier, Michel. 1964. *The Bureaucratic Phenomenon*. Chicago: University of Chicago Press.

Davis, David B. 1975. *The Problem of Slavery in the Age of Revolution, 1770–1823*. Ithaca: Cornell University Press.

Dawson, Alan. 1977. *55 Days: The Fall of South Vietnam*. Englewood Cliff: Prentice-Hall.

Deloche, Pascal, and Milton Thread. 1987. "Sauvés des Eaux." *Pélerin* Juillet 24:17-18.

Déaz-Briquets, Sergio, and Lisandro Pérez. 1981. "Cuba: The Demography of Revolution." *Population Bulletin* 36 (volume 1). Washington DC: Population Reference Bureau.

Desbarats, Jacqueline. 1985. "Indochinese Resettlement in the United States." *Annals of the Association of American Geographers* 4:522-38.

Dinnerstein, Leonard. 1982. *America and the Survivors of the Holocaust*. New York: Columbia University Press.

Dirks, Gerald. 1985. "Canadian Refugee Policy: Humanitarian and Political Determinants." Pp. 120-35 in *Refugees and World Politics*, edited by Elizabeth G. Ferris. New York: Praeger Publishers.

Documentation Française. 1988. *Etre Français Aujourd'hui et Demain, Tome 1*. Paris: Documentation Française.

_____. 1982. *Recensement Général de la Population de 1982: Les Etrangers*. Paris: La Documentation Française.

_____. 1966. *France Deals With Social Problems*. Paris: Documentation Française.

Documents Nord-Afriques. 1965. "Bilan Général de Rapatriement." *Documents Nord-Afriques* 608:np.

Doerner, William R. 1985. "Asians: To America with Skills." *Time* July 8:42–4.

Donelly, Harrison. 1982. "Welcome Mat Wearing Thin? Refugees Put Growing Strain on Welfare Programs; Critics Call for Cutbacks, Changes." *Congressional Quarterly Weekly Report* 33:1963–68.

Dowty, Alan. 1987. *Closed Borders: The Contemporary Assault on Freedom of Movement*. New Haven: Yale University Press.

Dunning, Bruce B. 1989. "Vietnamese in America: The Adaptation of the 1975–1979 Arrivals." Pp. 55–85 in *Refugees as Immigrants: Cambodians, Laotians, and Vietnamese*, edited by David W. Haines. Totowa: Rowman and Littlefield Publishers.

Dupin, Eric. 1990. *Oui, Non, Sans Opinion: 50 Ans de Sondages IFOP*. Paris: Inter Editions.

Dupont-Gonin, Pierre. 1979. "Migrations et Dévelopment: Des Réfugiés Hmong en Guyane." *Revue des Etudes Cooperatives* Fourth Quarter: 23–49.

Egawa, Janey, and Nathaniel Tashima. 1982. *Indigenous Healers in Southeast Asian Refugee Communities*. San Francisco: Pacific Asian Mental Health Research Project.

Eisenstadt, S. N. 1973. "Varieties of Political Development: The Theoretical Challenge." Pp. 41–72 in *Building States and Nations*, edited by S. N. Eisenstadt and Stein Rokkan. Beverly Hills: Sage.

Enloe, Cynthia H. 1986. "Ethnicity, the State, and the New International Order." Pp. 25–42 in *The Primordial Challenge: Ethnicity in the Contemporary World*, edited by John F. Stack. Westport: Greenwood Press.

Esping-Andersen, Gøsta. 1990. *The Three Worlds of Welfare Capitalism*. Princeton: Princeton University Press.

L'Express. 1979. "Sondage: Les Français et les Réfugiés du Sud-Est Asiatique." *L'Express* 28 juillet–3 août:38.

Fagen, Richard R., Richard A. Brody, and Thomas J. O'Leary. 1968. *Cubans in Exile: Disaffection and the Revolution*. Stanford: Standford University Press.

Fagin, Joe R. 1991. "The Continuing Significance of Race: Antiblack Discrimination in Public Places." *American Sociological Review* 1:101-16.

Fanning, Louis A. 1976. *Betrayal in Vietnam*. New Rochelle: Arlington House.

Fass, Simon. 1986. "Innovations in the Struggle for Self-Reliance: The Hmong Experience in the United States." *International Migration Review* 2:351–80.

Fawcett, James T. 1989. "Networks, Linkages, and Migration Systems." *International Migration Review* 2:671–80.

Fein, Helen. 1987. *Congregational Sponsors of Indochinese Refugees in the United States, 1979–1981*. Cranberry: Associated University Presses

Finnan, Christine R. 1981. "Occupational Assimilation of Refugees." *International Migration Review* 1:292–309.

Finnan, Christine R., and Rhona A. Cooperstein. 1983. *Southeast Asian Refugee Resettlement at the Local Level: The Role of the Ethnic Community and the Nature of Refugee Impact*. Menlo Park: SRI International.

Finney, John. 1975. "Kissinger Says U.S. may Shelter 70,000." *New York Times* May 15:1.

Flora, Peter, and Jens Alber. 1987. "Modernization, Democratization, and the Development of the Welfare State in Western Europe." Pp. 37-80 in *The Development of the Welfare State in Europe and America*, edited by Peter Flora and Arnold Heidenheimer. New Brunswick: Transaction Books.

Forbes, Susan S. 1985a. "Residency Patterns and Secondary Migration of Refugees." *Migration News* 1:3–18.

_____. 1985b. *Adaptation and Integration of Recent Refugees to the United States*. Washington, DC: Refugee Policy Group.

Fournier, Jacques, and Nicole Questiaux. 1980. *Traité du Social: Situtations, Luttes, Politiques, Institutions*. Paris: Dalloz.

Freeman, Gary P. 1986. "Migration and the Political Economy of the Welfare State." *Annals of the American Academy of Political and Social Science* 485: 51–63.

_____. 1979. *Immigrant Labor and Racial Conflict in Industrial Societies: The French and British Experience, 1945–1975*. Princeton: Princeton University Press.

Freeman, James A. 1989. *Hearts of Sorrow: Vietnamese-American Lives*. Stanford: Stanford University Press.

Friedline, Michael. 1986. "Resettlement [first panelist]." Pp. 44–47 in *Working With Refugees*, edited by Peter I. Rose. Staten Island: Center for Migration Studies.

Fritsch, Jane. 1989. "Cannibal or Savior: Viet Refugee Says He Was Both." *Los Angeles Times* February 24.

Gallagher, Denis, Susan Forbes, and Patricia W. Fagen. 1986. "Of Special Humanitarian Concern: U.S. Refugee Admissions Since Passage of the Refugee Act." *Migration News* 1:3–36.

Gallagher, Patrick L. 1980. *The Cuban Exile: A Socio-Political Analysis*. New York: Arno Press.

Gallup Opinion Index. 1979. "Most Americans Predict Good Reception for the 'Boat People.'" *Gallup Opinion Index* 170:8–11.

_____. 1975. "Majority Opposes Resettling Viet Refugees in the Country." *Gallup Opinion Index* 119:1–6.

Gallup Poll. 1981. "May 29, 1980: Immigration to the United States." Pp.120–24 in *The Gallup Poll: Public Opinion 1980*. Wilmington: Scholarly Resources.

_____. 1978a. "1973: May 13: Cambodia and Laos." Pp. 119–22 in *The Gallup Poll: Public Opinion 1972-1977, Volume II*. Wilmington: Scholarly Resources.

_____. 1978b. "1975: March 9: South Vietnam and Cambodia." Pp.440–41 in *The Gallup Poll: Public Opinion 1972–1977, Volume II*. Wilmington: Scholarly Resources.

_____. 1978c. "1975: April 23, South Vietnam." Pp.456–58 in *The Gallup Poll: Public Opinion 1972–1977, Volume II*. Wilmington: Scholarly Resources.

_____. 1978d. "1977: April 24, Illegal Aliens, Immigraton, and Identification Cards." Pp. 1048–53 in *The Gallup Poll: Public Opinion 1972–1977, Volume II*. Wilmington: Scholarly Resources.

Gallup Report. 1989. "Cults Lead List of Groups Unwelcome as Neighbors." *Gallup Report* 282/283:45–46.

GATREM Indochine. 1980. *Rapport Sur l'Accueil et l'Insertion des Réfugiés Pris en Charge par le GATREM-Indochine Periode du 1er janvier au 20 octobre 1980*. Limoges: GATREM Indochine.

Geschwender, James, Rita Carroll-Seguin, and Howard Brill. 1988. "The Portuguese and Haoles in Hawaii: Implications for the Origin of Ethnicity." *American Sociological Review* 53:515–27.

Gimbert, Cynthia J., and Maryann Semons. 1988. *Impact of Targeted Assistance on Refugee Economic Histories: Evaluation of the Refugee Targeted Assistance Grants Program (Phase III Final Report)*. Dover: Research Management Corporation.

Girard, Alain, Yves Charbit, and Marie-Laurence Lamy. 1974. "Attitudes des Français à l'Egard de l'Immigration Etrangère: Nouvelle Enquête d'Opinion." *Population* 6:1015–69.

Glazer, Nathan. 1986. "Welfare and 'Welfare' in America." Pp. 40–63 in *The Welfare State East and West*, edited by Richard Rose and Rei Shiratori. New York: Oxford University Press.

_____. 1983. *Ethnic Dilemmas*. Cambridge: Harvard University Press.

Goffman, Erving. 1961. *Asylums: Essays on the Social Situation of Mental Patients and Other Inmates*. Garden City: Anchor Books.

Gogler, Françoise. 1982. "Etat/Associations: La Distribution des Rôles." *Information Sociales* 8:34–37.

Gold, Steven J. 1992. *Refugee Communities: A Comparative Field Study*. Newbury Park: Sage.

_____. 1989. "Differential Adjustment Among New Immigrant Family Members." *Journal of Contemporary Ethnography* 4:408–34.

Gordenker, Leon. 1987. *Refugees in International Politics*. New York: Columbia University Press.

Gordon, Linda W. 1987. "Southeast Asian Refugee Migration to the United States." Pp. 153–74 in *Pacific Bridges: The New Immigration from Asia and the Pacific Islands*, edited by James W. Fawcett and Benjamin V. Cariño. Staten Island: Center for Migration Studies.

Gordon, Margaret S. 1988. *Social Security Policies in Industrial Countries: A Comparative Analysis*. Cambridge: Cambridge University Press.

Gourverneur, François. 1978. "Refugees from Indochina in South-Eastern France." *Migration News* 3:3–8.

Granville Corporation. 1982. *Final Report: A Preliminary Assessment of the Khmer Cluster Resettlement Project*. Washington, DC: Granville Corporation.

Greenberg, Nikki F. 1985. "Starting Over." *Newsweek* April 15:71.

Guillon, Michelle, and Isabelle T. Leonetti. 1986. *Le Triangle de Choisy: Un Quartier Chinois à Paris*. Paris: L'Harmattan.

Hage, Jerald, and Robert Hanneman. 1980. "The Growth of the Welfare State in Britain, France, Germany, and Italy: A Comparison of Three Paradigms." *Comparative Social Research* 30:45–70.

Haines, David W. 1988. "Kinship in Vietnamese Refugee Resettlement." *Journal of Comparative Family Studies* 1:1–17.

_____. 1987. "Patterns of Southeast Asian Refugee Employment: A Reappraisal of the Existing Research." *Ethnic Groups* 1:39–59.

_____. 1986. "Vietnamese Refugee Women in the U.S. Labor Force: Continuity or Change." Pp. 62–75 in *International Migration: The Female Experience*, edited by Rita J. Simon and Caroline B. Brettell. Totowa: Rowman and Allanheld.

_____. 1985a. "Refugees and the Refugee Program." Pp. 3–16 in *Refugees in the United States: A Reference Book*, edited by David W. Haines. Westport: Greenwood Press.

_____. 1985b. "Initial Adjustment." Pp. 17–35 in *Refugees in the United States: A Reference Book*, edited by David W. Haines. Westport: Greenwood Press.

_____. 1985c "Toward Integration into American Society." Pp. 37–55 in *Refugees in the United States: A Reference Book*, edited by David W. Haines. Westport: Greenwood Press.

_____. 1982. "Southeast Asian Refugees in the United States: The Interaction of Kinship and Public Policy." *Anthropological Quarterly* 3:170–81.

Haines, David W., Dorothy Rutherford, and Patrick Thomas. 1981. "Family and Community Among Vietnamese Refugees." *International Migration Review* 1:310-19.

Haley, P. Edward. 1982. *Congress and the Fall of South Vietnam and Cambodia*. Teaneck: Faileigh Dickinson University Press.

Hamel, Bernard. 1982. "Aperçu sur l'Implantation Asiatique dans le 13e Arrondissement de Paris." *L'Afrique et l'Asie Modernes* 135:23–32.

Hammer, Tomas. 1990. *Democracy and the Nation-State: Aliens, Denizens and Citizens in a World of International Migration*. Aldershot, UK: Avebury.

Hang, Nguyen M. 1985. "Vietnamese." Pp. 195–208 in *Refugees in the United States: A Reference Book*, edited by David W. Haines. Westport: Greenwood Press.

Hannoun, Michel. 1987. *L'Homme et l'Espérance de l'Homme: Raport sur le Racisme et les Discriminations en France*. Paris: Documentation Française.

Harwood, Edwin. 1986. "American Public Opinion and U.S. Immigration Policy." *Annals of the American Academy of Polical and Social Sciences* 487:201–12.

Hasenfeld, Yeheskel, and Jane A. Rafferty. 1989. "The Determinants of Public Attitudes Toward the Welfare State." *Social Forces* 4:1027–48.

Hasenfeld, Yeheskel, Jane Rafferty, and Mayer N. Zald. 1987. "The Welfare State, Citizenship, and Bureaucratic Encounters." *Annual Review of Sociology* 13:387–415.

Hassoun, Jean-Pierre. 1982. "Les Surprises de l'Insertion Rurale." *Information Sociales* 8:55–59.

Hastings, Elizabeth H., and Philip K. Hastings (eds.). 1991. *Index to International Public Opinion, 1989–1990*. New York: Greenwood Press.

Hatzfield, Henri. 1971. *Du Paupérisme à la Sécurité Sociale, 1850–1940: Essai Sur les Origines de la Sécurité Social en France*. Paris: Librairie Armand Colin.

Hayslip, Le Ly. 1989. *When Heaven and Earth Changed Places: A Vietnamese Woman's Journey from War to Peace*. New York: Doubleday.

Hein, Jeremy. 1991a. "Do 'New Immigrants' Become 'New Minorities'?: The Meaning of Ethnic Minority for Indochinese Refugees in the United States." *Sociological Perspectives* 1:61-77.

———. 1991b. "Immigrants, Natives, and the French Welfare State: Explaining Different Interactions with a Social Welfare Program." *International Migration Review* 3:592–609.

———. 1988. "State Incorporation of Migrants and the Reproduction of a Middleman Minority Among Indochinese Refugees." *Sociological Quarterly* 3:463–78.

Hemery, D. 1975. "Du Patriotisme au Marxisme: L'Immigration Vietnamienne en France de 1926 à 1930." *Le Movement Social* 90:3–54.

Herring, George D. 1986. *America's Longest War*. New York: Knopf.

Higgins, Joan. 1981. *States of Welfare: Comparative Analysis in Social Policy*. Oxford: Basel Blackwell.

Higley, John, and Michael G. Burton. 1989. "The Elite Variable in Democratic Transitions and Breakdowns." *American Sociological Review* 1:17–32.

Hirayama, Kasumi K., and Hasashi Hirayama. 1988. "Stress, Social Supports, and Adaptational Patterns in Hmong Refugee Families." *Amerasia Journal* 1:93–108.

Hirschman, Charles. 1983. "America's Melting Pot Reconsidered." *Annual Review of Sociology* 9:397–423.

Hirschman, Charles, and Morrison G. Wong. 1984. "Socioeconomic Gains of Asian Americans, Blacks and Hispanics: 1960–1976." *American Journal of Sociology* 3:584–607.

Horne, John. 1985. "Immigrant Workers in France During World War I." *French Historical Studies* 1:57–88.

Hume, Ellen. 1985. "Vietnam's Legacy: Indochinese Refugees Adapt Quickly in U.S., Using Survival Skills." *Wall Street Journal* March 21:1.

Huyck, Earl E., and Leon F. Bouvier. 1983. "The Demography of Refugees." *Annals of the American Academy of Political and Social Science* 467:39–61.

Indochina Resource Action Center. 1986. *Indochinese Community Leadership Covention: A Report*. Washington, DC: Indochina Resource Action Center.

_____. 1984. *Proceedings of the Refugee Financing Economic Development Conference*. Washington, DC: Indochina Resource Action Center.

_____. 1982. *The Cambodian Cluster Project: A Survey Report*. Washington, DC: Indochina Resource Action Center.

Indra, Doreen M. 1987. "Bureaucratic Constraints, Middlemen, and Community Organizations." Pp. 147–70 in *Uprooting, Loss, and Adaptation*, edited by Kwok B. Chan and Doreen M. Indra. Ottowa: Canadian Public Health Association.

Institute for Asian Studies. 1988. *Thailand: A First Asylum Country for Refugees*. Bangkok: Institute for Asian Studies, Chulalongkorn University.

Jaffré, Jérôme. 1986. "Les Surprises de la Droite." Pp. 57–66 in *Opinion Publiques*, edited by SOFRE. Paris: Callimard.

Jenkins, J. Craig and Barbara G. Brents. 1989. "Social Protest, Hegemonic Competition, and Social Reform: A Political Struggle Interpretation of the Origins of the American Welfare State." *American Sociological Review* 6:891–909.

Jenkins, Shirley. 1988. "Conclusion: The State and the Associations." Pp. 275–81 in *Ethnic Associations and the Welfare State: Services to Immigrants in Five Countries*, edited by Shirely Jenkins. New York: Columbia University Press.

Jenkins, Shirley, and Mignon Sauber. 1988. "Ethnic Associations in New York and Services to Immigrants." *Pp. 21–105 in Ethnic Associations and the Welfare State: Services to Immigrants in Five Countries*, edited by Shirely Jenkins. New York: Columbia University Press.

Jensen, Leif I. 1988. "Patterns of Immigration and Public Assistance Utilization, 1970-1980." *International Migration Review* 1:51–83.

Johnson, Phyllis J. 1988. "The Impact of Ethnic Communities on the Employment of Southeast Asian Refugees." *Amerasia Journal* 1:1–22.

Joly, Danièle, and Robin Cohen. 1989. *Reluctant Hosts: Europe and its Refugees*. Brookfield: Gower Publishing Company.

Jordon, Winthrop D. 1974. *The White Man's Burden: Historical Origins of Racism in the United States*. New York: Oxford University Press.

Kalergis, Mary M. 1989. *Home of the Brave: Contemporary American Immigrants*. New York: E. P. Dutton.

Kanjanapan, Wilawan. 1989. "The Asian-American Traditional Household."

Pp. 39–55 in *Ethnicity and the New Family Economy*, edited by Francis K. Goldscheider and Calvin Goldscheider. Boulder: Westview Press.

Karnow, Stanley. 1984. *Vietnam: A History*. New York: Penguin Books.

Kelly, Gail P. 1977. *From Vietnam to America: A Chronicle of the Vietnamese Immigration to the United States*. Boulder: Westview Press.

Kerpen, Karen S. 1988. "China's Refguee Program." Pp. 48–49 in *World Refugee Survey: 1987 in Review*. Washington, DC: American Council of Nationalities Service.

Khath, Phyrun. 1989. "My Life Structure." Pp.95–104 in *The Far East Comes Near: Autobiographical Accounts of Southeast Asian Students in America*, edited by Lucy N. H. Nguyen and Joel M. Halpern. Amherst: University of Massachusetts Press.

Khoa, Le Huu. 1985. *Les Vietnamiens en France: Insertion et Identité*. Paris: L'Harmattan.

Khoa, Le Xuan, and Diani D. Bui. 1985. "Southeast Asian Mutual Assistance Associations: An Approach for Community Development." Pp. 209–24 in *Southeast Asian Mental Health: Treatment, Prevention, Services, Training, and Research*, edited by T. C. Owan. Washington, DC: National Institute of Mental Health.

Khoa, Le Xuan, and John Vandeusen. 1981. "Social and Cultural Customs: Their Contribution to Resettlement." *Journal of Refugee Resettlement* 2:27-47.

Kohl, Jürgen. 1987. "Trends and Problems in Postwar Public Expenditure Development in Western Europe and North America." Pp. 307–44 in *The Development of the Welfare State in Europe and America*, edited by Peter Flora and Arnold Heidenheimer. New Brunswick: Transaction Books.

Kohn, Melvin L. 1987. "Cross-National Research as an Analytic Strategy." *American Sociological Review* 6:713–31.

Koizumi, Koichi. 1991. "Resettlement of Indochinese Refugees in Japan (1975–1985): An Analysis and Model for Future Services." *Journal of Refugee Studies* 2:182–99.

Lamphere, Louise. 1987. *From Working Daughters to Working Mothers: Immigrant Women in a New England Industrial Community*. Ithaca: Cornell University Press.

Lanphier, C. Michael. 1982. "Sponsorship of Refugees in Canada." *Migration News* 3/4:18–28.

Laroque, Michel. 1984. *Politiques Sociales dans la France Contemporaine: Le Social Face à la Crise*. Paris: Les Editions S.T.H.

Layton-Henry, Zig. 1990. "The Challenge of Political Rights." Pp. 1–26 in *The Political Rights of Migrant Workers in Western Europe*, edited by Zig Layton-Henry. London: Sage.

Ledgerwood, Judy. 1990. "Portrait of a Conflict: Exploring Changing Khmer-American Social and Political Relationships." *Journal of Refugee Studies* 2:135–54.

Leman, Christopher. 1980. *The Collapse of Welfare Reform: Political Institutions, Policy, and the Poor in Canada and the United States*. Cambridge: MIT Press.

_____. 1977. "Patterns in Policy Development: Social Security in the United States and Canada." *Public Policy* Spring:261–91.

Lewin and Associates, Refugee Policy Group, and Berkeley Planning Associates. 1986. *Assessment of the MAA Incentive Grant Initiative*. Berkeley: Berkeley Planning Associates. Washington, DC: Lewin and Associates; Refugee Policy Group.

Lieberson, Stanley. 1980. *A Piece of the Pie: Blacks and White Immigrants Since 1880*. Berkeley: University of California Press.

Light, Ivan. 1972. *Ethnic Enterprise in America: Business and Welfare Among Chinese, Japanese, and Blacks*. Berkeley: University of California Press.

Lipsky, Michael. 1980. *Street-Level Bureaucracy: Dilemmas of the Individual in Public Services*. New York: Russel Sage Foundation.

Loescher, Gil, and John A. Scanlan. 1986. *Calculated Kindness: Refugees and America's Half-Open Door, 1945–Present*. New York: Free Press.

Majka, Lorraine. 1991. "Assessing Refugee Assistance Organizations in the United States and the United Kingdom." *Journal of Refugee Studies* 3:267–83.

Marrus, Michael R. 1985. *The Unwanted: European Refugees in the Twentieth Century*. New York: Oxford University Press.

Marshall, T. H. 1964. *Class, Citizenship, and Social Development*. Chicago: University of Chicago Press.

Mason, Linda, and Roger Brown. 1983. *Rice, Rivalry, and Politics: Managing Cambodian Relief*. Notre Dame: University of Notre Dame Press.

Massey, Douglas S. 1990. "American Apartheid: Segregation and the Making of the Underclass." *American Journal of Sociology* 2:329–57.

Massey, Douglas, Rafael Alarcón, Jorge Durand, and Humberto González. 1987. *Return to Aztlan: The Social Process of International Migration from Western Mexico*. Berkeley: University of California Press.

Masud-Piloto, Félix R. 1988. *With Open Arms: Cuban Migration to the United States*. Totowa: Rowman and Littlefield.

May, Someth. 1986. *Cambodian Witness: The Autobiography of Someth May*. New York: Random House.

Mayer, Nonna, and Pascal Perrineau (eds.). 1989. *Le Front National à Decouvert*. Paris: Presse de la Fondation Nationale des Sciences Politiques.

McConnell, Scott. 1989. *Leftward Journey: The Education of Vietnamese Students in France, 1919–1939*. New Brunswick: Transaction Publishers.

McNeil, William H. 1986. *Polyethnicity and National Unity in World History*. Toronto: University of Toronto Press.

Meunier, Paul. 1974. "Les Vietnamiens de Paris: Beaucoup de Restaurants mais aussi un Drame Politique." *La Croix* novembre 16 et 17:1c.

Migrations Etudes. 1989. "Le Devenir des Réfugiés et Demandeurs d'Asile Ayant Sejouné dans les Centre Provisoire d'Hébergergement." *Migration Etudes* 4:1–8.

Mitchell, Christopher. 1989. "International Migration, International Relations and Foreign Policy." *International Migration Review* 3:681–708.

Mitchell, Roger. 1987. "The Will to Believe and Anti-Refugee Rumors." *Midswestern Folklore* 1:5–15.

Le Monde. 1975. "M. Giscard d'Estaing: Les Vietnamiens de Culture Française Pourront Etre Accuillis dans Notre Pays." Le Monde 9 mai.

Montero, Darrel. 1979a. *Vietnamese Americans: Patterns of Resettlement and Socio-Economic Adaptation in the United States*. Boulder: Westview Press.

_____. 1979b. "Vietnamese Refugees in America: Toward a Theory of Spontanious International Migration." *International Migration Review* 4:624–48.

Montero, Darrel, and Ismael Dieppe. 1982. "Resettling Vietnamese Refugees: The Service Agency's Role." *Social Work* January:74–81.

Moon, Anson, and Nathaniel Tashima. 1982. *Help-Seeking Behavior and Attitudes of Southeast Asian Refugees*. San Francisco: Pacific Asian Mental Health Research Project.

Morawska, Ewa. 1990. "The Sociology and History of Immigration." Pp. 187–238 in *Immigration Reconsidered: History, Sociology, and Politics*, edited by Virginia Yans-McLaughlin. New York: Oxford University Press.

Morgan, Edmund S. 1975. *American Slavery, American Freedom: The Ordeal of Colonial Virginia*. New York: W. W. Norton.

Morse, Arthur. 1968. *While Six Million Died: A Chronicle of American Apathy*. New York: Hart.

Mortland, Carol A., and Judy Ledgerwood. 1987. "Refugee Resource Acquistion: The Invisible Communication System." Pp. 286–306 in *Cross-Cultural Adaptation: Current Approaches*, edited by Young Y. Kim and William B. Gudykunst. Newbury Park: Sage.

National Association for Vietnamese American Education. 1989. *The New Generation of Indochinese Americans*. Program for the Tenth Annual Conference on Indochinese Education and Social Services, Chicago March: 16–18.

National Institute of Statistics. 1972. *Vietnam: Statistical Yearbook 1972*. Saigon: National Institute of Statistics.

Nee, Victor, and Jimy Sanders. 1985. "The Road to Parity: Determinants of the Socioeconomic Achievements of Asian Americans." *Ethnic and Racial Studies* 1:75–93.

Neuwirth, Gertrud. 1988. "Refugee Resettlement." *Current Sociology* 36:27–42.

New York Times. 1979. "Poll on Refugees: Mixed Views." *New York Times* July 15:16.

Ngor, Heng. 1987. *Heng Ngor: A Cambodian Odyssey*. New York: MacMillan Publishing House.

Nguyen, Liem T., and Alan B. Henkin. 1982. "Vietnamese Refugees in the United States: Adaptation and Transitional Status." *Journal of Ethnic Studies* 3:101–16.

Nichols, J. Bruce. 1988. *The Uneasy Alliance: Religion, Refugee Work, and U.S. Foreign Policy*. New York: Oxford University Press.

Niehaus, Marjorie. 1979. "Indochinese Refugee Exodus: Causes, Impact, Prospects." Appendix VI in *U.S. Senate, Refugee Crisis in Cambodia*. Hearings Before the Committee on the Judiciary, United States Senate, 96th Congress, 1st Session (October 31, 1979). Washington, DC: U.S. Government Printing Office.

Noiriel, Gérard. 1988. *Le Creuset Français: Histoire de l'Immigration XIX–XX Siecles*. Paris: Seuil.

Noli, Jean. 1987. "Vingt-cinq Ans Après: La Réussite des Pieds-Noirs." *Le Point* 756:110-15.

North, David S. 1983. "Impact of Legal, Illegal, and Refugee Migrations on U.S. Social Service Programs." Pp. 269–85 in *U.S. Immigration and Refugee Policy: Global and Domestic Issues*, edited by Mary M. Kritz. Lexington: Lexington Books.

North, David. S., Lawrence S. Lewin, and Jennifer R. Wagner. 1982. *Kaleidoscope: The Resettlement of Refugees in the United States by the Voluntary Agencies*. Washington, DC: Lewin and Associates.

OECD. 1988. *Continous Reporting System on Migration*. Paris: OECD.

Olney, Douglas. 1986. "Population Trends." Pp. 179–84 in *The Hmong in Transition* edited by Bruce T. Downing, and Amos S. Deinard. Staten Island: Center for Migration Studies.

Olzak, Susan. 1989. "Labor Unrest, Immigration, and Ethnic Conflict in Urban America, 1880–1914." *American Journal of Sociology* 6:1303–33.

Orbach, Michael K. and Janese Beckwith. 1982. "Indochinese Adaptation and Local Government: An Example from Monterey." *Anthropological Quarterly* 3:135–45.

Outre Mer. 1937. "La Citoyenneté Française et l'Elite Indochinoise." *Outre Mer* 1:75–77.

Owen, Carolyn A., Howard C. Eisner, and Thomas R. McFaul. 1981. "A Half-Century of Social Distance Research: National Replication of the Bogardus Studies." *Sociology and Social Research* October:80–97.

Papyle, Henry. 1973. *L'Implantation des Repatriés d'Algerie en France: D'Après les Resultats du Recensement Général de la Population de 1968*. Nice:No Publisher. [Document located in the INSEE Bibliothèque, Paris.]

Parais, Joseph. 1982. "Les Aides Complementaires à la Sortie du CPH." Pp. 1–4 in *Stage de Formation Destine aux Responsables des Centre Provisoires d'Hébergement pour les Réfugiés*, edited by France Terre d'Asile. Paris: France Terre d'Asile.

Parker, Ann, and Michael Alford. 1986. "Chris Hurford: Australian Minister of Immigration and Ethnic Affairs." *Refugees* 33:21–22.

Passel, Jeffrey S. 1986. "Undocumented Immigration." *Annals of the American Academy of Political and Social Science* 487:181–200.

Patterson, James. 1986. *America's Struggle Against Poverty, 1900-1985*. Cambridge: Harvard University Press.

Pedraza-Bailey, Silvia. 1985. *Political and Economic Migrants in America: Cubans and Mexicans*. Austin: University of Texas Press.

Pérez, Lisandro. 1986. "Cubans in the United States." *Annals of the American Academy of Political Social Sciences* 487:126–37.

Peters, B. Guy, and Patricia K. Davis. 1986. "Migration to the United Kingdom and the Emergence of a New Politics." *Annals of the American Acadmey of Political and Social Science* 485:129–38.

Piori, Michael. 1979. *Birds of Passage: Migrant Labor and Industrial Societies*. New York: Cambridge University Press.

Pompa, Gilbert. 1981. "Community Relations Service." Pp. 166–70 in *Annual Report of the Attorney General of the United States 1981*. Washington, DC: U.S. Government Printing Office.

———. 1980. "Community Relations Service." Pp. 169–73 in *Annual Report of the Attorney General of the United States 1980*. Washington, DC: U.S. Government Printing Office.

Portes, Alejandro. 1990. "From South of the Border: Hispanic Minorities in the United States." Pp. 160–84 in *Immigration Reconsidered: History, Sociology, and Politics*, edited by Virginia Yans-McLaughlin. New York: Oxford University Press.

Portes, Alejandro, and Robert L. Bach. 1985. *Latin Journey: Cuban and Mexican Immigrants in the United States*. Berkeley: University of California Press.

Portes, Alejandro and Jòsef Böröcz. 1989. "Contemporary Immigration." *International Migration Review* 3:606–30.

Portes, Alejandro, and Robert D. Manning. 1986. "The Immigrant Enclave: Theory and Empirical Examples." Pp. 47–68 in *Competitive Ethnic Relations*, edited by Susan Olzack and Joanne Nagel. Orlando: Academic Press.

Portes, Alejandro, and Rafael Mozo. 1985. "The Political Adaptation Process of Cubans and Other Ethnic Minoriteis in the United States." *International Migration Review* 1:35–63.

Portes, Alejandro, and Rubén Rumbaut. 1990. *Immigrant America: A Portrait*. Berkeley: University of California Press.

Portes, Alejandro, and John Walton. 1981. *Labor, Class, and the International System*. New York: Academic Press.

Public Opinion. 1982. "A Nation of Immigrants." *Public Opinion* June/July:34.

Pullen, Jean. 1986. "Resettlement [second panelist]." Pp. 48–51 in *Working with Refugees*, edited by Peter I. Rose. Staten Island: Center for Migration Studies.

Quadagno, Jill. 1987. "Theories of the Welfare State." *Annual Review of Sociology* 13:109–28.

———. 1984. "Welfare Capitalism and the Social Security Act of 1935." *American Sociological Review* 5:632–47.

Quinsat, Thierry. 1984. "Les Réfugiés: Des Immigrés pas commes les Autres." *Croissance des Jeunes Nations* 263:19–26.

Réach, Geneviève. 1967. "118 petits Eurasiens Venus du Vietnam Voué à l'Assistance Publique." *Le Droit de Vivre* janvier-février:10.

Reagan, Ronald. 1986. "Letter from the President." P. 2 in *World Refugee Survey: 1986 in Review*. Washington, DC: American Council for Nationalities Service.

Refugee Policy Group. 1987. "Assessment of the MAA Incentive Grant Initiative." *Migration News* 1:33–41.

Refugee Reports. 1990. "1990 Statistical Issue." *Refugee Reports* 12:5-13

———. 1989a. "Update." *Refugee Reports* 2:11.

———. 1989b. "1989 Statistical Issue." *Refugee Reports* 12:5-16.

———. 1988. "1988 Statistical Issue." *Refugee Reports* 12: Special issue.

_____. 1984. "1984 Statistical Issue." *Refugee Reports* 12: Special issue.

Refugees. 1988. "China." *Refugees* December:31.

Regards sur l'Acualité. 1980a. "Cent Cinquante Mille Réfugiés." *Regards sur l'Actualité* Avril:19–25.

_____. 1980b. "Conseil du 27 août 1980." *Regards sur l'Actualité* septembre-octobre:63.

_____. 1979."Communiqués des Conseils des Ministres, Conseil du 24 octobre 1979." *Regards sur l'Actualité* 12 (15 juin):58.

Reimers, David M. 1985. *Still the Golden Door: The Third World Comes to America*. New York: Columbia University Press.

Rimlinger, Gaston. 1971. *Welfare Policy and Industrialization in Europe, America, and Russia*. New York: John Wiley and Sons.

Robequin, Charles. 1944. *The Economic Development of French Indochina*. London: Oxford University Press.

Roberts, Alden E. 1988. "Racism Sent and Received: Americans and Vietnamese View One Another." Pp. 75–97 in *Research in Race and Ethnic Relations*, edited by Cora Marrett and Cheryl Leggon. Greenwood: JAI Press.

Robinson, Donald L. 1971. *Slavery in the Structure of American Politics, 1765–1820*. New York: Harcourt, Brace, Javanovich.

Robinson, Vaughan. 1985. "The Vietnamese Reception and Resettlement Programme in the U.K.: Rhetoric and Reality." *Ethnic Groups* 4:305–30.

Rogg, Eleanor M. 1974. *The Assimilation of Cuban Exiles: The Role of Community and Class*. New York: Aberdeen Press.

Rogge, J. R. 1985. "The Indo-Chinese Diaspora: Where Have All the Refugees Gone?" *The Canadian Georgrapher* 1:65–72.

Rokkan, Stein. 1975. "Dimensions of State Formation and Nation-Building: A Possible Paradigm for Research on Variation Within Europe." Pp. 562–600 in *The Formation of National States in Western Europe*, edited by Charles Tilly. Princeton: Princeton University Press.

Rose, Peter I. ed. 1986. *Working With Refugees*. Staten Island: Center for Migration Studies.

_____. 1983. "The Business of Caring: Refugee Workers and Voluntary Agencies." *Refugee Reports* June:1–6.

Ross, George. 1988. "The Mitterand Experiment and the French Welfare State: An Interesting Uninteresting Story." Pp. 119–38 in *Remaking the Welfare State: Retrenchment and Social Policy in America and Europe*. edited by Michael K. Brown. Philadelphia: Temple University Press.

Rudge, Philip. 1987. "Fortress Europe." Pp. 5–12 in *World Refugee Survey: 1986 in Review*. Washington, DC: American Council for Nationalities Service.

Ruggie, Mary. 1984. *The State and Working Women: A Comparative Study of Britain and Sweden*. Princeton: Princeton University Press.

Rumbaut, Rubén., 1989a. "Portraits, Patterns and Predictors of the Refugee Adaptation Process: Results and Reflections from the IHARP Panel Study." Pp. 138–82 in *Refugees as Immigrants: Cambodians, Laotians, and*

Vietnamese in American, edited by David W. Haines. Totowa: Rowman and Littlefield.

_____. 1989b. "The Structure of Refuge: Southeast Asian Refugees in the United States, 1975-1985." *International Journal of Comparative Public Policy* 1:97–129.

Rumbaut, Rubén and John R. Weeks. 1986. "Fertility and Adaptation: Indochinese Refugees in the United States." *International Migration Review* 2:428–65.

Salt, John. 1989. "A Comparative Overview of International Trends and Types, 1950-80." *International Migration Review* 3:431–56.

_____. 1981. "International Labor Migration to Western Europe: A Geographic Review." Pp. 133–57 in *Global Trends in Migration: Theory and Research on International Population Movements*, edited by Mary M. Kritz, Charles B. Keely, and Silvano M. Tomasi. Staten Island: Center for Migration Studies.

Santoli, Al. 1988. *New Americans, An Oral History: Immigrants and Refugees in the U.S. Today*. New York: Viking.

Scanlan, John A., and Gilburt Loescher. 1983. "U.S. Foreign Policy, 1959-80: Impact on Refugee Flow from Cuba." *Annals of the American Academy of Political and Social Science* 467:116–37.

Schnapper, Dominique. 1991. *La France de l'Integration: Sociologie de la Nation en 1990*. Paris: Editions Gaillimard.

Schuman, Howard, Charlotte Steeh, and Lawrence Bobo. 1985. *Racial Attitudes in America: Trends and Interpretations*. Cambridge: Harvard University Press

Shawcross, William. 1984. *The Quality of Mercy: Cambodia, Holocaust and Modern Conscience*. New York: Touchstone.

Sheehan, Neil. 1988. *A Bright Shining Lie: John Paul Vann and America in Vietnam*. New York: Random House.

Simon, Rita J. 1985. *Public Opinion and the Immigrant: Print Media Coverage, 1880–1980*. Lexington: Lexington Books.

Skocpol, Theda. 1989. "The Limits of the New Deal System and the Roots of Contemporary Welfare Dilemmas." Pp. 293–311 in *The Politics of Social Policy in the United States*, edited by Margaret Weir, Ann S. Orloff, and Theda Skocpol. Princeton: Princeton University Press.

_____. 1984. "Emerging Agendas and Recurrent Strategies in Historical Sociology." Pp. 356–91 in *Vision and Method in Historical Sociology*, edited by Theda Skocpol. Cambridge: Harvard University Press.

Skocpol, Theda, and Edwin Amenta. 1986. "States and Social Policies." *Annual Review of Sociology* 12:131–57.

Skocpol, Theda, and John Ikenberry. 1983. "The Political Formation of the American Welfare State in Historical and Comparative Perspective." *Comparative Social Research* 3:87–148.

Smith, Anthony D. 1986. *The Ethnic Origin of Nations*. New York: Basil Blackwell.

Smith, J. Owens. 1987. *The Politics of Racial Inequality: A Systematic*

Comparative Macro-Analysis from the Colonial Period to 1970. Westport: Greenwood Press.

Smith, Kevin B., and Lorene H. Stone. 1989. "Rags, Riches, and Bootstraps: Beliefs about the Causes of Wealth and Poverty." *Sociological Quarterly* 1:93–107.

Smyser, W. R. 1985. "Refugees: A Never-Ending Story." *Foreign Affairs*. Fall:154–68.

Snepp, Frank. 1977. *Decent Interval: An Insider's Account of Saigon's Indecent End Told by the CIA's Chief Strategy Analyst in Vietnam*. New York: Random.

Stack, Carol B. 1974. *All Our Kin: Strategies for Survival in a Black Community*. New York:Harper Torchbooks.

Starr, Paul D. 1981. "Troubled Waters: Vietnamese Fisherfolk on America's Gulf Coast." *International Migration Review* 1:226–38

Starr, Paul D., and Alden E. Roberts. 1982. "Attitudes Toward New Americans: Perceptions of Indo-Chinese in Nine Cities." Pp. 165–86 in *Research in Race and Ethnic Relations*, edited by Cora Marrett and Cheryl Leggon. Greenwood: JAI Press.

_____. 1981. "Attitudes Toward Indochinese Refugees." *Journal of Refugee Resettlement* 4:51-66.

Stein, Barry. 1986. "Durable Solutions for Developing Country Refugees." *International Migration Review* 2:264–83.

_____. 1979. "Occupational Adjustment of Refugees: The Vietnamese in the United States." *International Migration Review* 1:25–45.

Stephens, John. 1979. *The Transition from Capitalism to Socialism*. New York: McMillan Press.

Stern, Lewis M. 1981. "Responses to Vietnamese Refugees: Surveys of Public Opinion." *Social Work* July:306–11.

Strand, Paul J. 1989. "The Indochinese Refugee Experience: The Case of San Diego." Pp. 105–20 in *Refugees as Immigrants: Cambodians, Laotians, and Vietnamese in America*, edited by David W. Haines. Totowa: Rowman and Littlefield Publishers.

Strand, Paul J., and Woodrow Jones. 1985. *Indochinese Refugees in America: Problems of Adaptation and Assimilation*. Durham: Duke University Press.

Suhrke, Astri. 1983. "Indochinese Refugees: The Law and Politics of First Asylum." *Annals of the American Academy of Political and Social Sciences* 467:102–15.

Suhrke, Astri, and Frank Klink. 1987. "Contrasting Patterns of Asian Refugee Movements: The Vietnamese and Afghan Syndromes." Pp. 71–84 in *Pacific Bridges: The New Immigration from Asia and the Pacific Islands*, edited by James T. Fawcett and Bejanmin V. Carino. Staten Island: Center for Migration Studies.

Sullivan, Marianna. 1978. *France's Vietnam Policy: A Study in French-American Relations*. Westport,: Greenwood Press.

Sutter, Valerie O. 1990. *The Indochinese Refugee Dilemma*. Baton Rouge: Louisiana State University Press.

Sutton, Francis X. 1987. "Refugees and Mass Exoduses: The Search for a Humane, Effective Policy." Pp. 201–26 in *Population in an Interacting World*, edited by William Alonso. Cambridge: Harvard University Press.

Szymusiak, Malyda. 1986. *The Stones Cry Out: A Cambodian Childhood, 1975–1980*. New York: Hill and Wang.

Tafan, Peirre. 1986. "La Corse." Pp. 961–1117 in *Gépolitiques des Regions Françaises, Tome III*, edited by Yves Lacosta. Paris: Fayard.

Taft, Julia, David North, and David Ford. 1980. *Refugee Resettlement in the United States*. Washington, DC: New Transcentury Foundation.

Takaki, Ronald. 1989. *Strangers from Different Shores: A History of Asian Ameicans*. Boston: Little, Brown, and Company.

Thompson, Virginia. 1952. "The Vietnamese Community in France." *Pacific Affairs* 1:49–58.

Tiberghien, Frédéric. 1985. "La Protection des Réfugiés en France." *La Revue Administrative* 224:115–25.

Tillema, Richard G. 1981. "Starting Over in a New Land: Resettling a Refugee Family." *Public Welfare* 1:35–41.

Tilly, Charles. 1990. "Transplanted Networks." Pp. 79–95 in *Immigration Reconsidered: History, Sociology, and Politics*, edited by Virginia Yans-McLaughlin. New York: Oxford University Press.

_____. 1984. *Big Structures, Large Processes, Huge Comparisons*. New York: Russel Sage.

_____. 1978. "Migration in Modern European History." Pp. 48–72 in *Human Migration*, edited by William McNeill and Ruth Adams. Bloomington: Indiana University Press.

_____. 1975." Reflections on the History of European State-Making." Pp. 3–83 in *The Formation of National States in Western Europe*, edited by Charles Tilly. Princeton: Princeton University Press.

Tomasckovic-Devey, Barbara, and Tomasckovic-Devey, Donald. 1988. "The Social Structural Determinants of Ethnic Group Behavior: Single Ancestry Rates among Four White American Ethnic Groups." *American Sociological Review* 4:650–59.

Tran, Thanh Gian. 1964. "Les Vietnamiens en France." *France Migrations* 34:10–18.

Tran, Thanh V. 1991. "Sponsorship and Employment Status among Indochinese Refugees in the United States." *International Migration Review* 3:536–73.

U.S. Committee for Refugees. 1991. *World Refugee Survey: 1990 in Review*. Washington, DC: American Council for Nationalities Service.

_____. 1987. *Uncertain Harbors: The Plight of Vietnamese Boat People*. Washington, D.C.: American Council for Nationalities Service.

Vallet, J. Champigné. 1980. "Une Experiencé de Formation et d'Insertion en Mileau Rural: Borneau." *Migrants Formation* 41/42:54–58.

Vandeusen et al. [eight co-authors]. 1981. "Southeast Asian Social and Cultural Customs: Similarities and Differences." *Journal of Refugee Resettlement* 1:20–38.

Velasco, Alfredo F., Kenji Ima, Binh K. Stanton, and Beverley C. Yip. 1983. *Adjustment Strategies of the Vietnamese Refugees in San Diego,*

California: Six Ethnographic Case Histories. San Diego: Union of Pan Asian Communities.

Vernejoul, Robert. 1961. *Problèmes Poses Par la Reintegration des Français d'Outre-Mer dans la Communauté Nationale*. Paris: Centre Economicque et Social.

Viviani, Nancy. 1984. *The Long Journey: Vietnamese Migration and Settlement in Australia*. Melbourne: Melbourne University Pess.

Wain, Barry. 1981. *The Refused: The Agony of the Indochina Refugees*. New York: Simon and Schuster.

Waldinger, Roger, Howard Aldrich, Robin Ward and Associates. 1990. *Ethnic Entrepreneurs: Immigrant Business in Industrial Societies*. Newbury Park: Sage.

Wangen, Gérold de. 1985. "La Protection des Réfugiés en France: Bilan, Problèmes d'Aujourd'hui et Solutions Possible" *Droit Social* février:150–59.

_____. 1982. "Les Réfugiés en France: Les Structures d'Accueil, la Prise en Charge par la Collectivité Nationale: Objectifs et Moyens." Pp. 1–8 in *Stage de Formation Destine aux Responsables des Centres Provisoires d'Hébergement pour les Réfugiés*, edited by France Terre d'Asile. Paris: France Terre d'Asile.

_____. 1980. *France Terre d'Asile: Historique de l'Accueil et de la Formation Initiale des Réfugiés en France*. Paris: France Terre d'Asile.

Waters, Mary C. 1990. *Ethnic Options: Choosing Identities in America*. Berkeley: University of California Press.

Weber, Eugen. 1976. *From Peasants into Frenchmen: The Modernization of Rural France, 1870–1914*. Stanford: Stanford University Press.

Weir, Margaret, Ann S. Orloff, and Theda Skocpol. 1989. "Introduction: Understanding American Social Policies." Pp. 3–27 in *The Politics of Social Policy in the United States*, edited by Margaret Weir, Ann S. Orloff, and Theda Skocpol. Princeton: Princeton University Press.

Weiss, John. 1983. "Origins of the French Welfare State: Poor Relief in the Third Republic, 1871–1914." *French Historical Studies* 1:47–78.

Wenden, Catherine W. de. 1987. *Citoynneté, Nationalité et Immigration*. Paris: Arcantère Editions.

Whelan, Frederick G. 1988. "Citizenship and Freedom of Movement: An Open Admission Policy?" Pp. 3–39 in *Open Borders? Closed Societies?*, edited by Mark Gibney. New York: Greenwood Press.

White, Paul, Hilary Wincherster, and Michelle Guillon. 1987. "South-East Asian Refugees in Paris: The Evolution of a Minority Community." *Ethnic and Racial Studies* 1:48–61.

Wiesner, Louis A. 1989. *Victims and Survivors: Displaced Persons and Other War Victims in Viet-Nam, 1954–1975*. New York: Greenwood Press.

Wilensky, Harold. 1987. "Leftism, Catholicism, and Democratic Corporatism: The Role of Political Parties in Recent Welfare State Development." Pp. 345–82 in *The Development of the Welfare State in Europe and America*, edited by Peter Flora and Arnold Heidenheimer. New Brunswick: Transaction Books.

Wilson, Kenneth, and W. Allen Martin. 1982. "Ethnic Enclaves: A Comparison of the Cuban and Black Economies in Miami." *American Journal of Sociology* 1:135–60.

Wilson, Kenneth, and Alejandro Portes. 1980. "Immigrant Enclaves: An Analysis of the Labor Market Experiences of Cubans in Miami." *American Journal of Sociology* 2:295–319.

Wilson, William J. 1987. *The Truly Disadvantaged: The Inner City, the Underclass, and Public Policy*. Chicago: University of Chicago Press.

_____. 1980. *The Declining Significance of Race: Blacks and Changing American Institutions*. Chicago: University of Chicago Press.

Wolf, Shelly T. 1981. "Orientation Needs of Indochinese Refugees." *Journal of Refugee Resettlement* 2:52–57.

Wollny, Hans. 1991. "Asylum Policy in Mexico: A Survey." *Journal of Refugee Studies* 3:219–37.

Wright, Robert G. 1981. "Voluntary Agencies and the Resettlement of Refugees." *International Migration Review* 1:157–74.

Wyman, David. 1984. *The Abandonment of the Jews: America and the Holocaust, 1941–1945*. New York: Pantheon.

_____. 1968. *Paper Walls: America and the Refugee Crisis, 1938–1941*. Boston: University of Massachusetts.

Yancey, William, Eugene Erickson, and Richard Juliani. 1979. "Emergent Ethnicity: A Review and Reformulation." *American Sociological Review* 3:391–403.

Yarland, Barbara M. 1990. *Refugees without Refuge: Formation and Failed Implementation of U.S. Political Asylum Policy in the 1980s*. Lanham: University Press of America.

Yathay, Pin. 1987. *Stay Alive, My Son*. New York: Free Press.

Zinn, Howard. 1980. *A People's History of the United States*. New York: Harper and Row.

Zolberg, Aristide R., Astri Suhrke, and Sergio Aguayo. 1989. *Escape From Violence: Conflict and the Refugee Crisis in the Developing World*. New York: Oxford University Press.

Zucker, Norman L., and Naomi F. Zucker. 1989. "The Uneasy Troika in U.S. Refugee Policy: Foreign Policy, Pressure Groups, and Resettlement Costs." *Journal of Refugee Studies* 3:359–72.

_____. 1987. *The Guarded Gate: The Reality of American Refugee Policy*. New York: Harcourt Brace Jovanovich.

France Terre d'Asile

All documents in quotation marks are staff reports of visits to temporary settlement centers (CPH in French). These documents are in file 4.62.5 in the Centre de Documentation, France Terre d'Asile, Paris. All others are publications by FTDA.

1975. *Accueil des Réfugiés d'Indochine: Protocole*.

1976. *Rapport à l'Assemblé Generale du mars 1976*.

1979. *Notes sur les Centres Provisoires d'Hébergement*.

1980a. "Compte Rendu de Mission à Bordeaux le 7/11/1980 par Mr. Duverge."

1980b. "Compte Rendu du Voyage à Lille le 2/12/1980 par Mme. de Wangen et M. Parais."

1981a. *Dossier du Permanent d'un Centre de Transit.*

1981b. "Compte Rendu de Mission à Porte-Leucate le 24/2/1981 par M. Duverge."

1981c. "Compte Rendu du Deplacement à Limoges le 24/3/1981 par Mme. de Wangen."

1981d. "Compte Rendu de Mission à Rodez le 10/6/81 par M. Duverge."

1981e. *Le Dispositif d'Accueil de France Terre d'Asile.*

1981f. "Compte Rendu de la Visite du CPH de Douvaine par JP du 29 mai au 1er juin 1981."

1982a. "Compte Rendu du Voyage à Amboise le 29/1/82, Y. Ajchenbaum."

1982b. "Reunions des CPH le 17 mai 1982."

1982c. "Comptes Rendu de Mission à Troyes et Bar-sur-Aube le 14 mai 1982 par P. Duvergé."

1982d. "Reunions des CPH le 17 mai 1982."

1982e. "Compte Rendu de Reunion à Dourdan du 10 juin 1982."

1982f. "Compte Rendu de la Reunion à la Prefecture de Strasbourg le 30 juin 1982 (SW et JL)."

1982g. "Reunion des Responsables des Centres d'Hébergement le 20 sept 1982."

1982h. "Compte Rendu du la Mission à Fameck et Rosselange le 2 novembre 1982."

1983a. *Bilan de l'Accueil des Réfugiés du Mois de dècembre.*

1983b. "Compte Rendu de la Visite au CPH de Laon le 8.11.1983 par P. Duverge."

1983c. "Comtpe Rendu de la Rencontre avec AFTM le 22 février 83 par J. Lambalais."

1983d. "Compte Rendu de la Reunion à Mulhouse le 25/2/1983 par Jacque Lambalais."

1983e. "Compte Rendu de la Visite au CPH de Valdahon le 28 octobre 1983 par P. Duverge."

1984a. "Visite au CPH de Cerizay le 8 février 1984 par P. Duverge."

1984b. "Compte Rendu du Visite au CPH de Gien et à Orleans le 2 mai 1984."

1984c. "Compte Rendu de la Visite de CPH de Bordaux le 8/3/84 par P. Duverge."

1984d. "Visite au CPH de Cerizay le 8 février 1984 par P. Duverge."

1987. *Bilan de l'Accueil des Réfugiés du Mois de septembre 1987.*

1991. *La Lettre d'Informatin (No. 80): Les Operations d'Accueil de Réfugiés.*

French Government Documents

Most of these documents are in the file "Chrono Text Legislative," in the Centre de Documentation, France Terre d'Asile, Paris. All others are in the

Bibliothèque de la Documentation Française, Paris, except those marked with an *, which were provided by government officials.

Journal Official. 1964. *Accueil et Réinstallation des Français d'Outre-Mer.*
_____. 1976a. "Arrêté du 29 février 1976." P. 1687 in *Journal Officiel*, 17 *mars.*
_____. 1976b. "Décret no.76-526 du 15 juin 1976 portant Application des Articles 185 et 185–3 du Code de la Famille et de l'Aide Social Entendant l'Aide Sociale à de Nouvelles Catégories de Bénéfiaires et Relatif aux Centres d'Hébergement et de Réadaptation." *Journal Officiel*, 8 juin.
_____. 1983a. "Réfugiés Vietnamiens: Aide." *Journal Officiel*, Débats Senat, Questions et Reponses, 6 janvier.
_____. 1983b. "Des Réfugiés." *Journal Officiel*, Débats Assebmlée Nationale, Questions et Reponses, 25 avril.
_____. 1984a. "Décret no.84-216 mars 1984 pour l'Application de l'Article L.351–9 du Code du Travail." *Journal Officiel*, 31 mars.
_____. 1984b. "Circulaire du 28 juin 1984 Relative à l'Etat Civil des Réfugiés." *Journal Officiel*. 9 décembre.
___. 1985. "Immigration: Debat en Assembleé Nationale." Pp.1488–523 in *Journal Officiel*, Debats Assembleé Nationale, 7 juin.
_____. 1987. "Etrangers (Laotiens)." P. 830 in *Journal Officiel*, Debats Assemblée Nationale, Questions et Reponses, 16 février.
_____. 1988. "Décret no. 88-888 du 23 août 1988 Relatif aux Attributions de Secrétaire d'Etat auprès du Permier Ministre, Chargé de l'Action Humanitaire." Pp. 10,742–43 in *Journal Officiel*, Textes Generaux, Primier Ministre, 24 août.
Journal Officiel II (Assemblée Nationale). 1979. Rapport Fait au Nom de la Commission des Finances, de l'Economie Générale et du Plan sur le Projet de Loi des Finances pour 1980. Annex no. 1, Affaires Etrangères, Assembleé Nationale, 2 octobre, no. 1292.
Ministère des Affaires Sociales. 1985. Letter from the Direction de la Population et des Migrations dated January 21, 1985 [no addressee].*
Minstère de l'Interieur. 1976. "Telegramme Adressé par le Ministre d'Etat, Ministre de l'Interieur, Circ no.76-67 du 5 février 1976. Objet: Réfugiés d'Exême Orient."
Ministère de la Santé. 1975a. "Circulaire no. 25. AS du 27 mai 1975 Relative à l'Accueil en France Métroplitaine Ayant à la Suite des Evénments Récents Quitté le Cambodge et le Vietnam."
_____. 1975b. "Circulaire 38 AS du 31 juillet 1975 Relative à l'Accueil en France Métroplitaine de Personnes Ayant Dû Quitter le Cambodge, le Laos et le Vietnam."
_____. 1976. Letter to "Messieurs les Préfects, Direction Départmentale de l'Action Sanitaire et Social. Objet: Circulaire no. 42 du 15 juin 1976."
_____. 1979a. "Le 4 juillet 1979, Le Secrétaire d'Etat, Objet: Accueil des Réfugiés du Sud-Est Asia."
_____. 1979b. "Le 19 septembre 1979, Le Secrétaire d'Etat, Objet: Réfugiés du Sud-Est Asiatique."

_____. 1980a. "Circulaire no. 7 SS du janvier 1980 Relative aux Conditions d'Octroi de l'Allocation aux Adultes Handicapés aux Réfugiés et Apatrides."

_____. 1980b. Letter dated November 24, 1980, to "Monsieur Jean-Jacques Beucler, Ancien Ministre, Président du Comité Nationale d'Entraide Franco-Vietnamien, Franco-Cambodgien, Franco-Laotien."*

Ministère de la Solidarité Nationale. 1981. "Circulaire no. 81-3 le 29 juillet. Objet: Réfugiés du Sud-Est Asiatique."

_____. 1982. "Note le 17 mars sur les Problemes de Formation des Réfugiés en vue de Leur Insertion dans la Communauté Française."*

Ministère du Travail. 1975. "Circulaire no. 14–75 du 3 juin 1975 à MM. les Préfects de Région, les Préfects, les Directeurs Régionaux du Travial et de la Main-d'Oeuvre, les Directeurs Départementaux du Travail de la Main-d'Oeuvre."

_____. 1981. *Etude Concernant l'Installation des Réfugiés du Sud-Est Asiatique Hors des Grandes Agglomeration Urbaines.* Paris: SETEF.

United States Government Documents

U.S. Code. 1983. "Chapter 12–Immigration and Nationality." Pp. 947–1525 in *United States Code 1983, Volume 2.*

U.S. Commission on Civil Rights. 1987. *Recent Activities Against Citizens and Residents of Asian Descent.*

_____. 1988. *The Economic Status of Americans of Asian Descent: An Exploratory Investigation.*

U.S. Conference of Mayors. 1982. "Findings of U.S. Conference of Mayors Concerning Refugee Impacts." Appendix A in *Reauthorization of Refugee Act of 1980.* Hearings Before the Subcommittee on Immigration, Refugees, and International Law of the Committee on the Judiciary, House of Representatives, 97th Congress, 1st Session (April 22 and 28, 1982).

U.S. Congressional Research Service. 1980. *Review of U.S. Refugee Resettlement Programs and Policy.* A Report Prepared at the Request of Senator Edward M. Kennedy, Chairman, Committee of the Judiciary, United States Sentate.

U.S. Department of Commerce. 1990. *Statistical Abstract of the United States 1990.*

U.S. Department of Health, Education, and Welfare. 1975. "Policy Instruction: Action Transmittal SRS-AT-75-27, June 9 1975." Pp.141–49 in *Indochina Evacuation and Refugee Problems, Part V: Conditions in Indochina and Refugees in the U.S.* Hearing Before the Subcommittee to Investigate Problems Connected with Refugees Escapees of the Committee on the Judiciary, Senate, 94th Congress, 1st Session (July 24, 1975).

_____. 1978. *Indochinese Refugee Assistance Program: Report to Congress.*

U.S. Department of Health and Human Services. 1983. "Refugee Resettlement Program: Placement Policy." *Federal Register* 239 (December 12):55,300–02.

_____ Region VII. 1982. *Developing Refugee Leadership: Moving Towards Self-Sufficiency*. Kansas City: U.S. Department of Health and Human Services Region VII.

U.S. Department of State. 1982a. "Proposed Refugee Admissions for fy 1983." *Department of State Bulletin* December:56–63.

_____. 1982b. "Statement of Ambassador H. Eugene Douglas, U.S. Coordinator for Refugee Affairs before the Subcommittee on Immigrants, Refugees, and International Law of the House Judiciary Committee." [Mimeographed copy]

_____. 1986. *Report of the Indochinese Refugee Panel*.

_____. 1988. "Indochinese Refugees and Relations with Thailand." *Current Policy* no. 1052.

U.S. General Accounting Office. 1979. *Report to Congress: The Indochinese Exodus: A Humanitarian Dilemma*.

_____. 1983. *Greater Emphasis on Early Employment and Better Monitoring Needed in Indochinese Refugee Resettlement Program*.

U.S. House of Representatives. 1975a. *Indochina Refugees*. Hearings Before the Subcommittee on Immigration, Citizenship, and International Law of the Committee on the Judiciary, House of Representatives, 94th Congress, 1st Session (May 5 and 7, 1975).

_____. 1975b. "Enabling the United States to Render Assistance to, or in Behalf of, Certain Migrants and Refugees." Pp. 14,338–73 in *Congressional Record*. Proceedings and Debate of the 94th Congress, 1st Session (May 14, 1975).

_____. 1975c. *Indochina Refugee Children Assistance Act of 1975*. House of Representatives Report 94-719, House Reports, 94th Congress, 1st Session, Volume 1-10 (January 14-December 19, 1975).

_____. 1976. *Refugees From Indochina*. Hearings Before the Subcommittee on Immigration, Citizenship, and International Law of the Committee on the Judiciary, House of Representatives, 94th Congress, 1st Session (April 8,9,14; May 22; July 17, 22; October 8; December 18, 1975; and February 5, 1976).

_____. 1977a. *Indochina Refugees–Adjustment of Status*. Hearings Before the Subcommittee on Immigration, Citizenship, and International Law of the Committee on the Judiciary, House of Representatives, 95th Congress, 1st Session (May 25 and June 2, 1977).

_____. 1977b. *Extension of Indochina Refugee Assistance Program*. Hearings Before the Subcommittee on Immigration, Citizenship, and International Law of the Committee on the Judiciary, House of Representatives, 95th Congress, 1st Session (September 23 and 27, 1977).

_____. 1977c. "Immigration Status of Indochinese Refugees." Pp. 34,086–91 in *Congressional Record*. Proceedings and Debate of the 95th Congress, 1st Session (October 18, 1977).

_____. 1979a. *Refugee Act of 1979*. Hearings Before the Subcommittee on Immigration, Refugees, and International Law of the Committee on the Judiciary, House of Representatives, 96th Congress, 1st Session (May 3, 10, 16, 23, and 24, 1979).

_____. 1979b. *Departments of Labor and Health, Education, and Welfare Appropriations for 1980.* Hearings Before a Subcommittee of the Committee on Appropriations, House of Representatives, 96th Congress, 1st Session (Part 6).

_____. 1979c. "Refugee Act of 1980." Pp. 37,198–205 in *Congressional Record.* Proceedings and Debate of the 96th Congress, 1st Session (September 6, 1979).

_____. 1979d. "Refugee Act of 1980." Pp. 37,223–47 in *Congressional Record.* Proceedings and Debate of the 96th Congress, 1st Session (September 6, 1979).

_____. 1979e. *The Refugee Act of 1979.* Report to Accompany H.R. 2816, House of Representatives, 96th Congress, 1st Session, Report No.96-608.

_____. 1982a. *Reauthorization of Refugee Act of 1980.* Hearings Before the Subcommittee on Immigration, Refugees, and International Law of the Committee on the Judiciary, House of Representatives, 97th Congress, 2nd Session (April 22 and 28, 1982).

_____. 1982b. *Refugee Assistance Amendments of 1982.* House of Representatives, 97th Congress, 2nd Session, Report No. 97-541.

_____. 1982c. "Refugee Assistance Amendments of 1982." Pp. 3704–13 in *Congressional Record.* Proceedings and Debate of the 97th Congress, 2nd Session (June 21, 1982).

U.S. Interagency Task Force for Indochina. 1976. "Papers From the Interagency Task Force for Indochina." Appendix II in *Refugees From Indochina.* Hearings Before the Subcommittee on Immigration, Citizenship, and International Law of the Committee on the Judiciary, House of Representatives, 94th Congress, 1st Session (April 8,9,14; May 22; July 17, 22; October 8; December 18, 1975; and February 5, 1976).

U.S. Office of Refugee Resettlement. 1980. *Refugee Resettlement Handbook.*

_____. 1981 through 1991. *Report to Congress: Refugee Resettlement Program.* [published annually]

U.S. Senate. 1970. *Refugee and Civilian War Causality Problems in Laos and Cambodia.* Hearing Before the Subcommittee on Refugees and Escapees of the Committee on the Judiciary, Sentate, 91st Congress, 2nd Session (May 7, 1970).

_____. 1975a. *Indochina Evacuation and Refugee Problems, Part V: Conditions in Indochina and Refugees in the U.S.* Hearing Before the Subcommittee to Investigate Problems Connected with Refugees Escapees of the Committee on the Judiciary, Senate, 94th Congress, 1st Session (July 24, 1975).

_____. 1975b. "The Indochina Migration and Refugee Assistance Act of 1975." Pp. 14,839–64 in *Congressional Record.* Proceedings and Debates of the 94th Congress, 1st Session (May 16, 1975).

_____. 1977. "Indochina Refugee Adjustment Status Act." Pp. 33,065–70 in *Congressional Record.* Proceedings and Debate of the 95th Congress, 1st Session (October 10, 1977).

_____. 1979a. *The Refugee Act of 1979.* Hearings Before the Committee on the Judiciary, Senate, 96th Congress, 1st Session (March 14, 1979).

_____. 1979b. "Refugee Act of 1979." Pp. 23,243–55 in *Congressional Record. Proceedings and Debate of the 96th Congress, 1st Session* (September 6, 1979).

_____. 1982. *Refugee Assistance Amendments of 1982*. Sentate, 97th Congress, 2nd Session, Report No.97–638.

U.S. Social Security Administration. 1983. "Refugee Resettlement Program: Proposed Designation of Impacted Areas." *Federal Register* 239 (December 12):55,339–40.

U.S. Statutes at Large. 1975. "Public Law 94–23—May 23, 1975." *United States Statutes at Large, Volume 89.*

_____. 1976. "Public Law 94–405—September 10, 1976." *United States Statutes at Large, Volume 90.*

_____. 1977. "Public Law 94–145—October 28, 1976." *United States Statutes at Large, Volume 91.*

_____. 1980. "Public Law 96–212—March 17, 1980." *United States Statutes at Large, Volume 93.*

U.S. Superintendent of Documents. 1988. *1988 Catalog of Federal Domestic Assistance.*

Index